The Palesti

The Palestine–Israel Conflict
A Basic Introduction

Gregory Harms with Todd M. Ferry

Pluto Press

LONDON • ANN ARBOR, MI

First published 2005 by Pluto Press
345 Archway Road, London N6 5AA
and 839 Greene Street, Ann Arbor, MI 48106

www.plutobooks.com

British Library Cataloguing in Publication Data
A catalogue record for this book is available from the British Library

ISBN   0 7453 2379 0 hardback
ISBN   0 7453 2378 2 paperback

Library of Congress Cataloging in Publication Data applied for

10   9   8   7   6   5   4   3   2   1

Designed and produced for Pluto Press by
Chase Publishing Services Ltd, Fortescue, Sidmouth, EX10 9QG, England
Typeset from disk by Stanford DTP Services, Northampton, England
Printed and bound in Canada by Transcontinental Printing

for my brother, Jason

Contents

Appendices

Maps

Maps 2–5 courtesy of PASSIA.

Acknowledgments

I would like to offer profound thanks to: Scott Darley, Ben Nowicki, Shawn Mitchell, Annie Higgins, Jeffrey Ball (Dove Booksellers), Shany Shlomo, Lahan Sarid, Ali Abu Shawish, Naim Toubassi, Zaid Alayobi, Ryan Robinson, Jerilyn Tabor, Michael Pugh, Alfonso Flores V, Clement Cherian, Jan Larsen (the *Herald News*), and George David Miller. Many thanks are owed to Alex Lubertozzi and Jennifer Fusco at Prologue Publishing for much-needed direction and guidance. To Roger van Zwanenberg, Julie Stoll, David Castle, Robert Webb, Matthew Seal and everyone at Pluto Press I am thankful for realizing this project. I am grateful to Professor Arthur Goldschmidt Jr and Professor Charles D. Smith for their availability, honesty, and advice. I am indebted to my mother, Martha Harms, and George Savich for their early and much-needed help. Grant and Genevieve Harms (both of whom passed during the writing of this book, and a second dedication would go to them) and my father, Joseph and Diana Harms all provided me with humbling support and hospitality at the farm.

I am grateful for immediate and unbending support of this project to Mark Eleveld, who upon my initial consideration of the idea firmly encouraged me to get started. Special thanks go to my friend and colleague, Todd Ferry, who thoughtfully came along at the right time and whose knowledge and expertise made a superb contribution to this book. Vikram Sura, who I met in Jerusalem, has been a tremendous source of support and counsel ever since. For innumerable reasons I am indebted to Michael Slager, countless conversations with whom have sharpened my thinking on all manner of subjects (thanks, Michael). I owe an impossible amount of gratitude to Tom Jasper for his selfless generosity and encouraging fireside chats (and to Givon and Madison Jasper for helpin' their Uncle G).

Lastly, I am grateful to the people in Israel and Palestine who, far too numerous to list here, showed me hospitality, friendship, and openness during my time spent researching there in June 2002. It is in these qualities and people that their leaders can – and must – find an exemplar.

All those noted above contributed to this project in a multitude of ways, the sum total of which made this possible. For the existence of this book they have an equal share in its arrival; for the contents and any errors therein, I alone am responsible.

Gregory Harms

Preface

"Who's fighting and what for?"
Mick Jagger, Altamont Raceway, 1969

One would be hard pressed to pick up a newspaper, or turn on the nightly news, and not come across words and phrases like "West Bank" or "Yasser Arafat" or "Ariel Sharon" or "Arab–Israeli peace process." The Palestine–Israel conflict has become a permanent fixture in news media the world over. Though geographically tiny, it sends shockwaves around the globe. Oftentimes, in reaction to news of Israel and Palestine, you might hear people make remarks like, "Those people have been fighting for thousands of years!" Given the way the conflict is presented on the news – as a perpetual tallying of deaths on each side – it's not surprising that people commonly make such judgments. But like most things, what actually lies beneath the surface bears little resemblance to what it's presumed to be. So, where is someone to go and get a basic understanding of the most notorious conflict of the twentieth century? The evening news tells you almost nothing except for dutifully reported death tolls, the classrooms of American high schools are free of contamination with discussion of it (though the September 11 attacks have opened things up a bit), and though there are mountains of books on the subject, they tend to be five hundred pages long, or focused on an aspect of the conflict, or both. People with families and jobs typically don't have the time to pore over cumbersome monographs on history and political science.

I've been staring blankly at the shelves of the Middle East section in countless bookstores for years now, wondering to myself, Why are there zero books on the Palestine–Israel conflict that are around 150 pages long, start with the ancient history, and feature plenty of endnotes and suggested reading to guide the reader onward? Until now there has been one book that came close to this, and that is Ron David's *Arabs & Israel For Beginners*. David's text was the only of its kind, yet even with his contribution, and now this one, there still remains a gaping hole in the literature for general readers. The *Dummies* and *Idiot's Guide* series have made a large contribution to offering people with basic introductions to everything from surfing to the Civil War, but even their titles on the Middle East are 400 to 500 pages long – a bit heavy for a primer. During a discussion of this problematic lack of primer-level titles a friend of mine pointed out something rather interesting: The scientific community publishes a whole host of magazines and books dedicated to a general readership. People who have three kids and work forty-plus hours a week can learn about the latest breakthroughs and theories in cosmology and quantum physics, and have an almost endless supply of articles written clearly and simply so he or she can understand the various concepts without a PhD or reading a book that weighs ten pounds. This trend would be most welcome – and is desperately needed – in the realms of foreign affairs and political science, especially in the present case of the Middle East. This book aims at contributing to the thin supply of basic and comprehensive literature on the Palestine–Israel conflict.

In producing the book I could never find I merely had to look at what wasn't being made available to readers, namely, an introduction to the *entire* history of Canaan–Palestine–Israel, from the Paleolithic period to last week. As a result, the first half of this book has almost nothing to do with the conflict directly, but a basic knowledge of the region's deep history is critical, especially in light of what I have somewhat blandly labeled the "Thousand Year Myth."

The book is broken up into three sections. Section I addresses the background history of the region from the dawn of humankind to the final moments of the Ottoman Empire (early 1900s). Section II introduces the people involved in the conflict: the Palestinians and the European Jews who founded and established Zionism. Section III discusses the actual conflict, from its earliest moments on through to the current situation that covers newsprint and television screens. From section to section, common questions are addressed, and no prior knowledge is assumed on the part of the reader. Questions I've repeatedly encountered at lectures have given me a base for what the reader might be wondering: What's the West Bank? What does religion have to do with this? Why are Palestinians blowing up themselves, and others? What is Zionism? Were the Jews or Arabs there first? I have tried to include the commonly asked questions about the conflict, while trying to anticipate further curiosities and possible confusion. However, if I have overlooked something that you were hoping to have answered, or something I've discussed remains muddled, please tell me about it: <gharms@gmail.com>.

A word about bias and balance. The Palestine–Israel conflict generates suspicion about bias and side-choosing like none other. Accusations fly and tempers flare over the slightest indication of a person, book, or article leaning one way or the other. For you the reader, I suggest making every effort to keep an open mind and read critically, starting with this book. The Palestine–Israel conflict is not a sporting event where people pick a side and root accordingly (though many people do). It is a political conflict over which people lose lives. As someone who is maybe new to the conflict, try to examine the history and come to a balanced understanding of what is at stake, what the key issues are, and what could be done about it. "Objectivity" is a word that has almost lost its meaning, and has frequently come to suggest imposing symmetry where things aren't necessarily symmetrical, thus distorting the actual situation. In the role of historian, I have made every effort to present the history of the conflict in a balanced and actual light. My choice and cross-comparison of the literature on the subject was attempted with care; avoiding grossly polemical texts, I chose sources based on their quality of research and presentation of the facts. Though some texts can sway to one side, it's been my every attempt to look past the tilt and focus on the research and information. Regardless, however, of my efforts at handling sources critically, and writing with caution, the reader will ultimately be the judge of my success.

One final thought. Irrespective of how the conflict is presented, discussed, or written about, none of this is hard, not even a little. If you can follow a soap opera or a professional sport, though not very good analogies, you can follow and comprehend Middle Eastern affairs, politics, foreign policy, and the rest of it. It's as easy as it is important, and the world desperately needs us to understand it.

Gregory Harms
February 2005

Introduction

THE MIDDLE EAST

Though this book addresses the Palestine–Israel conflict particularly, it is important that we get our bearings and go in with an understanding of where it is we're talking about. You might already know that the Palestine–Israel conflict is a Middle Eastern issue, and that it involves Arabs and Jews, but what do these terms mean exactly?

The Middle East is a term we are all familiar with, given its political turbulence and the resultant saturated coverage of it in the news. Yet, getting down to discussing what it is precisely can lead to vacant stares and head scratching. The very term itself – "Middle East" – is confusing upon initial consideration (the middle of where, and east of what?). If you live in India it's hardly east, and if you live in Mexico, well, the term is pretty much useless. Clearly, these terms are relative to Western Europe, suggesting its global centrality. Let's start with the *Encyclopaedia Britannica*:

> [The Middle East consists of] the lands around the southern and eastern shores of the Mediterranean Sea, extending from Morocco to the Arabian Peninsula and Iran and sometimes beyond. The central part of this general area was formerly called the Near East, a name given to it by some of the first modern Western geographers and historians, who tended to divide the Orient into three regions. Near East applied to the region nearest Europe, extending from the Mediterranean Sea to the Persian Gulf; Middle East, from the Gulf to Southeast Asia; and Far East, those regions facing the Pacific Ocean.[1]

The designation of the Middle East changed around the time Great Britain established colonial control in Egypt in the 1880s, where it then began to include what had previously been labeled the Near East in the above quote. As for the term "Orient," this word is usually taken to connote far-eastern Asian imagery – jade dragons, ornate lamps with tassels, etc. However, the Orient (which means "east") is Asia taken in its entirety, from Israel to Japan, including a big southwestern chunk of Russia. So, technically, what we call the Middle East could (should) be called Western or Southwestern Asia. However, for the purposes of this book, we will carry on the Eurocentric tradition and call it the Middle East.

What countries make up the Middle East? Egypt, Israel–Palestine, Jordan, Syria, Lebanon, Iraq, Iran, plus the countries that comprise the Arabian Peninsula: Saudi Arabia, Yemen, Oman, United Arab Emirates, Qatar, Bahrain, and Kuwait. All these countries are also considered Arab countries, with the exception of Iran whose inhabitants are Persian, and Israel where most are Jewish. Turkey, Greece, Libya, Morocco, and the Sudan are sometimes considered Middle Eastern.

THE PEOPLE

Though we get into it in Chapters 1 and 2, an Arab is simply someone who speaks Arabic, and who has grown up in, and identifies with, Arab culture, which is also typically Middle Eastern. As *Britannica* puts it: "This diverse assortment of peoples defies physical stereotyping."[2] A Jew is a person who believes in the religious tenets of Judaism and may have some ethnic roots tracing back to what may have been an original population group from Canaan or Palestine. Much more will be said about these matters later. Likewise, we will also get into the particulars of Islam in Chapter 2, but just keep in mind that Muslims are people who practice Islam, and they may or may not be Arab. (Actually, most Muslims aren't Arab.) Let's look at the current numbers:[3]

- There are 1.3 billion Muslims worldwide. In comparison, there are 2 billion Christians, 900 million Hindus, and 360 million Buddhists (world population: 6.3 billion).[4]

- 20 percent of Muslims are Arab, and 95 percent of the world's 260 million Arabs are Muslim.
- The four countries with the most Muslims in them, in order of greatest to least, are Indonesia (181m), Pakistan (141m), India (124m), and Bangladesh (111m).
- The Middle Eastern countries listed in the previous section, with the exception of Israel, are about 90 percent Muslim. Israel is 80 percent Jewish.

Though I've used *National Geographic* here for the current data on Islam, I also suggest seeking out the most recent *World Almanac*. It's relatively inexpensive and dead handy for looking up these sorts of figures.

Okay, we're ready to begin our understanding of the Palestine–Israel conflict, so we can watch the news with critical confidence as well as correct, with gentle sophistication, those who proclaim the Thousand Year Myth. And if *you're* that person, don't be hard on yourself – you've made the first step. We're going to cover a little over a million years of history in 182 pages, which makes for an average of 7,692 years per page. Let's begin.

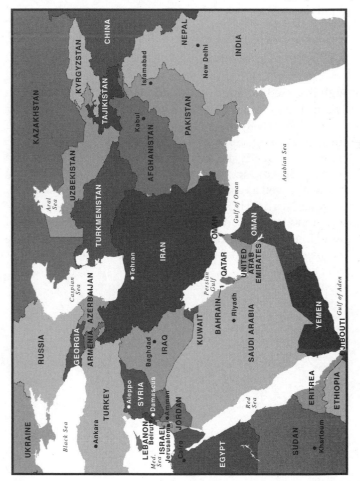

Map 1   The Middle East and Southwest Asia

1
Background History

The first three chapters will look at the regional history of Canaan and Palestine from the most ancient eras up to the eve of World War I: from the emergence of the Hebrews and the Arabs to Muhammad and the birth of Islam, the Crusades, the Mongols, and the Ottoman Empire. A sketch of where today's Palestinians and Israelis come from gives us a sense of context when we try to examine the Palestine–Israel conflict. It is important to keep in mind as a point of reference that *the ancient histories of the region have NO direct causal significance in the modern conflict*. Tempting as it is to assume the fighting stretches that far back, the conflict between the Palestinians and the Israelis goes back not even one hundred years. A survey of the history from the Paleolithic period to the decline and fall of the Ottoman Empire makes this apparent.

1

Ancient History: Canaan–Palestine
From the First Foot Falls to Rome

Todd M. Ferry

THE ANCIENT HISTORY OF PALESTINE

Why begin a book like this so far back in time from the present? First, we need to dispel the common misconception that the Palestine–Israel conflict is a struggle that has lasted for hundreds of years, millennia, or even since the time of Abraham's sons, Isaac and Ishmael. Second, it is important to show change over time. The history of the region goes back many thousands of years. Over that time, many peoples have populated the land of Palestine – not just Arabs and Jews – and they lived together, intermixed, intermarried, merged, and grew apart. Change is central to this story and so it will be constantly emphasized. Lastly, we need to be aware of the shared heritage of both peoples. Though Palestinians and Jews see themselves as different now, there is a remarkable congruence to their histories that should be remembered when considering the modern conflict and both people's claims to the land of Palestine.

Before we begin we need to say a word about the Bible.[1] The first place people often turn to for the history of ancient Palestine is the Bible, and indeed it has been the single most influential source. No doubt it offers a rare glimpse into the history of Israel as well as Israel's neighbors. But the Bible is religious literature written and compiled for reasons other than the purely historical. We know from critical study that it is a composite text made up of several books, each of which has its own religious, cultural, political, and personal (the writer's) perspective. It has also been copied, translated, and redacted (edited) by people with their own understanding of its meaning. In brief it has its own "spin" on history that may or may not reflect actual events and certainly not every side to the story.

There are other sources at our disposal. If our concern is for a fuller, more complete understanding of the ancient history of Palestine then archaeology, non-biblical texts, geography, and other interdisciplinary forms of study, should all have a hand in historical reconstruction. In this very general overview of the history of ancient Palestine we will attempt to bring in as much of these other sources as we can, while also drawing on histories of others who try to do the same. It all sounds complicated at first, and though reconstructing the history of ancient Palestine is a very complex matter, this chapter will attempt to make it easily understandable.

CHRONOLOGY AND GEOGRAPHY

Before we begin, a quick chronological and geographical note. Over thousands of years the cultures of Palestine changed. Conventional approaches break down the ancient history of the region into periods following technological change (Bronze Age, Iron Age, etc.) or some other dominant feature (Hellenistic Age, Roman Empire, etc.). These will be noted in the section headings as we go. We will also be using BCE (Before Common Era) and CE (Common Era) instead of the abbreviations AD (Anno Domini) and BC (Before Christ). The Common Era abbreviations are now the convention, in an attempt to avoid religious preferences.

Regarding geography, I have chosen to use "Palestine" as the most neutral and encompassing of modern names for the region (though this is certainly debatable).[2] For the ancient periods, I will start with the broad territorial term "Canaan," since it was one of the first recorded names for the region. Ancient Canaan covers an area slightly larger than the modern land of Palestine (including Israel, Gaza, and the West Bank), to encompass Lebanon, southern Syria, the eastern half of Jordan, and the Sinai Peninsula. As the many specific kingdoms (Israel, Philistia, Moab, etc.), empires (Assyrian, Neo-Babylonian, etc.), or provinces (Judaea, Samerina etc.) are established in the region, I will refer to them by what they were called in antiquity and describe them as we go. Don't worry, it's pretty straightforward.

SETTING THE STAGE

Over the course of several hundred thousand years known as the Paleolithic period (Paleolithic, "the stone age": 1.4 million years ago to 8500 BCE) human beings evolved, left Africa, and came to Palestine, developing their own unique cultures. During the following Neolithic period ("the new stone age": 8500–4300 BCE) they settled in villages, learned to domesticate animals and plants, and discovered clay could be manipulated into shapes and baked to form pottery – huge achievements in an amazingly short period of time. In the Chalcolithic period ("the copper and stone age": 4300–3300 BCE) their villages got larger, their homes more permanent, and they discovered how to make things for the first time with metal (copper). While all of this early pre-history is certainly important, it is really in the following periods that we know the most about the ancient history of Palestine and when we begin to see one of the most important cultures in the region develop. Here we will begin with our more detailed survey – in the Bronze Age.

THE BRONZE AGE AND THE CANAANITES
(Early: 3300–2000 BCE, Middle: 2000–1550 BCE, Late: 1550–1150 BCE)

By the beginning of the Bronze Age people in Palestine were living in well-fortified, walled cities. Palestine was becoming urban, and urbanism changed the social structure of ancient society. As is true for most of the ancient Near East, people lived in tribal societies where everything was based on kinship relations. You were part of a tribe, the member of a family, and the son of your father. Now with true urbanism, you could (though not everyone was) also be associated with a city or town. It is from the archaeological excavation of these cities (called "tells") that we have been able to learn so much about the ancient peoples of Palestine – and one people in particular during this period.

By the beginning of the Middle Bronze Age a whole new and important culture, called Canaanite culture, took hold of the region. The majority of peoples in Canaan spoke the same Semitic language, made similar styles of pottery and weapons and art from bronze (for which the period is named), and shared the same religion of many gods, whose head god, famously, was El (mentioned in the Bible). Ancient people even referred to the population of the region as "Canaanite." The term is used consistently throughout the Bible, and it is found in archives from Syria, Egypt, and Mesopotamia dating to the Middle Bronze Age and later.[3] Remember the Canaanites because they remain important for much of the following.

Now, the Canaanites were not alone. Palestine has always been the crossroads of the Near East; people came and went, passing through from one region to the next. It was an especially busy place during the Bronze Age. The Amorites, from Syria, are one group that migrated in and may have had a particularly profound effect on the Canaanite way of life. Joining with the local population, they brought new types of architecture and new artistic traditions to Canaanite culture. Movement between Canaan and Egypt was also quite common during this period (indeed, throughout Palestine's history), and for some unknown reason, perhaps because of famine or even pressure from the Amorite migration, some Canaanites moved south into Lower Egypt (the Delta region). Once in the Delta, they managed to take control of it and rule for over a hundred years as what would be called the Hyksos or "foreign" Dynasty.

The history of this period is very important for biblical historians. Many, including one of the most famous and influential archaeologists to study ancient Palestine, William F. Albright,[4] attempted to place the stories of the biblical

"Semitic"

The term "Semitic" derives from the biblical table of nations where Noah's son Shem is said to be the father of Arabs, Babylonians, Assyrians, Aramaeans, and Hebrews (Gen. 10). Historically it has been applied both as a linguistic and a cultural term. As a linguistic term it describes, very well, the similarities among a particular family of languages spoken in the Middle East. The Semitic languages are among a branch of the Afro-Asiatic language family, which includes such languages as (in historical order): Akkadian, Phoenician, Hebrew, Aramaic, Ethiopic, and Arabic, among many other lesser known and ancient languages, such as Ugaritic and Proto-Sinaitic. It might seem strange to think that Hebrew, Ethiopic, and Arabic are all related languages. There are many differences between them, but overall, the grammar, syntax, system of writing (for example right to left), the sounds, and even some roots and words are the same. As a linguistic term Semitic is useful, as a cultural term it is not. The problem with using Semitic to describe a culture is that the cultures referred to as Semitic are so diverse. Though they speak similar languages, the people are not at all the same. Sometimes the term is used to designate Jews singularly, but often in a derogatory way, making the term, again, not very useful to describe a people and culture. The best way to avoid all of this is to use Semitic only as a linguistic term and refer to each distinct group of people as they wish to be called.

patriarchs, Abraham, Isaac, Jacob, and Joseph, in the Middle Bronze Age period. Abraham and his family's journey from Ur to Harran and then south to Canaan is often tied to the Amorite migration. At first it seems the journey of Abraham might fit that description very well – but unfortunately, it is not that easy. There is no proof that what we call the Middle Bronze Age is the period the biblical writers had in mind, and while it seems to make a suitable backdrop for Abraham's life, other periods would work just as well. Neither do superficial similarities between Abraham and the Amorites prove that a historical Abraham existed. Most scholars suggest that he is more likely a mythical or literary figure of tradition to be remembered for his moral lessons and religious piety. The story of the patriarch Joseph's enslavement and later high position under Pharaoh is often linked to Hyksos rule over Egypt. Here again, we are in the same situation as with the Abraham story. A historical Joseph may or may not have existed, and though the parallels are intriguing, as of yet, little more can be said. The same is true of the other patriarchal figures. That is not to deny their religious significance; faith, of course, requires one to look beyond proof.

Early Indications of Israel

The Late Bronze Age began with a reversal of Canaanite / Hyksos fortunes in Egypt and, indeed, Canaan as well. Egypt chased the Canaanite / Hyksos dynasty out of the Delta, sending them running back to Canaan, but the Egyptians did not stop there. Surprisingly, they invaded Canaan, bringing all of it under Egyptian control. Pharaoh only loosely ruled the region, but governors were placed in the major cities along with small armies. We learn from letters (on clay tablets) sent from these governors of Canaan back to Egypt, however, that some native Canaanites would not bow down to their Egyptian masters. They turned their backs on Egyptian-controlled Canaanite society to become what the Egyptians called "bandits and marauders" or *Hapiru* in the language of the letters.

The similarity between this name and "Hebrew" has not gone unnoticed – and here we enter into the mystery of the first Israelites and where they came from. There is no archaeological or textual proof this early on for the people soon to be known as Israelites, but there are some fascinating hints as to its origins. These letters are the first major breakthrough. The two names Hapiru / Hebrew, it turns out, are not synonymous. The range and context of Hapiru in most letters suggests it was not used singularly for one ethnic group.[5] But the possibility remains that the Israelites are somehow related to the Hapiru and that they might have been an offshoot or formed a unified group under similar circumstances.

The Late Bronze Age affords us other tantalizing indications of the Israelites' origins. The *Shasu* who roamed the deserts of southeastern Canaan are another important group we know from Egyptian sources. Much like the Hapiru, they too were considered marauders and bandits and a general nuisance for Egypt's routes north into Palestine. Most intriguing about the Shasu, however, is that they worshipped a god by the name of *YHW,* or Yahweh. Moreover, and equally intriguing, the Shasu land, later called Edom in the Bible, contains within its bounds the traditional site of Mount Sinai.[6] Can this be coincidence? Here may be found a source for later Israelite Yahwism, but how the god might have passed from Shasu to the Israelites remains uncertain. Some have suggested Edomite–Shasu clans migrated into Canaan bringing the deity Yahweh with them, and that this may have taken place during the Israelite Exodus from Egypt.

We need to touch on the Exodus for a moment since the Late Bronze Age is the period most often suggested for a historical setting to the story. It is probably the most famous story in the Bible and central to the development of Judaism. Moses leads the Hebrews out of slavery and through the desert to Canaan, the promised land of milk and honey. However, despite what some have tried to show, evidence for the Exodus has yet to be discovered. The extra-biblical sources are conspicuously silent. No proof has yet verified the events within Egypt, the forty years spent by the Hebrews wandering the desert, nor even the existence of the great lawgiver Moses.

The last clue for the early origins of the Israelites comes at the very end of the period and is the most significant. A Pharaoh of Egypt named Merneptah (r. 1237–1226 BCE) conducted a campaign into Canaan listing the cities he conquered on a stone tablet called a stele. Appearing among these many cities is the word "Israel" after which is the Egyptian symbol for a people or tribe. It is called the "Israel Stele," and here is the first solid evidence for a people called Israel – but again, it is only so helpful. We have in it only the occurrence of the name and a general location, but it is the first inkling of a people we learn a great deal more about in the following periods.

EARLY IRON AGE AND ISRAEL
(Iron Age I: 1150–900 BCE)

Egypt, suffering from political and economic problems, pulled out of Canaan at the end of the Late Bronze Age. With Egypt's departure, what is often described as a "power vacuum" (lack of a political power structure) was left for the remaining peoples to attempt to fill. It is at this juncture in history that the famous kingdoms of the Bible take shape and battle to control the region. Just to the east the kingdoms of Moab, Ammon, and Edom are forming, on the southern coast the Philistines appear, to the north are the Phoenicians, and in the Highlands the Israelites emerge.

The Late Bronze / Early Iron Age is the traditional period of Israelite tribal and political formation. It is with this historical setting in mind that scholars have tried to answer the major question: Who were the Israelites and where did they come from? For the past several decades there have been three reigning models. They are significantly different, but each of them attempts to describe where the Israelites came from and how Israel became a kingdom.

The *Conquest Model* and the *Peaceful Infiltration Model* are both based on traditional biblical history.[7] The *Conquest Model*, articulated most adamantly by Albright (again), suggests the Israelites existed as described in the Bible's patriarchal stories. They then came to Canaan during the Exodus and invaded the region pretty much as it is recorded in the Book of Joshua. Albright's argument is detailed and originally made great strides in the study of biblical history by relying on archaeological evidence – not just the Bible. He studied the archaeological remains of sites known to be the biblical cities conquered in Joshua and showed a similar pattern of destruction for many of them dated to around the end of the Late Bronze Age. Archaeologists have since reassessed Albright's evidence and proven his interpretation of the data wrong. New evidence may arise to rekindle Albright's model, but until then, most scholars deny it any validity.

The *Peaceful Infiltration Model*, on the other hand, relies on the history of Judges and Samuel and goes into a little more detail. While rooted in biblical history, it also relies on social theory as well as ethnographic studies of nomadic desert tribes. In this model the Israelites were nomads from the surrounding regions who, over time, peacefully entered the highlands of Canaan and became settled there. As Egyptian power waned, the kingdoms of Palestine, including the burgeoning Israelites, began to assert themselves. The Philistines dominated Canaan at the time and began to push into the highlands from the other direction. In reaction to the Philistine threat, the now-settled nomads formed a confederacy of twelve tribes, Israel, then a nation under a king, Saul. They defended their land and conquered the Philistines, whereupon the rest of central Canaan fell under their power.

The *Peasant Revolt Model*[8] is significantly different. It applied Marxist social theory to Israel's origin. Typical of Marxist theory, the *Peasant Revolt Model* casts the Israelites as a subclass of Canaanite peoples united by their religious belief in the god Yahweh. They lived much like the Hapiru mentioned earlier, until they had enough. For either social or religious reasons they revolted (think early twentieth-century Bolshevik Revolution in Russia) and took over the Canaanite city-states, eventually uniting them as the kingdom of Israel.

The *Peasant Revolt Model* has been the most influential on modern scholarship because it claims a Canaanite origin for the Israelites. Biblical interpretation and more recent assessments of the archaeological evidence have now led scholars to view the first Israelites as indigenous to Canaan – they were Canaanites. They probably fit the description of the Hapiru, a conglomerate of Canaanite peoples from many different backgrounds, who reacted against the social structure of the Canaanite city-states. Most see this process culminating in a new group of people who regarded themselves as different from their Canaanite predecessors. They broke away from their native Canaanite heritage and gathered in the highlands of Canaan – the traditional land of Israel and the most likely place referred to in the Israel Stele – forming the early Israelite tribal population and later organizing to become the kingdom of Israel.

Canaanites and Israelites

Once we enter the period of Israelite history the continuing history of other Canaanite peoples is often overlooked by scholars. It should not be forgotten. Canaanite culture did not simply disappear with the rise of Israel and in actuality remained vibrant throughout the region. While the Israelite kingdom ruled its slice of Canaan, and even thereafter, non-Israelite Canaanites still populated most of the land. They persisted alongside the Israelites – again originally Canaanites themselves – maintaining the old Canaanite religion and the old Canaanite culture. The Bible clearly portrays this in its numerous mentions of Canaanite gods worshipped over Yahweh and in prohibitions against Israelites mixing with Canaanites. The Canaanites also persisted in areas outside of Israel's control, forming their own kingdoms that were very much equal to Israel in size and strength, just as powerful and just as important. The Canaanite kingdoms were, very briefly: Aram, Phoenicia, Moab, Ammon, and Edom. With the

---

Canaanite Kingdoms

Aram: Aram was located to the north and controlled nearly all of modern-day Syria. Homeland of the Aramaeans, it was one of Israel's greatest foes until the end of the Northern Kingdom of Israel. The Aramaeans spoke a Semitic language called Aramaic, which became the major language of the Near East from the seventh century until the Hellenistic Period (discussed later).

Phoenicia: Located on the northern coast, the Phoenicians were close friends of the early Israelite kingdom. According to the Bible, they even helped to build Solomon's temple. The Phoenicians trade all over the Near East, spreading merchant colonies across the Mediterranean region, even as far west as Spain. Legend has it they also spread alphabetic writing, a Semitic invention, to the Greeks – from which is descended the English alphabet.

Moab: Located east of the Jordan River, the Moabites were constantly at odds with the Israelite kingdoms of Judah and Israel. Moab controlled one of the largest fertile plains in ancient Canaan and much of the trade with kingdoms further east.

Edom: Located to the south and east of Judah, Edom was home to the Edomites and the Shasu people discussed previously. Edom shared a close relationship with Judah and was ruled by Judah until it revolted in the late ninth century BCE. It had a famous trading port on the Red Sea, now modern Eilat, and was known for its copper mines.

Ammon: Located east of the Jordan River near the modern city of Amman, the Ammonites were among the Israelites' earliest enemies in the Bible. This kingdom controlled a major portion of ancient Near Eastern trade across the great deserts. Nearly all the trade from Arabia and points east passed through its lands.

Philistia: The Philistines are the exception. They have no relation to Canaanite culture, but upon their arrival they were major players in Palestine's history. An Aegean people (from the region of the Aegean Sea), bringing with them their own Aegean culture, they arrived on the southern coast of Canaan sometime in the twelfth century BCE.

addition of Philistia, a kingdom of Aegean peoples on the coast of Canaan, these kingdoms shared Palestine with Israel (see box: Canaanite Kingdoms).

Each of these many kingdoms was equal in power and struggled to gain the upper hand over the others. Surprisingly, they remained mostly autonomous until foreign empires swept in from the east. Since the history of Israel is the best known of the kingdoms, and remains central to the rest of the book, it will serve as the example for what happened to all the inhabitants of Canaan when empire came. That is not to say that all the kingdoms of Canaan had the same experience, but only that each had to cope with a loss of autonomy and rule by a foreign power, just as Israel did.

ISRAEL AND THE EMPIRES
(Iron Age II: 900–539 BCE)

Early Israelite Monarchy (1000–925 BCE)

The United Kingdom of Israel was short lived. It lasted through three kings – Saul, David, and Solomon. Saul is known for establishing the nation, David for conquering the lands, and Solomon as the great administrator and builder. At the death of Solomon, around 925 BCE, the United Kingdom split into the two new kingdoms of Judah (in the south) and Israel (in the north). Never again were they to be united. It is clear that they still viewed each other as having a common heritage, but for the most part, they went their separate ways.

Assyrian Empire (900–609 BCE)

Shortly after 1000 BCE the kingdom of Assyria (in modern-day Iraq) began its dramatic rise to power, eventually to rule over almost the whole of the Near East. By the end of the eighth century BCE, all the old kingdoms of Canaan were conquered or made vassals and subsumed into the greater Assyrian Empire. At its height it ruled over an area making up parts of the modern states of Turkey, Egypt, Palestine, Syria, Iraq, and Iran. Much of its power rested in the fear of its ruthlessness.

Perhaps most representative of Assyria's brutal politics are the last days of the northern kingdom of Israel. Israel attempted to revolt and in response its capital, Samaria, was sacked in 720 BCE.[9] The city was completely destroyed. Those who were captured by the Assyrians were transported to Assyria and "the cities of Media" (modern-day Iran). Assyrian annals record 27,290 Israelites sent into exile at this time.[10] Israel was turned into an Assyrian province to be called Samerina and was repopulated with a mix of other conquered peoples over several years including Babylonians, Aramaeans, some "distant Arab tribes," and Philistines.[11]

A short time later Judah also attempted revolt (701 BCE). Luckily, it faced less dire consequences. Jerusalem, the capital of Judah, was not destroyed, but it was forced to pay out a huge tribute including silver and gold from the Jerusalem temple treasury.[12] Hezekiah, king of Judah, was left on his throne but large chunks of his kingdom were handed out to the Philistine city-states. The major city in Judah, Lachish, was sacked, a feat Sennacherib, king of Assyria, took great pride in. He devoted the relief-work of an entire room to the siege in his "palace without rival" in Nineveh. By the seventh century BCE a brief "Pax Assyrica" (Assyrian peace) under the dominion of the empire graced the region.

Neo-Babylonian Empire (612–539 BCE)

The quiet ended when the ancient and powerful city of Babylon (in modern-day Iraq) revolted from under the Assyrians. The Babylonians gradually gained ground and allies. The Assyrian Empire tried to defend itself but it had grown too large to control; it began to crumble and finally succumbed to the Babylonians in 612 BCE. The whole empire was taken over by the Babylonians without much trouble, at first.

Back in Palestine, Judah, seeing its chance, made an unsuccessful attempt to revolt against Babylon in 586 BCE. This time the outcome would be remembered as one of the most tragic events in Jewish history. In response, the Babylonians sacked Jerusalem, and the Temple to Yahweh built by King Solomon was destroyed. With the fall of Judah comes the end of the Israelite kingdoms. A large part of the population of Judah was transported to Babylon, and so began the period known in Jewish history as the Exile. The people continued on, only now primarily as a religious community. It is a formative period for Judaism, responsible for much of the codification of law and practice in the religion.

Persian Empire (539–332 BCE)

The Neo-Babylonian Empire did not last long. Cyrus "the Great," king of Persia, rose up in revolt and was able to take over the Babylonian Empire intact. It was good news for the exiled Israelites: they were allowed to return to Judah and to rebuild the Temple to Yahweh.[13] Traditionally, upon their return to Judah, they were called "Jews" – this is where the modern name originates. Judah, originally having no clear boundaries, became the highly administrated province of Judaea, extending over most of what is now modern Palestine.

The Jews shared Judaea with a host of other peoples whom had been transported there, or had moved there on their own accord over the previous few hundred years. The most predominant group was the Edomites, who had moved north when the Jews were exiled. There was a great deal of unrest between the two and throughout the region as peoples from all different lands butted heads over territory and trade. Persian administration of the empire, thick with bureaucracy, had broken down any further chance of the ancient kingdoms of Palestine, and the rest of the ancient Near East, returning to power. Ancient Near Eastern culture was being homogenized and by the Persian period identity had become an issue. As one prominent historian puts it:

> The country [Palestine] was populated by different groups of people who had lost their national identity, such as Philistines, Judahites, Samarians (including former Israelites and peoples that had been settled in Samerina by the Assyrians), Moabites, Ammonites, Edomites, Arabs, and in western and northern parts of the country the Phoenicians....[14]

After hundreds of years of rule by empire, the collapse and destruction of city-states and kingdoms, and the transportation of populations, a loss of national identity seems quite natural. Here too also marks the end of Canaanite culture. The old ways, Canaanite religion, language, art, architecture, and all else that once marked its originality disappeared to make way for the domination of Persian and, only a few centuries away, Greek and Roman cultures. Certainly some cultural distinctions remained intact, and religious identity would yet remain, especially for the Jews, but in the following period a great deal of assimilation takes place and indeed, is encouraged.

GREEK AND ROMAN PALESTINE

Alexander the Great and Hellenism (330–67 BCE)

Friction between the Persians and the Greeks brought to the fold one of the most memorable figures in ancient history, Alexander the Great. Alexander crossed from Macedonia, Greece into Asia in 334 BCE. Cutting his way through Persian territory, he conquered lands from Greece to Egypt and the borders of India. He brought his Greek culture with him, making concerted efforts to meld it with the different cultures of the peoples he conquered.

Shortly after Alexander's death (323 BCE) his generals sectioned up the empire, assuming first a "protectorate" role and then finally regressing into all-out war with one another for control of larger territories. The most important generals in the region of our concern were Antigonus, who took all of western Asia Minor (modern Turkey); Ptolemy, who took Egypt; and Seleucus, who eventually took all the region of greater Syria that was made to include Judaea. Over forty years of warring ensued until each new dynasty's territorial claims were recognized.[15]

These kings made conspicuous attempts to "hellenize" (make more Greek) the people in their territories. Hellenization under the Seleucid (Seleucus's) Empire had a profound effect on the native philosophy, religion, and culture of Palestine. Certain aspects of hellenization were willingly accepted and adopted by the people, but others were completely unacceptable – no matter how sternly they were imposed. One Seleucid king, Antiochus IV Epiphanes (r. 175–164 BCE) attempted to ban elements of Judaism altogether, even forcing sacrifice to pagan Greek gods at the Jewish Temple to Yahweh. This, coupled with the debilitating socio-economic conditions in rural Palestine at the time, led to the first of many Jewish revolts.

The Hasmonean Dynasty (166–37 BCE)

Judas Maccabeus ("the Hammer"), of the Jewish Hasmonean clan, led this first major revolt against the Seleucids. Their battles and diplomatic efforts are described in the books of Maccabees I–II. In brief, he and his followers fared well, eventually reclaiming Jerusalem in 164 BCE. One of their first tasks was to cleanse and rededicate the Temple to Yahweh, an event of great significance still celebrated every year by Jews as the feast of Hanukah. The Hasmoneans were able to carve out a small state of their own within the larger bounds of Judaea in an attempt to regain Jewish independence. Modern scholars call this the period of the Hasmonean Kingdom. It should be remembered, however, that the Seleucid Empire dominated the rest of Syria and Palestine, and control of the Hasmonean regions moved back and forth between the two powers for most of the second century BCE.

At the same time they were fighting with the Seleucids, the Hasmoneans were corresponding with the Romans. The Romans took a direct interest in the Hasmonean kingdom and its politics. Over the next half-century, as the Seleucid Empire finally collapsed, the Romans came to the fore.

Rome and Judaea (67 BCE–330 CE)

Between 67 and 63 BCE, Pompey of Rome took control of Syria (including Judaea) from the Seleucids without raising a finger. He entered Palestine shortly thereafter to quell a revolt led by the last of the would-be Hasmonean kings, and Judaea was made a client state. At the same time, back in Rome several parties were vying for control of the empire. Pompey and

Julius Caesar were the first to clash. Caesar won out, but after only a brief respite he was assassinated in 44 BCE. With Caesar dead another struggle for the Roman Empire took place, this time between Caesar's supporters Mark Antony and Octavian. Octavian would eventually become the first Roman Emperor, Augustus. In the middle of this chaos a civil war erupted among the remaining Hasmonean family over the position of high priest in Jerusalem. The Romans intervened again. This time they installed a king, Herod "the Great," in 37 BCE as king over all the territory of the Jews.

Herod was the son of the Roman Procurator (an employee of the Roman emperor in civil affairs), Antipater, and early on curried favor first with Mark Antony and the Roman senate, and later with Octavian. Herodian rule inaugurated some of the most grandiose building projects ever attempted in Palestine, many of which are still visible today. His palace-fortress at Masada and his renovation of the Jewish Temple to Yahweh in Jerusalem (it wasn't grand enough for Herod) are the two most cited examples.

At his death, Herod's kingdom was split among his family. Archelaus (r. 4 BCE–6 CE) received the largest territory but was later deposed for his brutality. His territory was transferred to a Roman Procurator who now controlled all the lands of the region, and Judaea was absorbed, as a minor province, into the larger Roman province of Syria. There would be no more Jewish kings.

It is in this setting that the life and teachings of Jesus of Nazareth took place. The revolutionary Nazarene and his followers should be viewed as one of many groups in Judaea reacting against poor treatment under Roman rule and the romanization–hellenization of Jewish culture. The more violent revolutionary groups were the Zealots and Sicarii. Their resistance to Roman rule eventually led to the outbreak of the first Jewish war against Rome (66–74 CE). The Jewish revolutionaries were brutally suppressed. When their main stronghold, the fortress at Masada built earlier by King Herod, was finally breached, many Jews committed suicide rather than be taken alive by the Romans. Jerusalem was also sacked in the name of Rome, and, most tragic of all, as a final act of retaliation the Jewish Temple to Yahweh, built in the Persian period and renovated by King Herod, was burned to the ground. All that remains now is the temple platform and its visible Western Wall (also called the "Wailing Wall," or in Hebrew the "Kotel"); it is Judaism's most sacred site and remains a place of pilgrimage and prayer for Jews all over the world.

Things remained relatively quiet until around 130 CE, when the Emperor Hadrian visited Palestine intent on rebuilding Jerusalem in the mold of a Greco-Roman city and to ban the Jewish practice of circumcision once and for all. It was a new and unappreciated attempt at hellenizing the region. To top it all off economic disparities were already high, stirring the people again to revolution. The second and last major Jewish war against Rome (132–135 CE) broke out under the charismatic leadership of Bar Kochba (sometimes called the Bar Kochba Revolt). It is uncertain whether the whole of Palestine took part, but Judaea was certainly at its center, and it paid a heavy price. The revolt was suppressed, but in a particularly bloody manner. Some scholars estimate that two-thirds of the Jewish population of Judaea was annihilated. The final result was that Jerusalem became a completely hellenized, Gentile (non-Jewish) city, rebuilt and renamed Aelia Capitolina. Jews were barred from entering the new city by imperial decree and threat of death. The Jews were scattered throughout the empire, eventually as far as Europe – thus beginning what is known as the Jewish diaspora (dispersion of people from their homeland). As a final insult, a shrine to Jupiter was built on the old site of the Temple to Yahweh in Jerusalem, and in the year 139 CE the name for the minor province of Roman Judaea was changed to Palaestina, from which comes the modern name Palestine. The following hundred years saw a codification of both Judaism and Christianity. The Jews wrote down their oral laws and commentary on the law in a book called the Talmud, and the Christians compiled the gospels and epistles into what became the New Testament. At the same time the Roman Empire was in decay and appeared headed for collapse. Between 235 and 275 CE Rome had 37 different emperors. It was the leadership of several emperors that revived the flagging empire, but one in particular changed the empire for good.

The Byzantine Empire (330 CE to the rise of Islam)

The Emperor Constantine (r. 313–337) brought order to the chaos of Rome's collapse by reordering the empire from the ground up. Perhaps his most famous innovation was to move the capital of the Roman Empire to a more central location – a smart move since Rome was now in charge of much of the Near East. Power over the empire was transferred from Rome to the city of Byzantium (hence the name Byzantine Empire), located on the Bosporus Straits (modern-day Turkey), around 330 CE, and eventually called Constantinople in honor of the emperor. He also took a special interest in Christianity; it was rumored he had a vision where he was directed to put the sign of the cross on his army's shields – he won every battle thereafter. Christianity was popular, but it was a bit surprising to the Romans to find the emperor promoting it to the status of a full-fledged, legal Roman religion (the Edict of Milan). The other pagan gods were still worshipped, but now Christianity had achieved the seal of Roman authority. It was no longer the religion of the poor, and its followers would no longer be hounded by imperial persecution (with a few exceptions). With the Christians in charge, the Jews of the empire were subject to yet more persecution, this time for the crucifixion of Jesus, but it was not constant, and at other times the Jews were granted quite a bit of autonomy. Palestine usually prospered under the Byzantine Empire. Jerusalem was hailed as the center for Christianity with Rome taking second place. Christian monuments began popping up all over Jerusalem. It was during this time that the site of Jesus's crucifixion and the remains of the true cross were discovered by Constantine's mother, Helena; the Church of the Holy Sepulchre was built on the site and still stands today. For the most part the Byzantine Empire remained relatively stable during its primacy with only the occasional war for more territory with the Persian Empire to the east – that is, until the rise of the Arab tribes and the new religion Islam, which was to become the leading faith in the region.

SUMMARY AND CONCLUSIONS

In view of what we now know about ancient Palestine, a few important points should be made in summary. First, the Palestine–Israel conflict is not thousands of years old. There is certainly no "blood feud" between Arabs and Jews dating back to the sons of Abraham. Secondly, the variety of cultures and the dramatic degree to which cultures have changed over time should also now be apparent. From the Canaanites to the Romans, these are the roots of ancient Palestinian and Jewish culture. Thirdly, Jews, the descendants of the ancient Israelites, are as such also descendants of the ancient Canaanites, the peoples of Canaan, now modern Palestine. And indeed, by one name or other, the Jews have populated the land for thousands of years. But, what we have not yet emphasized and what needs to be made explicit, is that the native Palestinians of today are also descendants of the ancient Canaanites. "Palestinian" is a regional ethnic term for a people who have lived in the land of Palestine for thousands of years, from Canaanite to Phoenician or Moabite or Edomite, etc., to the same people under Roman, then Greek, then Byzantine, and then Arab occupation, intermarrying with these other populations, but continuing on just the same. The Palestinian–Arab culture of today is a result of a later seventh–century influx of Arab tribes who brought with them the religion of Islam, Arabic culture, language, and the intermixing of Arab peoples with the population of Palestine – all of this will be discussed in the following chapter. But modern Arab Palestinians are, in effect, also originally descendants of the indigenous Canaanite population that continued in time alongside the first Israelites, then the Jews, and then the Roman–Judaeans of ancient Palestine, into modern history. The Palestinians are descendants of the ancient Canaanites – by a different name and a different culture – just as are the Jews. I choose to emphasize this relationship to show first, that for a long time

Israel and the other Canaanites lived in relative peace, and second, that both Jews and Palestinians have viable ancient claims to the land – in essence the same claim – that, indeed, converge in the ancient past.

Suggested Reading

For a strongly biblical interpretation of Palestine's history, consider Hershel Shanks, ed., *Ancient Israel: from Abraham to the Roman destruction of the temple* (Washington, DC: Biblical Archaeology Society, 1999). A valuable work focusing on archaeology in Palestine is Amihai Mazar, *Archaeology of the Land of the Bible: 10,000–586 BCE* (New York, NY: Doubleday, 1992). For a classic review of biblical interpretation and history, see J. Maxwell Miller and John H. Hayes, *A History of Ancient Israel and Judah* (Philadelphia, PA: The Westminster Press, 1986). Helpful studies on the origins of Israel include: John J. McDermott, *What Are They Saying About the Formation of Israel?* (Mahwah, NJ: Paulist Press, 1998); and William G. Dever, *Who Were the Early Israelites and Where Did They Come From?* (Grand Rapids, MI: William B. Eerdmans Publishing Co., 2003). A work on the Canaanites worth looking at is Jonathan N. Tubb, *Canaanites* (Norman, OK: University of Oklahoma Press, 1998). For a challenging but eye-opening placement of the ancient narrative in a modern context, see Keith W. Whitelam, *The Invention of Ancient Israel* (London, New York: Routledge, 1996).

2

Muhammad, Islam, and the Arab Empire

Note: As we saw in Chapter 1, there wasn't much mention of Arabs, as they don't make their way into the eastern Mediterranean portion of the Middle East until after Muhammad and the founding of Islam, which we will cover in this chapter. However, the Arabs were always present in the history of ancient Palestine, but primarily as itinerant traders and artisans, moving from the Arabian Peninsula (modern-day Saudi Arabia) along trade routes north in Palestine. Early possible reference to an Arabian tribe in Palestine is the story of the queen of Sheba, probably a Sabaean queen from southern Arabia, paying a visit to King Solomon (1 Kings 10:1–10). The first clear mention of Arabian tribes in history is in Assyrian and Babylonian texts. These suggest Arab populations moving all over the place during the first millennium. By all accounts, however, it is not until after the seventh century CE that the Arabs take a leading role in Palestine's history, as we will now see.

PRE-ISLAMIC ARABIA

Most considerations of the Arab Middle East are subsumed within its religious context (Islam). But although rarely regarded, the history of the Arabs before the emergence of Muhammad and the Islamic faith (more on that later) is a rich and interesting one that sets the stage for everything we know as "Middle Eastern" or "Muslim" or "Arabian."

Most likely a group who share ancestry with the Semitic peoples mentioned in the first chapter – the Hapiru, the Amorites, etc. – no one is totally certain where the Arabs came from, or when they appeared as a distinct group. According to scripture and legend the Arabs are descendants of Ishmael, who was the son of Abraham and his maid Hagar; his wife Sarah was having difficulty bearing him a son, but then finally gave birth to Isaac. But for the purposes of this book, an effort will be made to stay as close to archaeological evidence as possible, in which case we'll have to shrug our shoulders a little for lack of evidence.

Our discussion of the Arabs begins on the Arabian Peninsula, what its inhabitants sometimes refer to as *Jazirat al-'Arab*, "the Island of the Arabs."[1] Though a peninsula in actuality, if one considers the northern region that connects Arabia to modern-day Iraq and Jordan – the Nufud desert – it might as well *be* water. It is here that we encounter people engaged in two distinct styles of living in an otherwise frequently unforgiving environment: settled people living by means of agriculture, and nomadic pastoralists.

The latter group, known as the Bedouin, could be considered the Arabian in his quintessential form. These tribes of nomads roaming the Arabian Peninsula from oasis to oasis are the embodiment of adaptation to desert life. It was the domestication of the camel that allowed the Bedouin to travel deep into the punishing deserts of Arabia. A process that took place between 3000 and 1000 BCE, the domestication of the Arabian dromedary (one-humped camel) created the ideal animal companion. With its padded feet, short body-hair, a storage of reserve fat in its hump, and its ability to drink 25 gallons of water in half as many minutes – and then rely on it for days on end, up to five in the summer and 25 in the winter – this creature provided the Bedouin with a full-service vehicle. Historian Philip K. Hitti elucidates just how full-service they were:

> It is the Bedouin's constant companion, his *alter ego*, his foster parent. He drinks its milk instead of water (which he spares for the cattle); he feasts on its flesh; he covers himself with its skin; he makes his tent of its hair. Its dung he uses as fuel, and its urine as a hair tonic and medicine.[2]

So it was that the Bedouin navigated the desert, moving from one oasis to the next, subsisting on a diet of dates, milk, and the meat produced from their herds of goats and sheep (collectively referred to as *ghanam*).[3] With this minimal lifestyle, the Bedouin Arab never took much interest in cultural pursuits such as painting or architecture, but poetry on the other hand is something that dwelt deep within his heart and soul.

> The beauty of man lies in the eloquence of his tongue.
>
> *old Arab adage*[4]

Sometimes referred to as the public register, or *diwan*, of the Arabs, pre-Islamic poetry was an expression of all aspects of nomadic desert life. The Bedouin poet, never putting his verses on paper, captured, orally recorded, and thus archived, the "expression of their collective memory."[5] One poetic form worthy of note is that of the *qasida*, or ode, which was up to one hundred lines long and rather complicated in its various metering. It was in these odes that tales of travel, battles, love lost, and the Bedouin's relationship with the desert were thus recorded and handed down the generations. Also in these poems was the expression of what is called *muruwwah*:

> ... bravery in battle, patience in misfortune, persistence in revenge (the only justice possible at a time when no governments existed), protection of the weak, defiance toward the strong, hospitality to the visitor (even a total stranger), generosity to the poor, loyalty to the tribe, and fidelity in keeping promises. These were the moral principles that people needed in order to survive in the desert, and the verses helped to fix the *muruwwah* in their minds.[6]

Superlative examples of Bedouin poetry (of those that have survived) have been named the "suspended poems," or *Mu'allaqat*, which were later collected as the "Seven Golden Odes" and eventually appeared in English. Considered masterpieces of the art form, these poems were, legend has it, awarded the highest honor at the Fair of Ukaz.[7] The twenty-day fair at Ukaz was an annual event where poets would exhibit, compete, and test their prowess in the art. This festival took place in the early spring of the lunar calendar when fighting was taboo, and also featured trade, commerce, and exhibitions of various kinds.

It being pre-Islamic Arabia, one might wonder who, or what, the people of Arabia were worshipping. Among the sedentary people along the west coast, as well as various tribes throughout the peninsula, there was a small presence of Judaism and a number of sects of Christianity. For most Arabs of the time, both desert and oasis alike were populated with deities, sacred objects, and demons, or *jinn*. Particular practices and beliefs in this pagan animism varied. Regarding their degree of spirituality, the sedentary Arabs had far more developed belief systems than their nomadic neighbors. The Bedouin tends to be religious up to a point, but has a low tolerance for gods and deities that fail to cooperate. In the words of Hitti, "religion sits very lightly indeed on his heart."[8]

Let's pull back for a moment. The above description of Arabia holds accurate for at least a few thousand years. Over these few thousand years we cross the threshold of the eras, from BCE to CE. At this threshold, Jesus of Nazareth is being born, and the empires of Rome and Persia (Iran) are large and dominant. The Persians, ruled by the Sasanids, held sway over the area of today's Iran, Iraq, Afghanistan, and Pakistan. The Romans, on the other hand, after moving their capital from Rome to the "new Rome" or Constantinople in 330, exerted their fair share of power over the Middle East as well.[9] With Arabia stuck in the middle of this, obviously there were some points of contact and a degree of cultural exchange between these powers. Ethiopia, to the southwest of Arabia in Africa, also possessed a significant amount of power, which also added to the mix. Now each of these powers – Rome, Persia, and Ethiopia – paid a client tribe for military assistance. As a result, this created a good deal of fighting in the peninsula between the three client tribes of the outside powers. It was against this socio-political backdrop that the Prophet Muhammad arrived and would one day be known to the followers of Islam as "the Seal of the Prophets."

Islam

Islam (meaning "surrender" or "submission") is one of the largest religions in the world, second in size only to Christianity. Its 1.3 billion followers, or Muslims, devote themselves to Allah (God, or "the one") and study of the Qur'an, Islam's sacred text. The word of God was made available via revelations channeled through the archangel Gabriel to the Prophet Muhammad. For Muslims, the prophethood of Muhammad is a continuation of the prophetic traditions also found in Judaism and Christianity: Adam, Abraham, Moses, and Jesus (all of whom appear in the Qur'an). The act of submission to Allah is carried out through practice of the Five Pillars of Islam: (1) *shehadah*, or the profession that "there is no god but God; Muhammad is the Prophet of God"; (2) *salah*, the five daily prayers performed while facing toward Mecca, the birthplace of Muhammad and holiest city of Islam; (3) *zakat*, or almsgiving to the poor and underprivileged; (4) *sawm*, the month-long holiday of dawn-until-dusk fasting called Ramadan; and (5) the annual pilgrimage, or *hajj*, to the Great Mosque in Mecca, required of every Muslim at least once in their lives, though lenience toward the poor is granted.

MUHAMMAD

On the west coast of Arabia, in the town of Mecca, around the year 570, Abu al-Qasim Muhammad ibn Abd Allah ibn Abd al-Muttalib ibn Hashim was born. This being his full name, he is simply known as Muhammad. His father, Abd-Allah, died before the young Muhammad was born, which left the grandfather, Abd al-Muttalib, who was head of the clan of Hashim (a branch of the ruling Quraysh tribe), as the child's guardian. Muhammad's mother, as was customary among Meccan families, sent the young Muhammad away to spend a couple years in the healthy climate of the desert, under the care of a wet-nurse, to live and travel with the Bedouin. At the age of six, the young Muhammad lost his mother, and two years later his grandfather died. Left an orphan, Muhammad was then under the care of his uncle, Abu-Talib, who became the new head of the Hashemite clan. Abu-Talib, a caravan merchant, took the young Muhammad on journeys into Syria where the boy learned the ropes of commerce and trade. But learn as he did, being an orphan in Mecca left one with few options for upward mobility. The social fabric of Mecca was such that, unlike the Bedouin, people were left to their own devices in an "every man for himself" set of circumstances. Beyond having enough to eat, Muhammad had no capital to launch him on any kind of career. In short: he was stuck.

But as luck would have it, and perhaps accompanied by a bit of intent given his situation, Muhammad met a moneyed woman by the name of Khadija while on a trade journey in his mid-twenties. Khadija entrusted her caravan to Muhammad and, being so impressed with his honesty and skill, proposed marriage to him. (No, this was not customary.) It is estimated that Muhammad was 25 years old, and fifteen years her junior. Despite her age, she bore him six children, four daughters and two sons, both of whom died in infancy. Muhammad never took any other wives during his relationship with Khadija.

Muhammad now had things in order: a wife he loved and the money he needed. But with these needs met and the attendant sense of stability that goes with it, Muhammad still found himself lacking a sense of fulfillment. Having endured the hardships of his youth and now seeing Mecca through adult eyes, he grew disturbed and dismayed with the condition of his society. In stark contrast to the familial solidity of the Bedouin clans lay a Mecca of materialism, greed, and ravenous individualism. This weighed heavy on Muhammad's heart. In an attempt to sort through his thoughts and feelings, Muhammad took to meditating in a cave in the hills near his neighborhood. During one of his moments of meditation, around the year 610, a strange feeling came over Muhammad. He had a vision of an angelic being and heard a voice:

> Recite in the name of your Lord who created – created man from clots of blood.
> Recite! Your Lord is the Most Bountiful One, who by the pen taught man what he did not know.
>
> (Qur'an 96:1–5)[10]

Understandably, Muhammad was unsettled by this experience and ran home to Khadija, where she assuaged his fears and covered him with a coat. Khadija consulted a cousin of hers, who reassured her that Muhammad was not in a state of madness but, on the contrary, had experienced revelations from God. With this steadfast support at home, Muhammad found the confidence and resolve to heed the revelations spoken to him by the being whom Muhammad later identified as the archangel Gabriel. (A point to consider: it is common for women in Arab countries to play an extremely subservient role, but it was a woman's wisdom and support that was probably responsible for Muhammad embarking on his life as a prophet in the first place.) For the rest of his life, Muhammad would frequently receive such revelations, the accumulation of which would later become what is known as the Qur'an.

By 613 Muhammad was preaching to the public and proselytizing his fellow Meccans. He developed a small following initially. Most of Muhammad's followers were young men in their twenties and thirties who were from middle-class families. As his following grew and his influence strengthened, the leading families of the Quraysh tribe grew irritable with Muhammad and his preaching. Posing a threat to their power and their financial interests, the Quraysh began to make Muhammad feel unwelcome in Mecca. The heat continued to rise. In addition, in 619 Khadija and Abu-Talib both died. Losing his strongest sources of support, Muhammad was rendered vulnerable. It was time to leave Mecca.

During the pagan pilgrimage to the Ka'bah in 620, Muhammad was approached by some men from Yathrib (eventually known as Medina), an oasis about 200 miles north of Mecca. These men expressed their support and faithfulness, promising to return to Yathrib and pave the way for the Prophet's arrival. By September 24, 622, Muhammad and about 70 followers emigrated to Yathrib. This emigration, or *hijrah* (which also translates as "the severing of kinship ties"), marks the beginning of Islamic history, falling on the precise date July 16, 622.

Once settled in at Yathrib, the name of the oasis was changed to Medina (*madinat al-nabi*, "the city of the Prophet"). Initially, Muhammad acted as an arbiter settling disputes between a few of the pagan tribes of Medina. He was a skilled politician and was known for his honesty. But in this early period there were trials and tribulations more daunting for the Prophet

---

Qur'an

The Qur'an (meaning "recital" or "recitation"; also spelled Koran) is, for Muslims, the infallible word of God as it was communicated by the angel Gabriel to Muhammad. The text is composed of 114 chapters, or *surahs*, which contain the various revelations. The *surahs* are generally organized according to size, in order of decreasing length; the shorter *surahs* at the end of the book are some of the earlier revelations. Functioning as a source of moral and spiritual inspiration, the Qur'an's teachings addressed the social ills of Arabia in Muhammad's time. Treatment of orphans, women, and the underprivileged are addressed, along with the severe rampant corruption in Mecca.

> ... the Quran places the chief emphasis on the religious aspect of the troubles of Mecca. It calls on men to acknowledge the power and goodness of God their Creator and to worship Him. Thereby they will be denying the omnipotence and the omni-competence of the wealthy man. The Quran thus provides a corrective – a more satisfying corrective – to the 'presumption' and 'pride in wealth' which it regards as the root of the materialistic humanism underlying the social malaise of the times.[11]

It must be remembered that the Qur'an was not assembled until decades after Muhammad's death. Ever since, the Qur'an has been considered the superlative model of classical Arabic prose.

---

than presiding over feuds. The Muslim emigrants that came with Muhammad from Mecca were not skilled in agriculture, and Medina's economy was almost solely based on crops of dates, cereals, etc. In an effort to pull their own weight and support themselves while living in Medina, the emigrants took to raiding Meccan caravans – another skill they lacked, being from a sedentary culture. Most of these raids were dismal failures, but with practice they began to accrue successes.

Also a matter of significance was Muhammad's "break with the Jews." Of the eleven or so clans that made up Medina, three were Jewish, and at one time they had had control

---

Ka'bah

In Islam's holiest city of Mecca, and in Mecca's holiest mosque – the Great Mosque – lies Islam's holiest object, the Ka'bah. Arabic for "cube," the Ka'bah predates Islam, previously serving as a place of pagan worship, and is believed to have been built by Adam, and then rebuilt by Abraham. When Muslims face Mecca to pray five times a day, it is toward the Ka'bah that they are facing.

of Yathrib. Though distinct by their adherence to Judaism, these Jews were probably indistinguishable from any of the other clans in Medina at the time.[12] It was with respect that Muhammad viewed Christians and Jews, recognizing them as "People of the Book." Believing himself to be a continuation of the Abrahamic pedigree, or lineage – Abraham, Moses, Jesus – Muhammad looked to these Jews as potential supporters. Some indications of deference shown to these clans at the time were the observance of the Jewish fast of Yom Kippur, or the Day of Atonement, and Muhammad's choice of Jerusalem as the Muslim *qiblah*, the direction in which one faced during prayer. But despite Muhammad's efforts, the Jewish clans were never quite convinced of his prophethood and challenged the legitimacy of his preaching. Eventually, Muhammad would change the *qiblah* to Mecca (where it remains today) and exchange the fast of Yom Kippur for the month-long fast of Ramadan. Muhammad's break with the three Jewish clans was a political and strategic maneuver motivated by the dissent from these clans, along with the support provided by them to a number of Muhammad's enemies. This rift would eventually result in the expulsion of two of them (the Qaynuqa and an-Nadir clans). The fate of the third, the Qurayzah clan, was rather worse. The men were executed and the women and children sold into slavery. Other much smaller groups of Jews were allowed to remain.

Some readers learning of this event may do so with raised eyebrows, thinking: "Aha! So *that's* the beginning of the conflict between the Jews and the Arabs!" Well, no. But first and foremost, this event concerning the Qurayzah clan is historically verified and cannot be ignored. However, it should be remembered that in seventh-century Arabia, tribal and clan warfare was quite common. Yet, by all accounts this sort of policy was rare for Muhammad. The whole purpose of his preaching was to unite the people of Arabia and move society away from this sort of barbarism. Then, such acts in ancient Arabia were perpetrated with the general understanding that they might generate a response; attacks took the form of a challenge. Most instances where people were shown "mercy" were actually carried out to avoid retaliation. Muhammad, in this event, caused little shock in his brutality, but surprised everyone by his fearlessness of reprisal.

In March 628, Muhammad decided to make a pilgrimage to Mecca with roughly 1,500 men. They made their way to Hudaybiya, just north of Mecca, where they were met by a defensive Meccan military presence, acting under the assumption that Muhammad possessed hostile intentions. A truce was established between the two sides and the Muslims were allowed to return the following year for the pilgrimage. After the pilgrimage in 628, allies of Mecca attacked allies of Muhammad. Deeming this a breach of the Hudaybiya treaty, in January 630 Muhammad advanced on Mecca with a force of 10,000. Overwhelmed by this show of force, Mecca allowed Muhammad to enter and occupy the city, which he did peacefully, meeting almost no resistance. Without Muhammad's insistence, most Meccans converted to Islam. With this major victory and a series of smaller ones, Muhammad's power grew exponentially. By the end of 630 Muhammad led the strongest military force in Arabia, now predominantly Islamic and unified with its capital in Medina.

By 632 Muhammad's health was failing, though he did manage to lead the pilgrimage to Mecca in that year. It would be his last and has come to be known as the "pilgrimage of farewell." On June 8, 632, in the presence of his wife Aisha, Muhammad died. Abu-Bakr, Muhammad's best friend and Aisha's father, is quoted as saying: "O ye people, if anyone worships Muhammad, Muhammad is dead, but if anyone worships God, He is alive and dies not."[13]

THE ARAB EMPIRE

With the passing of Muhammad, his followers found themselves uncertain what to do. Having no sons who lived past infancy, the Prophet was left without a successor. And leaving in place no system of administration or organization, the Muslim community needed someone to replace Muhammad. It was Abu-Bakr who was chosen to be the Prophet's successor, or caliph (which comes from *khalifa* in Arabic, meaning "to succeed").

The caliph was not a prophet and did not receive revelations. He was merely a leader of the community. Abu-Bakr (r. 632–634) was confronted almost exclusively with administrative and political issues, both of which grew quite difficult with the passing of Muhammad. The solidity of the Muslim community quickly degenerated into chaos and infighting. Abu-Bakr, and his successor Umar (r. 634–644) implemented a tried and true notion: the best way to create solidarity is to focus the group's attention outside itself. This was achieved by moving north to conquer lands held by the Byzantine and Persian empires. With the fighting that had been going on between the two empires they were both greatly weakened and their territories were ripe for the picking. In a decade the Arab armies won control of Rome's Middle Eastern holdings: Palestine, Syria, Egypt, and Cyrenaica (a region in the eastern portion of modern-day Libya). The Persian Empire would eventually fall and all its provinces acquired by the Arabs. In the matter of a century, the Arab Empire stretched from Spain (its westernmost territory), across North Africa and the whole of the Middle East, to the western border of China. Over the course of the Rashidun caliphate (comprised of the first four caliphs, known as "the rightly guided" caliphs) and two main dynasties, the Umayyad and the Abbasid (sometimes referred to as the High Caliphate),[14] the Arab Empire retained its power for over six centuries. The Abbasids were in power from 750 to 1258. However, after the relatively unified rule of the Umayyads (661–750) and some 200 years into the Abbasid era (950), things were winding down and the empire was becoming fractured and disintegrated. The empire as it stood from Abu-Bakr to the tenth century is a story of frequent revolts, dissent, assassinations, and more revolts. But what happened culturally during this time was something quite noteworthy.

The invaders of the desert brought with them no tradition of learning, no heritage of culture, to the lands they conquered. In Syria, in Egypt, in al-'Iraq, in Persia, they sat as pupils at the feet of the peoples they subdued.[15]

Coming from a rather unsophisticated and simple, but not barbaric, style of living, the Arabs made their way into these foreign lands and encountered highly cultured societies and happened upon classical literature, Hellenistic thought, Byzantine institutions, Roman law, Syriac scholarship, and Persian art.

> At first these resources were appropriated directly, with little reshaping. Before long, however, they were more selectively utilized, combined into novel patterns that served as both resources and stimulus to creative Muslim scholarship. The result was not simply a montage of bits and pieces of disparate culture. It was a new creation with its own distinctive pattern, infused with a new spirit and expressing a new social order.[16]

So the mission of the Muslims was not domination in the sense of one power moving in and exerting total control and subjugating the native populations. The Arabs had entered Persia, Spain, Africa, and the Middle East and established a synthesis between their pan-Islamic intentions of expansion and the cultural and intellectual resources of the people they were conquering. What resulted was that the diverse and varied cultures spanning the territory of the empire came into contact with one another by virtue of being under the same rule. Their cultural practices – music, art, science, and literature – were no longer confined to a specific region, but instead contributed to a larger culture. With capitals in Cordoba in Spain, Cairo in Egypt, Damascus in Syria, and Baghdad in Iraq, these cities became centers of high culture, boasting achievements in science and art that were, at the time, unrivaled anywhere else in the world. It was this Arab Golden Age that would inspire and create the impetus for the Renaissance.

3

The Crusades to the Ottoman Empire

Note: Phrases like "the Crusades" and "the Ottoman Empire" are commonly associated with high school and college history courses, of which you'd probably rather not be reminded. Remaining sensitive to this I've endeavored to keep this chapter short and somewhat lively – though thousands of people being hacked to pieces doesn't need much spicing up. Nevertheless, this chapter attempts to lay out in a quick and clear manner a huge expanse of history that connects the ancient with the modern.

THE CRUSADES (1095–1291)

Over the course of the second half of the first millennium, a nomadic people coming most likely from Central Asia and Mongolia entered Persia. These people, known as the Turks, eventually made their way into Persia and the Middle East. During the expansion of the Arab Empire, the Turks, in their southern migration, came into contact with the Arabs. They were actually part of the Abbasid era discussed in the previous chapter, and quickly converted to Islam.[1]

One of the more historically noteworthy tribes were the Seljuks. This dynasty, in 1044, defeated and supplanted the prior Ghaznavid dynasty, and with an initial alliance with the Abbasids eventually gained control of all the region covering modern-day Turkey, Syria, Palestine, Iraq, Iran, and Afghanistan. But this rapid expansion of Seljuk control unnerved the Byzantine emperor Alexius Comnenus. (Bear in mind that as the Seljuks expanded into modern-day Turkey they were approaching Constantinople where the Byzantine Empire's capital was located.) In 1095, Alexius contacted the pope in Rome, Urban II, with an appeal for help.

Alexius and Urban were anything but friends, but Pope Urban saw an advantage in Rome coming to the aid of the Byzantine emperor. Along with saving the day and rescuing Christians in the east, as well as opening up Palestine and the routes of pilgrimage, Urban could establish the supremacy of the papacy over the entirety of the Christian Church. Later in the same year Urban gave a speech at the Council of Clermont calling upon all Christians, rich and poor, to leap to the aid of the eastern Christians. Though what he said precisely is unknown (there are accounts but they were written years later) it is safe to assume the speech was a masterpiece of oratory and persuasion. Appealing to a range of motives – from religious to racist – the pope cultivated a mass hatred for the "wicked race" of Muslims and urged that the Holy Land be regained and the infidels exterminated. Fired with a zeal for honor, spiritual salvation, acquisition of wealth, and adventure, the crowds cried *"Deus volt!"* (God wills it).

In the following year, 1096, an army of 15,000 knights headed for Constantinople. After turning back the encroaching Turks, most of the army continued with the original plan of marching on to Jerusalem. The crusaders took Jerusalem in a six-week siege, in 1099. An account by one crusader gives a glimpse into what ensued:

> The amount of blood that they shed on that day is incredible.... Some of our men (and this was more merciful) cut off the heads of their enemies; others shot them with arrows, so that they fell from towers; others tortured them longer by casting them into flames. Piles of heads, hands, feet were to be seen in the streets of the city.... It was a just and splendid judgment of God that this place should be filled with the blood of unbelievers, since it had suffered so long from their blasphemies.[2]

Killing Muslims and Jews – men, women, and children alike – the First Crusade managed to drive back the infidels, or

"Saracens" as the crusaders referred to Muslims and Arabs, from Constantinople and liberate the Holy City of Jerusalem. A little over half a century later, the Turks launched a counteroffensive to regain Jerusalem, and under the leadership of the legendary Saladin (Salah al-Din in Arabic), who was of Kurdish decent, took the Holy City back in 1187.

After the First Crusade there were countless other expeditions, only a few of which have actually been enumerated by historians. The Second Crusade (1147–49), encouraged by the French monk St Bernard of Clairvaux, was short-lived and resulted in a pitiful attempt to take Damascus; in a five-day siege it was over. The Third Crusade (1189–92) was inspired by Saladin's recapture of Jerusalem. Preached by Pope Gregory VIII but led by the French king Philip II and England's Richard I (also known as Richard the Lionheart), this crusade attempted to reach Jerusalem, but went to and defeated Acre (a town in northwestern modern-day Israel) in 1191. Richard and Saladin, between who there was reported mutual respect, then signed a treaty that lasted five years.

The Fourth Crusade (1202–4) is a story of the crusaders planning to make their way to Egypt via the Mediterranean Sea. However, their intentions were sidetracked in Venice, and the crusaders instead helped the Venetians attack their rivals – who, incidentally, were Christian. After doing so, the crusaders, along with the Venetians, further changed their objectives and stormed Constantinople. In a somewhat peculiar turn of events, the crusaders were attacking the very place that had appealed to their forefathers for help!

The year 1212 witnessed the involvement of children in what is called the Children's Crusade. A peasant boy by the name of Stephen of Cloyes gathered approximately 30,000 French and German kids and set out from Marseilles. Vulnerable to ruthless merchants, the children were promised free passage to the Holy Land, but instead were sent to slave markets in North Africa. A second Children's Crusade that came out of Germany suffered a similar fate.

The Fifth Crusade (1218–21) took place in Egypt and, after a modicum of initial success, failed; this was to be the last crusade where the papacy played an active role. The Sixth Crusade (1228–29) wasn't much of a crusade at all, and instead ended up being a diplomatic visit by the Holy Roman Emperor Frederick II, resulting in a truce and a partial surrender of Jerusalem and Bethlehem. However, the Muslims soon reoccupied both places. A treaty in 1244 restored Christian possession, but Egyptian Muslims and some Turkish allies took Jerusalem once again, leading to the Seventh Crusade.

Another attempt at Egypt, this time by King Louis IX of France, resulted in his own capture, and release. Deciding he hadn't had enough, Louis led another expedition in 1270 – the Eighth Crusade – this time to Tunisia in North Africa. Upon his arrival plague began to wipe out his troops and then eventually him too. Aside from an attempt by Prince Edward (1271–72) at coming to Louis's assistance, a bit too late, Louis's Crusade is considered the last. By 1291 the Christians had lost the last of their strongholds (Acre). Some low-key attempts at regaining various territories continued for a short while, but by 1291 what we know as the period of the Crusades was over.

Aside from initial and temporary success, all subsequent seven Crusades resulted in failure. What the crusaders brought home with them, on the other hand, were the cultural and scientific achievements of the Middle East. While the Arabs, Persians, and Jews were making breakthroughs in art and science, Europe was mired in the stagnancy of the Middle Ages. Upon the return of the crusaders to their homelands, an impetus was created that would eventually result in the Renaissance.

For the Muslims, victory failed to outweigh some of the costs (this is referred to as a *pyrrhic* victory). Two hundred years of warfare had left its imprint on the region. Another aspect of the expensive victory of the Muslims was their vulnerability to other potential invading forces, though it did increase cultural cohesion and willingness to resist. While the Crusades were winding down, and the region being sufficiently softened up from years of strife, the Muslims were visited by another foreign presence – one without pretense of purpose.

THE MONGOL INVASION

During the initial years of the Fifth Crusade (1218–21), the Muslim Middle East suffered another bloody invasion, this time by the Mongols and their leader, Genghis Khan. A nomadic people from north of the Gobi Desert (located in modern-day Mongolia, north of China), the Mongols were originally tribal hunters and herders but in the early thirteenth century formed a confederation under the leadership of Genghis (also spelled Chingis, Chingiz, Jenghis, and Jenghiz, though the spelling of his real name, Temujin, is relatively constant). He was preoccupied with taking over China, but was sidetracked by a plea for help from the Turks in modern-day Kyrgyzstan (northeast of Afghanistan). They had fallen under the control of a rival Mongol confederation, the Kara-Khitay. After dealing with this group, Genghis's momentum inspired a wholesale invasion of Southwest Asia and Persia. What ensued was genocidal slaughter and destruction of entire cities and populations.

> They slaughtered 700,000 inhabitants of Merv; their engineers broke the dams near Gurganj to flood the city *after* it had been taken; they poured molten gold down the throat of a Muslim governor; they carried off thousands of Muslim artisans to Mongolia as slaves, most of them dying on the way; they stacked the heads of Nishapur's men, women, and children in pyramids; and they even killed dogs and cats in the streets.[3]

After Genghis's death in 1227, one of his grandsons, Hulegu, decided to move the conquest further west with the intent of driving his forces all the way through the Middle East as far as Egypt.

In 1256 Hulegu ploughed through the territories of Iran, Iraq, and Syria. By 1258 the Mongols had reached Baghdad and laid waste to libraries, mosques, and centuries worth of physical history. Estimates vary, but it's safe to say that a million people were slaughtered during the siege (though Christians and Jews were spared). Along with the destruction of the city and many of its people, the caliphate in Baghdad was also toppled: the Abbasid caliph and all the males of his house, after surrendering, were rolled into carpets and trampled to death by horses. The stench of the corpses throughout the city finally drove Hulegu and company out of Baghdad. The city would never recover.

Again, momentum carried the Mongols toward the Mediterranean and Egypt. In 1259–60 Hulegu's forces took the Syrian cities of Aleppo and Damascus, with Jerusalem next on the list. However, during the years the Mongols spent moving west, a powerful new group known as the Mamluks was rising in Egypt. Originally the Mamluks (meaning "slave" or "owned men") were a military force raised by the Abbasid caliphs of the ninth century by forcing non-Muslim boys into military training. Yet they grew into a formidable power in Egypt. Moving on Jerusalem the Mongols were stopped in their tracks by the Mamluks from Egypt, meeting defeat at the Battle of Ayn Jalut in September of 1260. Thus the Mamluks became the masters of Syria and Palestine, while Hulegu withdrew to Iraq and Persia. While in control of Syria and Palestine the Mamluk forces drove the last of the crusaders out in 1291, and remained in power until 1517.

THE OTTOMAN EMPIRE (1299–1922)

The genesis of the Ottoman Empire took place between the disintegration of the Byzantine Empire, the disintegration of Seljuk power, and the invasion of the Mongols. With the Byzantine Empire reeling from the unexpected effects of the Fourth Crusade (when the crusaders attacked Constantinople), and the Seljuks' defeat in 1243 by the Mongols, tribes of warrior nomads called *ghazis* slipped through the cracks into Anatolia (modern-day Turkey).

In an attempt to escape the Mongols (as well as seek material gain and expand the boundaries of Islam) these *ghazi* nomads occupied eastern and central Anatolia, and then eventually formed principalities in the contested border regions west and north. One of the weaker and less significant of these was the principality run by Osman I (ca. 1258–1324?).

Located right at the edge of the Byzantine defense perimeter, Osman's principality was engaged in constant battle with the empire. After a number of military successes it began to attract the attention of other tribes who soon pledged their loyalty. Osman's growing military might created the needed conditions for vast expansion, which is exactly what he and his son, Orhan (r. 1324?–60), initiated. Those belonging to the principality of Osman and Orhan were to become known as Osmanlis, or Ottomans.

Over the next number of rulers, or sultans, the Ottomans conquered the Balkans in Eastern Europe. In 1453, a watershed year in Ottoman history, Constantinople was finally, after many previous attempts, taken by Sultan Mehmet II (r. 1451–81). Constantinople would henceforth be called Istanbul. Through vast reconstruction programs instituted by Mehmet II and his successors, it was restored to the splendor of its best years under Byzantine rule. Under the sultanates of Selim I (r. 1512–20) and Suleyman the Magnificent (r. 1520–66), the Ottoman Empire underwent its greatest expansion. By the end of Suleyman's rule, the Ottoman Empire covered the territories of Hungary, Yugoslavia, North Africa, Egypt, Syria (including what is now Israel and Palestine), Iraq, Iran, and the western rim of Arabia. Suleyman the Magnificent's sultanate (the tenth) marks the zenith of the Ottoman Empire.

By the sixteenth century the Ottoman Empire was the largest and most powerful empire in the world. Far from homogeneous, the empire consisted not just of Turks, but also Arabs, Armenians, Greeks, and Slavs. Istanbul, by this time, was a cosmopolitan melting pot of 700,000 inhabitants representing all three monotheistic faiths: 58 percent were Muslim, 32 percent were Christian, and 10 percent were Jewish.[4] With this broad range of cultural and religious diversity, the Ottoman Empire chalked a good deal of its success up to the flexibility of its administrative policies. Management methods like the *millet* system allowed the different religious groups a significant amount of autonomy. Millets were communities of non-Muslims granted the freedom to continue their faith-specific policies regarding education and legal issues with minimum interference. The relative autonomy of these communities reduced the likelihood of resistance; even the religious leaders of the various communities were kept intact, but were assigned the responsibility of being tax farmers for the Ottomans. The primary concerns of the Ottomans were taxes and stability, and this system kept both concerns successfully addressed.

The sixteenth and seventeenth centuries saw a loss of steam for the Ottoman Empire. The international tide was changing, which forced the Ottomans into new and unfamiliar territory. Economic competition with neighboring powers, in particular Europe, created new patterns of commerce and trade that eventually reduced hitherto economic independence of the Ottoman Turks to a state of utter dependence. (Europe had undergone steady and significant development from the Renaissance onward, eventually arriving at the Industrial Revolution.) Along with these external changes the Ottomans also experienced changes from within. Less effective sultans, deterioration of institutional integrity – corruption, merit-based systems replaced by nepotism, etc. – and decentralization of the power structure served only to weaken the empire politically, militarily, and economically.

Attempts at reform were undertaken to westernize various institutions, including the military. Most notable of the reformers were sultans Selim III (r. 1789–1807) and Mahmud II (r. 1808–39). Shortly after Mahmud II, the era of intense reformism known as the Tanzimat took hold. During this period a new literary movement involving poetry and journalism gave rise to a group (more in name than in substance) called the Young Ottomans. The Young Ottomans were interested in reforms that reconciled the westernizing attempts of the Tanzimat with Ottoman/Islamic traditional foundations. They called for a constitution. The Ottoman Constitution of 1876 was suspended before the ink was dry due to, among other things, a Russian invasion. Shortly thereafter, a number of opposition groups formed a movement called the Young Turks. This movement and its secret society called the Committee of Union and Progress (CUP) inspired a coup in 1908 that restored the 1876 constitution and eventually overthrew the government. Despite good intentions the Young Turks inherited, and couldn't handle, internal instability, external strife including large losses of territory (especially in Eastern Europe), and two coups – one that removed the CUP from power and one that restored it. Ottoman pursuit of reform, democracy, and statehood was finished. With World War I a few years away, the 600-year-old empire was soon to go the way of every empire before it.[5]

II
Pre–conflict

Chapters 4 and 5, addressing Zionism and Palestine, will set the conflict's stage by examining the two involved groups. First we'll look at the tribulations and persecution of Europe's Jews and the resultant birth of Zionism. Secondly, a description of Palestine between the years of 1882 to 1914 will help us glean a sense of what things were like at the twilight of the Ottoman Empire: the political climate, the people, how they lived, etc. Chapter 6 then traces the developments over World War I and World War II that gave rise to what we will finally arrive at in Section III.

4

Jewish Persecution and Zionism

The world resounds with outcries against the Jews,
and these outcries have awakened the slumbering idea.

Theodor Herzl, The Jewish State[1]

THE TRIBULATIONS OF EUROPEAN JEWRY

In Europe, the emerging concept of nationalism was also taking hold of Jewish communities; at first in Eastern Europe, but eventually spreading from London to Moscow. Recall from Chapter 1 that the Jews were spread throughout much of Europe after being expelled by the Romans in the second century. Historian David Vital succinctly states: "The distinguishing characteristic of the Jews has been their Exile."[2] As a result of living among other cultures and in order to maintain cultural identity living in a diaspora, an element of Jewish consciousness for 1,900 years has been to return to Eretz-Israel (Land of Israel), or Zion. From a theological perspective the Jews were cast out of Eretz-Israel and into exile for transgressions against Yahweh. Therefore, some believe the Jews are serving a penance and awaiting redemption from God. Jewish redemption and return to Eretz-Israel can only, as a matter of course, be divinely provided on Judgment Day, when the Messiah comes to bring peace to all nations. The return from exile has survived as a religious notion, but the idea of a homeland was never considered an actual political ideology until the nineteenth century. But as the above quotation by Theodor Herzl (more on him later) indicates, some Jews in the late 1800s began to see a potential political reality in the Promised Land.

To get an idea of the evolution of European Jewry during the eighteenth and nineteenth centuries, we can more or less look at Europe along its Eastern/Western axis.

> To the Jew as a man – everything: to Jews as a nation – nothing.
>
> *Count Stanislas Clermont-Tonnerre*
> *to the French Assembly, October 12, 1789*

As a result of the French Revolution (1789) and its Declaration of the Rights of Man, France became a place where Jews were included as citizens under the "preservation of the natural and imprescriptible rights of ... Liberty, Property, Safety, and Resistance to Oppression."[3] Over the next half-century Western Europe offered the possibility of assimilation (blending into the surrounding culture) for Jewish people. Many western Jews chose this route and assimilated into the cultures among which they lived, becoming more European and less culturally distinct. This phenomenon greatly increased social and legal equality, and reduced suspicion and xenophobia (fear of the foreign) of Jews, though sporadic instances of anti-Semitic violence still persisted. Jews were sometimes still viewed as aliens and used as scapegoats for social, political, and economic maladies. All in all, things were better for western Jews than for eastern Jews.

In Eastern Europe, where the large majority of world Jewry (75 percent) was located, Jews were faring far worse. The change

---

Anti-Semitism

The term "anti-Semitic" was coined around this time (1879) by the German journalist, Wilhelm Marr. The term indicates a shift in thinking; from that of religious hatred to that of racist hatred. So even if Jews fully merged into the surrounding culture and played by the rules, they were still viewed as Jews biologically. But, as was covered in Chapter 1, a Semite is someone who belongs to a particular language group, one that includes a variety of peoples – including Arabs. So the terms "anti-Semite" and "anti-Semitic" are technically misnomers.

in philosophy in Central and Western Europe did not take root in Russia and Eastern Europe. With the partitioning of Poland (1772–95) between Austria, Prussia, and Russia, Russia's Jewish population was greatly expanded by Jews inherited from the annexed territory.

> To the tsarist government, no less than to the backward, largely illiterate native peasantry, the Jews were regarded in terms of their medieval stereotype: as Christ killers, well poisoners, or at best as usurious traders and parasitic middlemen.[4]

Confronted with having to deal with this influx of undesired people, the government, in an effort to keep Jews from infiltrating mainland society, decided to concentrate them in Russia-controlled Poland. Passed in 1791 (but formally instituted in 1794) the Pale of Settlement was created. Essentially a vast ghetto stretching from the Black Sea to the Baltic Sea, Jews were confined to certain areas and cities within this territory and endured severe restrictions. One of the most brutal aspects of life in the Pale was its military conscription *ukase* (edict). These recruitment policies ordered Jewish children as young as eight to be taken from their parents by press-gangs and forced into 25 years of military service – more or less a death sentence.[5]

The reign of Czar Alexander II (r. 1855–81), however, saw a relaxation of governmental policies and the institution of reforms that benefited the Jews as well as the Russian citizenry. This period of slight liberal reform ushered in a movement of Jewish enlightenment known as the *Haskalah*. With students being able to attend university in Moscow, a minor easing of Pale restrictions, and the birth of a literary movement among Jewish students and intellectuals, Russian Jewry began to examine its own culture more closely. Issues of modernity, traditional religiosity, cultural insularity, and Gentile (non-Jewish) society, especially Western culture, came to the fore. Jews began to question and reassess their cultural role. "Be a Jew at home and a man in the street" became a slogan that enshrined the prevailing sentiment of the Haskalah poets and writers.[6] There was much discussion and published philosophizing about the pros and cons of assimilation and secular modernity, as well as more traditional Torah-based solutions to the plight and problems of Jewish people. Though there were improvements under Alexander II (including the termination of conscription of children), life was far from easy and anti-Jewish sentiment was a fixture of Russian thinking, from the ruling elite to the peasantry. Then, in 1881, things got worse.

In March, a group of young revolutionaries assassinated Alexander II. The reign of Alexander III brought a shockwave of anti-Semitism along with it. Blamed for the assassination (in fact only one of the assassins was Jewish), the Jews suffered severe reinstitution of restrictions, expulsion from Moscow, strict quotas for students, and transference from the countryside to the already overcrowded city slums. Aside from political backlash the Russian peasantry, with tacit support from the government, also acted out its contempt with waves of attacks and riots known as pogroms. These pogroms were acts of profound violence that shook Russian Jewry to its roots. A dispatch describing one such attack that took place on Passover, April 1882 reads as follows:

> On the tenth, at three o'clock in the afternoon, the riot began; the Jewish inhabitants … prepared to defend themselves; whereupon the municipal authorities had them dispersed by troops who beat them with rifle-butts. On the eleventh, at eight o'clock in the morning, 600 peasants from the surrounding country recommenced the attack and maintained it without further obstacle. It was a scene of pillage, murder, arson, and rape to make one tremble with horror; 700 Jews were injured, 40 seriously, 3 were killed [the figures were later corrected: 211 injured of whom 39 seriously, 9 killed]; girls were raped; all houses inhabited by Jews, with 16 exceptions, were demolished [later corrected: 976 houses, 253 shops, and 34 public houses]; all household furniture was broken or burned; everything destroyed. The Jews are dying of hunger.[7]

A four-year period of fear and violence more or less totally destroyed any hopes or illusions of emancipation and equality. The harsh restrictions of the Pale, anti-Semitic hatred, attacks, and the attendant poverty, misery, and fear that went along with this treatment, brought Russian Jewry to the psychological brink. From the beginning of the pogrom years to the turn of the century, hundreds of thousands of Jews emigrated from Russia to Western Europe, South America, Palestine, and to a large extent the United States. Escape seemed the only viable option under such circumstances. In the background, however, the notion of escape was being focused and tempered with thoughts of nationalism. Russia's implied hopes that "one-third will die out, one-third will leave the country, and one-third will completely dissolve in the surrounding population" had indeed awakened the slumbering idea.[8]

THE BIRTH OF ZIONISM

In a nutshell, the impulse of Jewish desire for a national homeland was motivated, almost exclusively, by what they suffered and endured in Russia. This desire for a safe haven state is the very essence of Zionism. The term "Zionism," coined by the Austrian author and publicist, Nathan Birnbaum, didn't become·the formal label for this idea until the mid-1880s. The concept of Zionism, as an actual political strategy, began to germinate several years earlier.

As early as 1839 a rabbi from near Belgrade by the name of Yehuda Alkalai published a text entitled *Darchai Noam* (*Pleasant Paths*) in which he propounded the colonization of the Holy Land. A contemporary of Alkalai's from East Prussia, Rabbi Zvi Hirsch Kalischer, published similar writings regarding redemption through action. In 1862 a German Jew by the

---

"Zion"

The background and origin of the term "Zion" is somewhat obscure. The name refers to both the city of Jerusalem as well as the hill on which it was built. In the Bible the term is mentioned in both Old and New Testaments, such as Mount Zion. As the *Encyclopaedia Britannica* states: "Mount Zion is the place where Yahweh, the God of Israel, dwells (Isaiah 8:18; Psalm 74:2), the place where he is king (Isaiah 24:23) and where he has installed his king, David (Psalm 2:6). It is thus the seat of the action of Yahweh in history."[9] Zion can also denote heaven and the Jewish people.

name of Moses Hess (a classmate of Karl Marx, incidentally) reacted to the recurrent anti-Semitism around him by authoring *Rome and Jerusalem*. Now a classic of Zionist literature, it wasn't significantly considered until Zionism was fully developed years later. But its thesis concluded that Jewish return to the Land of Israel was requisite for true emancipation.

Aside from these initial instances, the longing for statehood didn't become pronounced until the pogrom years (1881–84). With the crushing blow of these years on Russian Jews, the Haskalah became a distant memory, its light all but snuffed out. Nevertheless, a number of students, writers, and intellectuals who remained motivated decided to apply its achievements to a desperately practical end.

By the 1870s Zionist groups and clubs began to sprout up throughout the Pale, such as the Hovevei Zion (Lovers of Zion) – later a confederation called Hibbat Zion (The Love of Zion). These circles engaged in various activities, social and political, but the ideological substrate of these organizations was singular and to the point: living in Russia is intolerable and the solution is Eretz-Israel. Hibbat Zion would eventually come under the leadership of the physician Leo Pinsker, who in 1882 published *Autoemancipation*. Pinsker's text was the first substantive analysis and formulation of the Jewish question, suggesting that the world's anti-Semitism was incurable and that a homeland was the only vehicle of deliverance – though he was not insistent on Palestine, and suggested other possibilities including North America. Regardless, *Autoemancipation* became the manifesto of the Hibbat Zion and was fairly well received, placing Pinsker at the heart of the burgeoning movement.

Another group working at around the same time was the BILU, an acronym from the biblical passage Isaiah 2:5: "O house of Jacob, come ye and let us walk in the light of the Lord."[10] A group of students from Kharkov (in Ukraine), the BILU in 1882 organized and committed to establishing agricultural settlement communes in Palestine. Fourteen members set out for Eretz-Israel that same year, but achieved very limited success and ended up returning to Europe, ultimately in failure.

Also at this time (1882 was a big year) a large wave of immigration called the First Aliyah ("Ascent") occurred. Between 1882 and 1903, 25,000 Jews entered Palestine. Though some were motivated ideologically, most were simply fleeing Russia and Eastern Europe and headed for the larger cities as opposed to settlements in the hinterland. All in all, Zionism was just getting off the ground and lacked any real political organization. What movements and groups did exist were comprised of small numbers with a modicum of planning and strategy, and less than a modicum of financing. Some of the settlements were propped up solely by the philanthropy of western Jews, wealthy men like Moses Montefiore and the financier, Baron Edmond de Rothschild. Zionism up until the 1880s lacked the cohesion and the engine of a full-blown political movement that would give sufficient force to Zionism's goals, but a 30,000-word pamphlet published in 1896 changed all that.

THEODOR HERZL AND POLITICAL ZIONISM

Oddly enough, the one who would end up gluing it all together and giving Zionism a unified voice and a politically structured agenda came not out of Russia or Eastern Europe, but Austria. Born in Budapest, Hungary in 1860 to an assimilated and well-to-do banking family, Theodor Herzl grew up in liberal European environs. In his late teens, he and his family moved to Vienna, where he attended university and became a lawyer. Disillusioned with the study of law Herzl became interested in journalism, eventually taking a position as Paris correspondent at the prestigious Austrian paper, *Neue Freie Presse*. (Herzl was also something of a playwright, but never garnered much attention in that endeavor.)

For many years Herzl was unfamiliar with the plight of Russian Jewry or the fledgling Zionist movements that were being preached and practiced, his concern being European Jewry. Herzl's contemplation of this matter grew into obsession, and then the "Dreyfus Affair" brought his feelings and thoughts on the issue to a head. Captain Alfred Dreyfus, a French Jew and officer in the French army, was arrested in 1894 for selling military intelligence to the Germans. The case became a conflagration in French society, and anti-Semitism in liberal France came to the surface. Herzl, covering the event as a journalist, was most moved by French mobs shouting *"Á mort les Juifs!"* (Death to the Jews). Dreyfus was convicted and sentenced to life imprisonment on Devil's Island, a French penal colony off the northeast coast of South America and a former leper colony. It wasn't until 1899 that Dreyfus was given a presidential pardon, and not until 1906 that he was fully vindicated and allowed to resume his post. But the effect the affair had on France was immense, and the effect it had on Herzl equally so.

Herzl began work on formalizing a solution to Jewish discrimination, and, in 1896, produced *The Jewish State (Der Judenstaat)*. It was a short pamphlet (under one hundred pages) that spelled out in style and force of conviction what would become the principal statement of Zionism. Though not asserting anything conceptually innovative or new, Herzl was putting a face on the cause.[11] What was unique was an assimilated European intellectual promoting the notion of the Jews removing themselves from their situation. For Herzl, and many others, it was an incurable and hopeless situation, one that gave rise to an "inescapable conclusion."[12]

> A nation is everywhere a great child, which can certainly be educated; but its education would, even in most favorable circumstances, occupy such a vast amount of time that we could, as already mentioned, remove our own difficulties by other means long before the process was accomplished.[13]

On particular issues Herzl diverged from "traditional" Zionist groups like Hibbat Zion. His strategy was to proceed diplomatically and seek the support and cooperation of the power elite and the wealthy, Jewish and non-Jewish alike. Rather than trickle-immigration, an international avowal and acknowledgment should be in order to initiate mass settlement. Moreover, Herzl wasn't totally dedicated to Palestine and was open to the possibility of Argentina as a potential Jewish homeland. Irrespective of these differences, Zionists were still in support of Herzl and the program he had laid out, coupled with the increased exposure of *The Jewish State*, which was being smuggled into Russia in defiance of its censorship. Herzl's name and legend were growing. On August 29, 1897, a congress was called to assemble in Basel, Switzerland to lay the foundation of a Zionist organization.

Akin to a town hall meeting the congress crowded into an auditorium and convened for three days. At the end of three days of speeches, reports, and arguments, a definitive program was penned for the newly formed World Zionist Organization:

> The aim of Zionism is to create for the Jewish people a home in Palestine secured by public law. The Congress contemplates the following means to the attainment of this end.
>
> 1. The promotion, on suitable lines, of the colonization of Palestine by Jewish agricultural and industrial workers.
> 2. The organization and binding together of the whole of Jewry by means of appropriate institutions, local and international, in accordance with the laws of each country.
> 3. The strengthening and fostering of Jewish national sentiment and consciousness.
> 4. Preparatory steps towards obtaining government consent, where necessary, to the attainment of the aim of Zionism.[14]

The declaration of principles known as the "Basel Declaration" clearly stated the intentions of the congress while at the same time trying not to create concern or panic about a "Jewish State" in Ottoman Palestine; the word "home" was used to prevent, or at least allay, those fears. The congress was deemed a success, especially by Herzl, who had this to say in his diaries: "Were I to sum up the Basel Congress in a word – which I shall guard against pronouncing publicly – it would be this: At Basel I founded the Jewish State."[15]

With the foundation laid and everyone on board the issues that came to the fore were securing capital and international recognition for a charter in Palestine. Herzl embarked on a diplomatic tour to address this small but daunting list of needs. Trips to Constantinople were made in an attempt to strike a deal with Sultan Abdul Hamid. Looking for Ottoman approval for Zionist settlements in Palestine, Herzl, in 1901, extended the offer of helping the sultan with Ottoman debt. The meetings proved fruitless. In 1902 Herzl turned to the British for support, only to be presented with the option of settling in a territory in British East Africa. The British colonial secretary, Joseph Chamberlain, in 1903, offered "Uganda," which was in reality the area that would later become Kenya. Herzl considered it, though mostly in order not to jeopardize his relationship with the British. News of the offer caused not a little tumult in the Sixth Zionist Congress. It split Zionists everywhere into two polarized camps: one urging practicality, and the other idealism – a home in Palestine. All hell broke loose, and Herzl desperately tried to put the pieces back together. But time ran out for Theodor Herzl, who died on July 3, 1904 at the age of 44.

Though never achieving the international support he hoped for, Herzl left the World Zionist Organization in a good position. With a bank established, and the direction, momentum, and ideological clarity that the group needed, the Zionist movement was now a unified and organized political force. The Seventh Zionist Congress of 1905 picked up where it left off (after putting to bed the Uganda issue) and forged ahead resolute.

5

Palestine

From the dawn of civilization to the fast-approaching period of the modern era and World War I, we've seen the word Israel used in connection with a kingdom that developed in the Levant. Later, we saw the term used in conjunction with the longed-for Jewish homeland in scripture and its appropriation by Zionist ideology regarding the actual establishment of a homeland in Eretz-Israel. With the name Israel we've established some familiarity. The name Palestine, however, needs more clarification.

Determining the "what" and the "when" of Palestine can be an ambiguous issue. Looking at a modern map one would have great difficulty finding a country labeled "Palestine." Even if you had a map from the second half of the nineteenth century you would still experience the same difficulty. On top of that, it isn't until 1922 that the name Palestine is conferred with any "official" status, which we'll get to in the next chapter. So what is all this talk of Palestine about? As for the derivation and origination of the name, the *Encyclopaedia Britannica* says the following:

> The word Palestine derives from Philistia, the name given by Greek writers to the land of the Philistines, who in the 12th century BC occupied a small pocket of land on the southern coast, between modern Tel Aviv–Yafo [Tel Aviv–Jaffa] and Gaza. The name was revived by the Romans in the 2nd century AD in "Syria Palaestina," designating the southern portion of

the province of Syria. After Roman times the name had no official status
until after World War I and the end of Ottoman rule....[1]

Into the late-Ottoman years, Palestine was not a singular
administrative geopolitical entity. Its organization changed
over the course of the nineteenth century, but by the end
of the century it was divided into three districts, or *sanjaks*:
Jerusalem, Nablus, and Acre, all of which had been a part
of the *vilayet* (governorate) of Syria. These names correspond
to towns that can certainly be located on a map, but in the
1880s they pertained also to districts named after the towns.
In 1887 Jerusalem became an independent *sanjak*, and those of
Nablus and Acre were transferred to the new *vilayet* of Beirut,
created in 1888. So until World War I, southern Palestine was
under the administration of Jerusalem, while the north was
controlled by Beirut. But these divisions notwithstanding,
the whole of the territory west of the Jordan River and south
of the *vilayet* of Beirut was referred to as "Palestine." All the
concerned groups in our discussion – Arabs, Jews, and Ottoman
officials – referred to the geographic area as Palestine, with the
Ottoman government using the term *Arz-i Filistin* (the "Land
of Palestine") in their official correspondence.[2]

At the turn of the century, however, things were beginning
to change in the *sanjaks*. At the twilight of the Ottoman
Empire, and the years leading up to 1914, notions of European-
style nationalism were starting to swirl among the Arab
communities. It is important to remember that our present-
day concept of nationality – that is, a group of people who
live within internationally recognized borders, acknowledge
the same flag, use the same currency, carry the same passport,
etc. – was unknown to the various tribes, confederations, and
empires of the millennia covered so far.

Nationalism in the European sense was almost unknown among the Arabs
at the end of the nineteenth century. Personal loyalties were therefore to
family and religion and, at another level, either to the Ottoman Empire
(probably a somewhat abstract concept for the most) or to the much
more concrete framework of town or village. In the years before 1914 a

discrete Palestinian "patriotism" (rather than a full nationalism) emerged, in large part as a reaction to Zionism.[3]

Nationalism as a way of thinking deepened over time as a result of the culture's evolution, in particular, the development of the region's trade and commerce, and its subsequent engagement with Western European markets. Palestinian Arabs began to look further than their villages and farms, and started to think and feel collectively. As the years progressed toward World War I the developing Palestinian identity was met with increasing changes in landholding patterns, an issue that lay at the very center of that identity.

THE LAND

For the most part, life in Palestine during the thirty or so years between 1882 and 1914 was much like it had been for centuries: farming was how a living was made. With a small minority in the cities, most Palestinians lived a rural life where *fellahin* (peasant laborers) tended to their fields as a means of feeding their families. Olives, cotton, grains, melons, citrus – including the legendary oranges of Jaffa – are some of the crops that the *fellahin* grew, cultivated, and sent to market.

For generations these peasant families worked the land as a cooperative, practicing usufruct, or communal ownership. Yet, as mentioned, in the mid-nineteenth century change was upon the Ottoman Empire. In an attempt to stabilize the empire, especially in the Arab provinces where revenue was being lost in mismanagement, the Tanzimat principles (see Chapter 3) were applied to Syria and Palestine with increasing determination. The Ottoman Land Code of 1858 was one measure taken to address this loss of revenue.

In an effort to regulate landholdings, the new code demanded that land be attached to a clear title or deed of ownership, thus ensuring a direct and easy system of taxation. Though this policy was instituted slowly, over the course of decades, it eventually had a profound effect on landholding patterns in the region. As peasants often could not withstand the imposed

tax burden, the *fellahin* frequently registered their lands with
wealthy notables and village shaykhs, who would then in turn
pay the taxes. Doing so also kept a family's name off the tax
rolls, the means by which the Ottomans used to find and
conscript children into the military. All the same, the *fellahin*
continued farming with the presumption that their rights to
the land had not changed. Registration was thought of merely
as a formality. Though some of the new landowners were local
Palestinian landlords, and occasionally *fellahin*, most were
absentee landlords, and of these most were non-Palestinian.
Many from this group were Christian merchants and notables
from Beirut, along with some Europeans. Eventually it started
to become apparent that this registration wasn't just so much
paperwork. The *fellahin* claim to the land was caught in a
lose–lose predicament: register your family and risk losing the
land owing to insufficient means to pay your taxes, or have
a landlord register for you and risk losing the land through
purchase to a third party. With the Zionist movement in
high gear and making its way to Palestine, a motivated and
willing third party was fast approaching, namely, European
and Russian Jews.

JEWISH–ZIONIST IMMIGRATION

A land without a people for a people without a land.

Zionist slogan[4]

Before Zionist immigrants began to arrive in 1881, a small
minority population of Jews already resided in Palestine, some
of who had been there as long as any of the native Arabs.

*Note: On the eve of Zionist immigration, there were roughly 400,000
Muslims, 43,000 Christians, and 15,000 Jews living in Palestine
as Ottoman citizens, non-Jews making up 96 percent of the total
population.*[5]

The two main Jewish groups living in Palestine at the time
(mainly in the towns) were the Sephardim and the Ashkenazim,

together constituting the Old Yishuv ("old settlement").[6] The Sephardic Jews were Arabic-speaking Ottoman citizens who were integrated into the culture and, for all intents and purposes, had decent relations with the native Christians and Muslims. The Ashkenazim, on the other hand, weren't altogether integrated into the surrounding culture (though some spoke Arabic) and consisted mostly of deeply religious Europeans who came to Palestine to pray as well as die. Ashkenazic Jews probably had a more difficult time being accepted. Jews in general were seen as second-class citizens regardless, though on the average they fared far better in Muslim countries than in Christian ones. What the Ashkenazim and the Sephardim shared in common at the dawn of the twentieth century, however, was a concern about Zionist immigration. Both groups feared the unsettling of their places in Palestinian society that would be brought on by massive influxes of Russian and European Jews.

The First Aliyah (1882–1903), as we covered in Chapter 4, saw the immigration of 25,000 Jews into Palestine. But this group was mostly made up of people who were far more interested in parting company with Russia than anything ideological. As much as half would leave Palestine upon arriving, observing the lack of developed land and opportunity.[7] Many of the immigrants were surprised to find little cultivable land available, on the one hand, and the presence of another culture on the other. After a three-month stay in Palestine in 1891, Ahad Ha'Am (pen name of Asher Ginzberg), a prominent Eastern European Jewish essayist and Zionist leader, wrote the following in a piece entitled "Truth from the Land of Palestine":

> We abroad are used to believing that Eretz Israel is now almost totally desolate, a desert that is not sowed, and that anyone who wishes to purchase land there may come and purchase as much as he desires. But in truth this is not the case. Throughout the country it is difficult to find fields that are not sowed. Only sand dunes and stony mountains that are not fit to grow anything but fruit trees – and this is only after hard labor and great expense of clearing and reclamation – only these are not cultivated.[8]

The Second Aliyah (1904–14) consisted of 30,000 Jews and resulted in an equal, and maybe greater, return rate than that of the first,[9] but the immigrants in this wave arrived with a larger sense of political purpose. The Jews of the second wave of immigration were steely in their resolve and fired with socialist zeal. The majority was secular and gave little thought to what some saw as the religiosity of their situation.

> Back home they had denied or denounced both Jewish tradition and czarist government as well as God. They were no more subdued before Ottoman writ and Arab custom. They brought with them an air and swagger of rebelliousness. They were revolutionaries, come to create a new heaven and a new earth....[10]

With focused intent the immigrants of the Second Aliyah continued what the earlier immigrants had inaugurated, somewhat feebly. They acquired as much land as possible so as to begin to "create for the Jewish people a home in Palestine."[11] Through the "conquest of labor," Zionists at the turn of the century applied a philosophy slightly divergent from many of the earlier immigrants, namely, an emphasis on establishing settlements that would operate exclusively on Jewish labor. In other words, the *fellahin* who had just been reduced to tenant farmers as a result of the Ottoman land laws and Zionist land purchases would now be unwelcome on the land altogether. As clarified by Dr Arthur Ruppin, head of the Palestine Office of the Zionist Organization, which was in charge of colonization:

> Land is the most necessary thing for our establishing roots in Palestine. Since there are hardly any more arable unsettled lands in Palestine, we are bound in each case of the purchase of land and its settlement to remove the peasants who cultivated the land so far, both owners of the land and tenants.[12]

From 1878 to 1908, 400,000 dunams (1 dunam is 0.25 acres) were purchased out of a total 27 million dunams.[13] The Zionists were off to a small but significant start, and with the increase of establishment came an increase in ideological determination. Needless to say, the native population who had been operating according to the same communal system for generations (centuries worth) grew dismayed and fearful of the changes that were taking hold.

THE SEEDS OF CONFLICT

So, you can see where this is headed. Jews from Russia, Eastern Europe, and to a degree Western Europe, treated none too kindly in their respective countries, have decided to remove themselves from a bad situation. The Zionist forefathers chose Palestine primarily for religious significance (though many of them were not practicing Jews), but somewhat deliberately neglected to note the presence of a fully developed indigenous population – one that had already cultivated most of the available arable land. Though perhaps somewhat behind the times, the Palestinians were making a go at catching up. In 1908 the revolt of the Young Turks within the Ottoman Empire brought, among other developments, freedom of the press. Two Palestinian newspapers came out during this time, *Filastin* in 1908 and *al-Karmil* in 1911. With a functioning press, a new voice in parliament as a result of Ottoman reforms, and a growing reaction to Zionist immigration and land purchases, a Palestinian nationalist movement was beginning to germinate. Irrespective of any particular level of cultural development, home was home, and had been for centuries. Vladimir Jabotinsky, an influential militant Zionist, who we'll meet in the next chapter, had this to say later in 1923, though its pertinence is timeless:

> [The Palestinians] look at Palestine with the same instinctive love and true fervor that any Aztec looked upon Mexico or any Sioux looked upon his prairie. Palestine will remain for the Palestinians not a borderland, but their birthplace, the center and basis of their own national existence.[14]

In terms of their growing sense of distinction, the die had been cast. However, this emerging nationalist mindset of the

Palestinian Arabs was soon to be placed in a set of circumstances that would forever change them as a people and a culture. To the list of masters that have ruled over Palestine – Assyrians, Persians, Greeks, Romans, Arabs, Seljuk Turks, Crusaders, Mamluks, and Ottoman Turks – we will add another in the next chapter.

Note: The population of Palestine on the eve of World War I was 657,000 Muslims (including 55,000 nomads); 81,000 Christians; 60,000 Jews (including 21,000 non-Ottoman citizens), totaling 798,000.[15]

6
World War I to World War II
The Genesis of Conflict

Note: In this chapter things get a little involved. Featured are going to be a good deal of names and dates: of people, international agreements, documents, committees, etc. Though it may look slightly overwhelming on the surface, each section in this chapter will simply revolve around the two main concerns for a country involved in a war, namely, how the war is going and what can be gained when it's over.

Decisions made during the period covered in this chapter molded the Middle East into, more or less, what it is today. At the beginning of World War I, the countries of Lebanon, Israel, Jordan, Iraq, and Kuwait and the Arabian Peninsula states didn't exist; the region consisted of Greater Syria, Palestine, and Arabia. The Middle East was casually carved up with a stick in the sand by foreign (European) powers, and with no concern for the people or cultures living in the newly created geopolitical designations. Colonel Edward Mandell House, an aide to President Woodrow Wilson, seeing France and Great Britain divide up their spoils at the end of World War I made a comment more prophetic than he probably realized: "They are making [the Middle East] a breeding place for future war."[1]

WORLD WAR I (1914–18)

An examination of "the Great War" (as it was originally called) is beyond the scope of our discussion, but for this section the period of the war's duration coincides with a period of great significance in the history we're concerned with – hence the section names in this chapter. For a quick rundown: On August 1, 1914, Germany declared war on Russia, inaugurating an international upheaval that would set the Allies (Great Britain, France, Russia, Japan, and, in 1917, the United States) against the Central Powers (Germany, Austria-Hungary, and the Ottoman Empire). The Ottoman Empire, as we have seen, was not long for this world – being referred to as the "sick man of Europe" – and Great Britain and its ally France were quite aware of this. Perched and eager, Britain and France focused on those portions of the Ottoman Middle East they could each walk away with at the end of the war. Transforming these strategically desired portions, or "spheres of influence," into colonial assets was the driving force of the decisions made, especially by Britain, during the war.

Though allied with Germany, the Ottoman Empire at first played it neutral. But despite Allied attempts to persuade the Ottomans to remain so, the Turks entered the war on Germany's side in November 1914. Once the Ottoman Empire sided with the Central Powers, the Bosporus Strait was then closed, choking off Russia's import/export lifeline. Within a year, Russia's supplies were fearfully low and the threat of its pulling out of the war loomed over France and Britain; Russia's withdrawal would create Germany's ability to focus its attention on the western front. At the same time, Britain grew concerned about its capacity to protect its colonial interests, namely, keeping the Suez Canal (the canal between the Sinai Peninsula and Egypt), as well as its access to oil in present-day Iraq and southwestern present-day Iran. One step toward addressing these concerns, and appeasing the Russians, was the Constantinople Agreement (March 1915), which satisfied Russian desire for postwar control of Constantinople, the Dardanelles, the Bosporus Strait, and the surrounding territory – essentially the northwest chunk of present-day Turkey. In return, France and Britain would gain the whole of the Middle East that was under Ottoman control. So that was settled.

It is important to keep in mind that the Allied countries were not, by virtue of their allied relationship, pals. Britain, France, and Russia didn't trust one another for anything, and in some instances they saw the other as a potential future enemy. Now that it had been agreed that the Middle East was to be the sphere of influence for Britain and France, Britain worked overtime to keep France somewhat content while not having to concede any territory thought to be strategically valuable to London. Britain realized that in order to protect its interests the Arabs, who were more than ready to part company with their Ottoman masters, might come in handy in destabilizing the Ottoman Empire *for* them.

What follows is a string of promises and agreements between Britain and the Arabs, and between Britain and France, which when we get done will make absolutely no sense – and that's exactly what was intended.

1. The Hussein–McMahon Correspondence (1915–16)

The British high commissioner in Cairo, Sir Henry McMahon, and Sharif Hussein of Mecca sustained an exchange of letters from mid-1915 to January 1916. In these letters was discussed the particulars regarding an agreement between the Arabs and Great Britain. Britain wanted the Arabs to revolt against the Ottoman Turks, and Hussein wanted guarantees from McMahon that the British would pick up the tab as well as help the Arabs attain independence. The issue of boundaries was addressed – one that historian Arthur Goldschmidt describes as, "one of the toughest issues in modern Middle Eastern history" – in terms of working out just what was meant and intended.[2] McMahon, while willing to "recognize and support the independence of the Arabs in all the regions within the limits demanded by the Sherif of Mecca," included some exceptions.[3] To keep France from getting nervous the British included them in territorial considerations, all the while maintaining certain areas deemed vital to British interests. McMahon stated the following:

> The two districts of Mersina and Alexandretta [northwest Syria] and portions of Syria lying to the west of the districts of Damascus, Homs, Hama and Aleppo cannot be said to be purely Arab, and should be excluded from the limits demanded.[4]

The cities of Damascus, Homs, Hama, and Aleppo run south to north in a rather straight line through western Syria. This would suggest that the land referred to in McMahon's letter would pertain to present-day Lebanon and the Syrian coast. Arab interpretation was in line with this thinking, but the British later maintained that the use of the word "districts" suggested that the land west of the *district* of Damascus (the capital of Greater Syria) included present-day Jordan, and therefore would exclude from independence the land west of the Jordan River, namely, Palestine. In the Hussein–McMahon correspondence Palestine is never mentioned by name.

2. The Sykes–Picot Agreement (1916)

Meanwhile, in November 1915, Great Britain approached France to settle postwar divisions of the Middle East. Representing France was Francois Georges-Picot, a French diplomat, and representing Great Britain was Sir Mark Sykes, a member of Parliament. Between France's serious interest in Syria and Britain's increasing presence and involvement in the Middle East, negotiation was necessary to allay concerns between the two powers. Similar to the Constantinople Agreement in March, the powers were carving up something that wasn't dead yet. In a secret treaty that was ratified in May 1916 (the Sykes–Picot Agreement wouldn't be published until after the war) Paris and London divided between themselves the whole of the Middle East, designating areas as zones of direct control and spheres of indirect influence. The indirect spheres, where Britain and France would be guaranteed priority in enterprise and local loans, were to be the sites of the independent state(s) promised to Sharif Hussein. Palestine, except for the far south and the ports of Haifa and Jaffa, which went to Britain, was to remain an international entity, the administration of which was to be determined later. Needless to say, the Sykes–Picot Agreement and the Hussein–McMahon correspondence had little in common and made for future disagreement, as we shall see.

3. The Balfour Declaration (1917)

Foreign Office
November 2nd, 1917.

Dear Lord Rothschild,
I have much pleasure in conveying to you, on behalf of His Majesty's Government, the following declaration of sympathy with Jewish Zionist aspirations which has been submitted to, and approved by, the Cabinet.

"His Majesty's Government view with favour the establishment in Palestine of a national home for the Jewish people, and will use their best endeavours to facilitate the achievement of this object, it being clearly understood that nothing shall be done which may prejudice the civil and religious rights of existing non-Jewish communities in Palestine, or the rights and political status enjoyed by Jews in any other country."

I should be grateful if you would bring this declaration to the knowledge of the Zionist Federation.

Yours sincerely,
ARTHUR JAMES BALFOUR[5]

Read it again for good measure. The Balfour Declaration is without a doubt the most controversial document to come out of the entire history of the Palestine–Israel conflict. Interpretations of its meaning, and views of its legitimacy, vary widely and greatly, to say the least. In the form of a letter from the foreign secretary, Arthur Balfour, to Lord Walter Rothschild, a leader of the British Jewish community, the British in one fell swoop made an impact on the region that still resonates today.

With the war growing in intensity, both Britain and France were concerned about Russia staying in the war and hopeful that the United States would enter it on the side of the Allies. The resulting rationale was this: If Britain extended a declaration of support for Zionism, influential Russian and American Jews would then help the Allies achieve these goals of Russian persistence and American entrance. Until now,

Palestine wasn't deemed vital to British strategic concerns. But with a new government (December 1916) and new prime minister, Lloyd George, Great Britain began to re-evaluate its objectives. Palestine would serve as a buffer between British and French territories, thus protecting Britain's control of the Suez Canal and Egypt. But two things stood in the way that the Balfour Declaration's support of Jewish self-determination fixed, at least on paper: (1) The Russian Revolution of 1917 ushered in Bolshevik rule, which was against imperial hegemony (domination); and (2) US President Wilson's denunciation, also, of imperial hegemony and his support of national self-determination, eventually formalized in the declaration of his Fourteen Points. In other words, by helping the Zionists establish a national home in Palestine, the British could claim to be aiding self-determination as well as provide justification for imperially setting up shop in Palestine. As Lord Balfour stated to the war cabinet in October 1917, where the declaration was approved:

> The vast majority of Jews in Russia and America, as indeed all over the world, now appeared to be favorable to Zionism. If we could make a declaration favorable to such an ideal, we should be able to carry on extremely useful propaganda both in Russia and in America.[6]

The Balfour Declaration was the product of much debate and lobbying on the part of Zionists, anti-Zionists Jewish groups, and the British government. In an effort to satisfy the Zionists, anti-Zionists, the Americans, the Arabs (who were still fighting the Ottoman Turks), and the Hussein–McMahon promises, the final version of the Balfour Declaration used deliberately imprecise language, for example, the establishment of a *national home* for the Jews *in* Palestine. For Zionists, this was interpreted as a Jewish *national state*, while for anti-Zionists, Sharif Hussein, and Woodrow Wilson – all of whom accepted the declaration – this meant a Jewish protectorate or sanctuary *located in* Palestine. Chaim Weizmann, an extremely influential Zionist close to the British government (and eventual first president of the state of Israel), indicated: "[The wording] would mean exactly what we would make it mean – neither more nor less."[7] Edwin Montagu, British secretary of state for India and member of the Jewish anti-Zionist camp in the discussions, maintained:

> I assume that it means that Mohammedans [Muslims] and Christians are to make way for the Jews ... you will find a population in Palestine driving out its present inhabitants, taking all the best country.... Palestine will become the world's Ghetto.[8]

Montagu also argued that Jews and Judaism were a culture and not a nation, and to create one would increase European anti-Semitism by suggesting that Jews were something distinct and apart.

Summary ... So Far

In June of 1916, the Arabs began their revolt against the Ottoman Turks. With British provision of arms and advisers, the best known of whom was T. E. Lawrence ("Lawrence of Arabia"),[9] and the leadership of Hussein's son, Faisal, the Ottomans were defeated and the Armistice of Mudros was signed on October 30, 1918. This ended the Middle Eastern portion of the war. In light of the Sykes–Picot Agreement and the Balfour Declaration, promises to Sharif Hussein looked less than genuine, yet this didn't stop Britain from making more promises to the Arabs – which in turn were contradictory to Sykes–Picot and the Balfour Declaration. Aside from the promises of self-determination and independence made to the Arabs, some earlier on-the-side promises are noteworthy: (1) The Baghdad Proclamation of March 1917 promised independence to Arabs of present-day Iraq when British forces took Baghdad; (2) the "Declaration of the Seven" in June 1918 promised independence to Arab lands that were independent before the war, or had been liberated by Arabs forces; and (3) in December 1917, between the first two promises, General Edmund Allenby, after occupying Palestine and while heading toward Syria, made the following declaration:

The object of war in the East on the part of Great Britain was the complete and final liberation of all peoples formerly oppressed by the Turks and the establishment of national governments and administrations in those countries deriving authority from the initiative and free will of those people themselves....[10]

If we add all this up – Hussein–McMahon, Sykes–Picot, Balfour, and the odd promise of independence here and there – we're left with a pile of documents and promises, one of which seems to have no greater legal or official legitimacy over any other. On top of that, the issue of interpretation, of at least Hussein–McMahon, Sykes–Picot, and Balfour, seems to suffer from the same confusion.

At eleven o'clock, on the eleventh day of the eleventh month of 1918, World War I ended. Germany and the Allies signed the armistice at Compiègne, in France. But things in the Middle East were just getting warmed up.

INTERWAR PERIOD (1919–39)

The Paris Peace Conference (1919) put an official end to the war, and gave rise to a number of treaties between the Allied powers and their enemies. The Treaty of Versailles, which addressed Germany's responsibilities, also provided for the birth of the League of Nations (the predecessor to the United Nations). The League's chief advocate and architect was President Wilson, who had included plans of such an international body in his Fourteen Points. This program was a peace plan he created near the end of the war to address matters of postwar intentions on the part of the Allies. Regarding Ottoman territory, Point 12 called for the "absolutely unmolested opportunity of autonomous development" of those territories.[11]

The League of Nations was an international apparatus whose function was to prevent, through diplomacy and conflict negotiation, the kind of upheaval and violence that embodied World War I. In its defining document, known as the Covenant, the League created the mandate system. A system of guardianship, the mandate assigned a "mandatory" power to those territories and nationalities judged soon-to-be capable of sovereignty, but were in need of tutelage and further development. Article 22 of the Covenant begins with the following paragraph:

> To those colonies and territories which as a consequence of the late war have ceased to be under the sovereignty of the States which formerly governed them and which are inhabited by peoples not yet able to stand by themselves under the strenuous conditions of the modern world, there should be applied the principle that the well-being and development of such peoples form a sacred trust of civilisation and that securities for the performance of this trust should be embodied in this Covenant.

Article 22 then goes on to say:

> Certain communities formerly belonging to the Turkish Empire have reached a stage of development where their existence as independent nations can be provisionally recognized subject to the rendering of administrative advice and assistance by a Mandatory until such time as they are able to stand alone. *The wishes of these communities must be a principal consideration in the selection of the Mandatory.*[12] [Emphasis added.]

Now it must be borne in mind that France and Great Britain were not thrilled about Wilson's policies of self-determination and "unmolested opportunity of autonomous development." Molestation was the very intention of these two nations, but Wilson's power and prestige as a statesman made it difficult for Paris and London to fly in the face of said policies. As the last sentence of the above-quoted passage of Article 22 states quite clearly, the people of Greater Syria (which includes Jordan), Palestine, and what is modern-day Iraq, were to have a say in who their mandatory power was to be. Needless to say, Britain and France weren't keen on this either.

The King–Crane Commission (1919)

To determine the "wishes of these communities" an American delegation called the King–Crane Commission was sent to the Middle East to make such a determination. Headed by

Henry King, president of Oberlin College, and Charles Crane, a Chicago businessman, the commission toured Syria and Palestine (but not Iraq) through June and July of 1919, making its report in August. Though beginning the tour in favor of Zionism, extracts from the report indicate a change of view:

- If ... the strict terms of the Balfour Statement are adhered to ... it can hardly be doubted that the extreme Zionist Program must be greatly modified. For a "national home for the Jewish people" is not equivalent to making Palestine into a Jewish State; nor can the erection of such a Jewish State be accomplished without the gravest trespass upon the "civil and religious rights of existing non-Jewish communities in Palestine."
- If that principle [Wilson's principle of self-determination] is to rule, and so the wishes of Palestine's population are to be decisive as to what is to be done with Palestine, then it is to be remembered that the non-Jewish population of Palestine – nearly nine-tenths of the whole – are emphatically against the entire Zionist program.
- No British officer, consulted by the Commissioners, believed that the Zionist program could be carried out except by force of arms ... That of itself is evidence of a strong sense of the injustice of the Zionist program.
- For the initial claim, often submitted by Zionist representatives, that they have a "right" to Palestine, based on an occupation of two thousand years ago, can hardly be seriously considered.[13]

The commission would go on to suggest limited Jewish immigration, the creation of one state of Greater Syria (including Palestine), and the United States as the mandatory power, with Great Britain as a secondary option. The King–Crane report, however, would not be published for several years after its submission to the Paris Peace Conference. With its threat to French and British imperial interests, and with Wilson's absence in trying to gain Senate support of the Treaty of Versailles (which he never did, thus the US was never part of the League of Nations), the report died on the vine. Balfour's comments at the end of the King–Crane investigation are revealing:

For in Palestine we do not propose even to go through the form of consulting the wishes of the present inhabitants of the country ... Zionism, be it right or wrong, good or bad, is rooted in age-long traditions, in present needs, in future hopes, of far profounder import than the desires and prejudices of the 700,000 Arabs who now inhabit that ancient land.[14]

It was at the San Remo Conference (April 1920; League of Nations ratification took place in July 1922) that the mandates were distributed. Great Britain was given mandatory responsibility over Palestine (with inclusion of the Balfour Declaration in the mandate), Transjordan (later Jordan), and Iraq. The French were assigned Syria and Lebanon.[15]

Note: This marks the beginning of the modern Middle East, as it exists on maps today. The countries of Lebanon, Syria, Jordan, Palestine (which mostly becomes Israel), and Iraq, are all relatively young, each having existed as part of an Ottoman whole only eighty years ago.

Right before ratification of the mandate, Britain was already busying itself with imperial concerns, which necessarily meant a departure from the mandate. Winston Churchill, then colonial secretary, issued the white paper of June 1922, which denied that Palestine was to become, like Zionist leader Chaim Weizmann had indicated, as Jewish as England is English.[16] The paper also maintained that the Jewish national home mentioned in the Balfour Declaration was to be founded *in* Palestine. Churchill, in an attempt to calm Arab apprehensions in Palestine, was toning down the spirit of the Balfour Declaration while not throwing it out the window altogether. He hoped to smooth things over and reduce conflict in Palestine, thus making it more manageable from a colonial vantage point. The Zionists hesitantly agreed to the white paper, the Arabs rejecting it owing to its continued acknowledgment and support of the Balfour Declaration.

Palestine at the end of World War I was something of a mess. It was used as a staging area early in the war, and shortly thereafter it became a battleground. To make matters worse, the crop yield had been poor through weather, locusts, etc., so the economy was in sad shape, and the people were hungry and malnourished. To that we add an increasingly agitated and hostile Arab population (almost 90 percent of Palestine) who viewed Zionism, Jewish immigration, and the Balfour Declaration as attempts to create a Jewish state at their expense, ultimately to result in their dispossession.

Great Britain, on the other hand, was looking to sustain its colonial control of Palestine, and thus needed to justify indefinite presence in light of Wilson's policies. Conflict was necessary (to make the justification), but not too much of it (to keep the effort and price down). To do this required a juggling act, keeping both groups, Arabs and Jews, somewhat appeased. Much of Britain's leadership was one or more of the following: (a) sympathetic to the Zionist cause, (b) under the anti-Semitic assumption that being in league with the Jews would benefit Britain financially, or (c) of the view that the Zionist presence in Palestine gave Britain the perfect justification for being there in the first place. Generally, however, the military personnel and officials in Palestine tended, more often than not, to find sympathy with the Arabs. They felt that Zionist goals would ultimately jeopardize Britain's colonial standing, and encountered the oftentimes abrupt and adverse air of the determined European and Russian Jews who were trying to create a safe haven state there. But try as Britain did to strike a balance, the incompatible interests of the Arabs (independence), the Zionists (a Jewish state), and Great Britain (colonial control) created an untenable situation that eventually – and unsurprisingly – turned violent.

The Western Wall (see Chapter 1), located in Jerusalem, is a remaining segment of the outer wall of the second Jewish temple; Herod rebuilt Solomon's temple during the time of Christ. Today's wall is part of Herod's reconstruction, and is now the holiest site of Judaism. The wall is part of the perimeter that contains the Temple Mount, as it is known to Jews and Christians, or Haram al-Sharif (Arabic for "Holy Sanctuary"), as it is known to Muslims. For all three religions, this is the site where Abraham attempted to slay his son, Isaac (Genesis 22:1–18; Qur'an 37:102–10). For the Muslims, also, the Western Wall is where Muhammad tethered his horse, al-Buraq, before making his nocturnal journey to Heaven. Preceded by Mecca and Medina, the Haram al-Sharif is the third holiest site of the Islamic faith, and houses the Dome of the Rock and the al-Aqsa mosque. Needless to say, the British and the League of Nations were aware of all this and thus included in the mandate a policy to preserve the status quo in this realm. But tensions were building among Arabs and Jews, and were to play out where these two peoples ostensibly differed, and at a place where emotions are prone to run higher than elsewhere.

In the summer of 1928, Jews customarily praying at the wall brought benches and a screen that separated worshippers according to gender. Arousing Arab indignation, Palestinians approached the British authorities to remove the screen. This sparked a series of provocations from Arab and Zionist leaders, which further upset their own people and agitated the other. A year went by, and in the summer of 1929 the aggravation came to a head, producing riots in Jerusalem that eventually spread to other towns. The violence lasted roughly a week, resulting in the deaths of 133 Jews and 116 Arabs. Most Arabs were killed by British reinforcements. Some of the bloodiest attacks were perpetrated by the Arab rioters, who often killed unarmed Orthodox Jews of the Old Yishuv. A number of Jews in Hebron were aided during the attacks and hidden by their Arab neighbors. The British sent a commission to investigate the underlying causes of the riots, which created the following list of more commissions and white papers:

1. The Shaw Report (September 1929)

This commission was headed by Sir Walter Shaw, and found the reasons for the conflict and unrest to be the aggravated landless class of Arabs, who were fearful of Zionism and dispossession. The commission suggested controlled Jewish immigration, a precisely laid-out Arab policy, and the cessation of evicting Arabs from land transfers. The Zionists were dismayed with Shaw's conclusions and demanded the formation of a new commission. Jewish immigration was temporarily suspended, and British Prime Minister Ramsay MacDonald sent a new commission.

2. The Hope–Simpson Commission (1930)

Headed by Sir John Hope-Simpson, this inquiry attributed the violence to Zionist labor policies; the policy of making Jewish-bought land inalienable created Arab unemployment. The conclusions and recommendations were more or less identical to the Shaw Report and were incorporated into the following white paper.

3. The Passfield White Paper (1930)

This white paper suggested limits on Jewish immigration, and concessions regarding the settling of landless Arabs. The Zionists were furious. Weizmann, along with other senior Zionist leaders and prominent members of the British and American Jewish communities, threatened and put immense pressure on the MacDonald government. In a letter to the House of Commons, MacDonald repudiated the white paper.

What occurred next was the Arab Revolt. A list of what inspired the uprising, which spanned 1936 to 1939, would include the following: (1) dismissal of the 1929/Western Wall inquiries; (2) a generation of young people (Jewish and Arab) who grew up in the mandate and were more literate and politically minded; (3) a worldwide depression; (4) rising Arab unemployment; and (5) increased Jewish immigration as a result of Adolf Hitler's rise to power in 1933. The first phase (April–November 1936) was the shorter and less violent of the two phases that would make up the Arab Revolt. The first featured a general strike, a boycott on Jewish goods, and violence committed against Jews and British alike. The British in turn promised a new commission of inquiry – though commissions were beginning to lose their appeal. In conjunction with a lack of Arab success, and the significant British suppression of the revolt, Arab leadership called off the strike and the violence subsided. This ended the first phase. The promised commission would result (again) in the following three commissions and white papers:

I. The Peel Commission (1937)

The list of reasons for the Arab anger and violence expressed in the revolt that was provided by the Peel Commission report bears much resemblance to the previous reports we've covered in this chapter. As the report itself enumerates:

The underlying causes of the disturbances of 1936 were –

1) The desire of the Arabs for national independence; 2) their hatred and fear of the establishment of the Jewish National Home.

These two causes were the same as those of all the previous outbreaks and have always been inextricably linked together. Of several subsidiary factors, the more important were –

1) the advance of Arab nationalism outside Palestine; 2) the increased immigration of Jews since 1933; 3) the opportunity enjoyed by the Jews for influencing public opinion in Britain; 4) Arab distrust in the sincerity of the British Government; 5) Arab alarm at the continued Jewish purchase of land; 6) the general uncertainty as to the ultimate intentions of the Mandatory Power.[17]

The commission deemed the mandate unviable and ultimately suggested that the solution to the conflict was partition of Palestine into separate Arab and Jewish states. The Jews were allocated 20 percent of the country, the area comprised of the north and the upper coast. The Arabs were given the rest of mandatory Palestine, with it becoming part of Transjordan.

The Zionist leadership wasn't altogether pleased with this report, but it was a start and they accepted it. The Arabs were outraged. From September 1937 to January 1939 they made that very clear by carrying out the second phase of the Arab Revolt. For a year and a half Palestine became lawless. Arab violence found not only Jewish and British victims, but Arab victims as well. Notable Arab families were accused of conspiracy and corruption and were subjected to attacks. With the breakdown of leadership, the Arab Revolt became fragmented, chaotic, and ultimately ended in failure. Given the chaos in Palestine and its threat to Britain's position there,

London needed to diffuse Arab unrest. In the shadow of an approaching second world war against fascism and the Nazis – who were beginning to issue propaganda in the Middle East in an attempt to undermine the British and court Arab favor – the British needed to reassess their policy toward the Arabs. Hence, we continue with the list.

2. The Woodhead Commission (1938)

In an attempt to appease the Arab population, both inside and outside of Palestine, the Woodhead Commission was set up to re-evaluate the Peel Report's suggestion to partition Palestine. The report asserted that, "... the political, administrative, and financial difficulties involved in the proposal to create independent Arab and Jewish States inside Palestine are so great that this solution of the problem is impracticable."[18] Nevertheless, three partition plans were included in this report, all of them allocating significantly less land to the Zionists. Zionist response was predictably negative, and the British then issued *another* white paper, which made quite an impact.

3. The 1939 White Paper

After a failed attempt at resolving the conflict in a roundtable meeting in London, known as the St James Conference, the British announced their new policy on May 17, 1939, declaring that, "... His Majesty's Government believe that the framers of the Mandate in which the Balfour Declaration was embodied could not have intended that Palestine should be converted into a Jewish State against the will of the Arab population of the country."[19] The document then goes on to cite Churchill's White Paper of 1922 as proof! (So many documents, papers, and promises had been generated at this point that the British, and anyone else for that matter, could hand-pick documents to suit a variety of agendas.) The white paper envisaged a Jewish national home in Palestine, with controlled Jewish immigration for five years, and the implementation of Arab–Jewish self-governing institutions. The 1939 White Paper was rejected by both sides: the Zionists maintained it contravened the mandate, and the Arabs wanted immediate independence, period. But by this time World War II was about to commence and Great Britain, along with the rest of the world, was focusing its energies on the approaching global turmoil.

WORLD WAR II (1939–45)

Note: For our discussion, brevity is necessary in describing the events of this war. It may seem odd to mention only briefly the plight of Europe's Jews in the Holocaust, but this event has more to do with European history and less with Middle Eastern affairs. The effects were certainly felt in Palestine – increased Jewish immigration, changes in British policy, etc. – but a substantive treatment would be reaching beyond our purview. A brief review will suffice.[20] Sworn in as chancellor in 1933, Adolf Hitler immediately began the installation of the Nazi Party, or the Third Reich, in Germany. He soon began developing policies to purify Germany, and the "bloodlines" of its people. Jews were viewed as a social and political threat to German society, and thus were defined as a race that had to be purged. What started with denial of basic civil rights and deprivation of citizenship escalated into the "final solution of the Jewish question." Over the course of World War II, the Nazis executed six million Jews, along with homosexuals, the mentally retarded and insane, and gypsies, also collectively numbering in the millions.

On September 1, 1939, the Second World War began with Germany's invasion of Poland. The next five years featured destruction and bloodshed the likes of which the world has never seen in its entire history. When the Allies (mainly Great Britain, France, the USSR, and later, the United States) and the Axis powers (mainly Germany, Japan, and Italy) finished battling one another, the death toll reached between 40 and 50 million people. If you killed every man, woman, and child in New York City, Chicago, and Los Angeles, you'd only kill half as many people.

Great Britain's primary concern, needless to say, was its involvement in the war, and the 1939 White Paper made it very clear that what London valued most in Palestine was stability, which meant appeasing the Arab population. This of course came at the expense of giving the Zionists short shrift, leaving them none too pleased by the arrangement. Zionist–British relations plummeted during World War II and would never recover. Jewish terrorism became aimed at British buildings and personnel. The most notorious terrorist groups were the Irgun and LEHI.[21]

Zionism as an ideology became more militant, a methodology endorsed by David Ben-Gurion, head of the Jewish Agency and eventually Israel's first prime minister. In contrast was Chaim Weizmann, then head of the World Zionist Organization, who preferred gradualism and diplomacy. Weizmann's diplomatic approach, however, was pushed aside by Zionist leaders like Ben-Gurion and, earlier, Vladimir Jabotinsky. Along with increasing militancy was growing Jewish-American interest in Zionism and Palestine. Especially in light of the Holocaust's atrocities, news of which emerged in 1942, American Jews began to support Zionism. The Biltmore Conference in New York City (May 1942) was one of the catalyzing events that brought Jewish-American support to Zionist organizations. The conference maintained that Palestine should be opened for unlimited immigration under Jewish monitor, and that it also be established as a Jewish Commonwealth. Between the alliance of American and European Zionists and news of the Holocaust, support and publicity began to grow for the Zionist movement.

At the end of World War II Britain was broke and beleaguered. Zionists were digging in and growing bolder, as well as becoming more organized and determined. Things for the Arab population remained fairly constant and quiet throughout the war. They even enjoyed a slight economic boost, though remaining virtually leaderless after the revolt and riots of the late 1930s. Filling this vacuum was the leadership of the surrounding Arab states, who met in Alexandria, Egypt (October 1944) and created a pact called the Alexandria Protocol. This meeting would eventually lead to the formation of the Arab League, an organization that still exists today. In the Alexandria

Protocol Palestine was the subject of a resolution that stated the following:

> Palestine constitutes an important part of the Arab world and that the rights of the Arabs [Palestinian] cannot be touched without prejudice to peace and stability in the Arab world....
>
> The Committee also declares that it is second to none in regretting the woes that have been inflicted upon the Jews of Europe by European dictatorial states. But the question of these Jews should not be confused with Zionism, for there can be no greater injustice and aggression than solving the problem of the Jews of Europe by another injustice, that is, by inflicting injustice on the Palestine Arabs of various religions and denominations.[22]

The Arab League eventually helped Palestine toward something of a unified leadership, but the protocol fell on deaf ears the world over. The events of World War II had brought the plight of the Jews to international light, and permanently attached Palestine to this unspeakable chapter in history.

III
Conflict

Like anything else, the preparatory work always takes the most time, which is what we've been doing for the first two sections of the book. But as the end of Chapter 6 portends, the elements in Palestine – native Arabs, Zionist Jews, and British colonialism – formed an admixture that was not likely to find its own equilibrium, at least not in any gentle kind of way. You have your work cut out for you in Chapter 7. It covers 1947 to 1967, which forms the nucleus of the Palestine–Israel conflict; it is perhaps the most important (and longest) chapter in the book. Go slowly, take your time. Chapter 8 is full of wars, but also sees the reemergence of the Palestinians, who get scooted aside a little in Chapter 7. The ninth and tenth chapters bring us up to date, reviewing the recent turmoil of the last ten years. If an eleventh chapter is ever added to this book, let us hope it's a happier one.

7

1947–1967
Conflict: Partition, Israeli Statehood, and the Six-Day War

Note: What's been developing in the last chapter will now become actual and official in this chapter. The conflict in which "those people have been fighting for thousands of years" really goes back about as far as the film Miracle on 34th Street, *and the first airing of the children's television show* Kukla, Fran and Ollie; *if you were born before 1948, you're older than Israel. In the twenty years covered in this chapter, Israel as a nation-state emerges; Palestine is reduced to 20 percent of its post-World War I size; and the Arab–Israeli conflict between Israel and the surrounding Arab nations is born. And by chapter's end, in 1967, we will arrive, for all intents and purposes, at present history in which the region is still embroiled.*

POSTWAR AND THE TWILIGHT OF THE BRITISH EMPIRE

The end of World War II brought with it a redistribution of global political power. Where Western Europe had been the sole power, the US and the Soviet Union were now the two "superpowers," both with little in the way of competition from anyone else. Great Britain, much to the contrary, found itself out of money and unable to sustain its imperial presence across West Asia. With Britain's announcement (February 1947) that it was pulling out of various colonial holdings, including Palestine, the US was handed the baton and became London's replacement in the Middle East. By this time, Russia had grabbed up all of Eastern and Central Europe, and began looking toward the Middle East, Turkey and Iran in particular. This caused concern in the Harry S. Truman administration (Roosevelt died April 1945), and on March 12, 1947, the White House announced the Truman Doctrine.

The intent of this policy was to contain Russian expansion – and the feared specter of communism – by economically supporting countries (mainly Greece and Turkey) that were deemed potential prey for the Soviets. The resultant balance of power and rivalry between the United States and the USSR led to what became known as the "Cold War." Also in response to the developing Cold War psychology was the creation of the Marshall Plan. The US feared that the beleaguered and unstable economies of Western Europe would tempt voters in these countries to tend toward communism. By instituting this economic and military reconstruction plan the US could further cultivate democracy – and alliances – thus inoculating the rest of Europe from potential Soviet influence.[1] As far as views on communism were concerned, the US and Great Britain were in agreement, but their views and interests concerning the Palestine question were divergent. This brings us to the crossroads of the epilogue of British colonialism and the prelude of direct and long-term American involvement in the Middle East.

As historian Charles D. Smith concisely states: "Immigration became the nexus of British–American–Zionist interactions."[2] Great Britain, in trying to cling to what colonial control it could, began reassessing its strategy. With the 1939 White Paper still intact, the British were also concerned about their oil holdings in the Persian Gulf, a commodity that the British economy was most interested in. Given these preoccupations, the British were more inclined to make gestures toward the Arabs so as not to rock the boat; vast immigration into Palestine would unnerve the Palestinians and thus not serve British needs. The Truman White House was torn on the matter and decided to shoot down the middle. The president felt personally obligated to do something for the displaced Jews – an obligation that would also help things domestically ("Gentlemen, I have no

Arabs among my constituents."). The US State Department, on the other hand, had its eye on Soviet expansion and decided that currying Arab favor was in America's best interest. Truman, more verbally supportive of the Jews than he actually was, asked the British to allow 100,000 Jewish refugees into Palestine. This obviously didn't serve British interests, and naturally resulted in delay at London's end. The British devised a committee that would attempt to solve the immigration/refugee impasse: the Anglo-American Committee of Inquiry (AAC).

Six British and six American delegates formed the twelve-man committee, which would interview Jewish refugees in America and Europe. What they decided (May 1946) was the following: 100,000 immigration certificates to be issued; rejection of partition of Palestine; relaxed future immigration; removal of restriction on Jewish land purchases; and the illegalization of discriminatory Zionist labor laws. Great Britain would continue the role of administrator, thus continuing the British mandate. The following groups were unsatisfied with the AAC report: the British, the Americans, the Zionists, and the Arabs. (The Americans and the Zionists were supportive of the immigration certificates, the British and the Arabs were not – all for different reasons, of course.) In a final effort the British, predictably, created another committee: the Morrison–Grady Committee. The report of Morrison–Grady suggested, again, the 100,000 certificates along with partition of Palestine into semi-autonomous cantons (districts or zones), and the eventual creation of a binational state with the British overseeing administrative concerns; in other words, a continuance of the mandate. London found this solution palatable but met resistance from the other three parties. By this time, however, the sun had set on the British Empire.

1947: PARTITION

In February 1947, the British handed Palestine to the United Nations. The reasons for this decision are somewhat speculative, but within a narrow range of possibilities. London's lack of economic willpower to carry on is certainly one reason.

That Britain may have been hoping the UN would simply decide to prolong the mandate and maybe support some of Britain's recent proposals is another.[3] As historian Benny Morris summarizes, British relations with the US were certainly a consideration:

> Most historians agree that given the Cold War context, in which the need for Anglo-American amity was seen as paramount, and Britain's insolvency, Whitehall [London] could ill afford to alienate Washington over a highly emotional issue that, when all was said and done, was not a vital British interest.[4]

The UN set up the United Nations Special Committee on Palestine (UNSCOP), an eleven-member team composed of representatives from eleven different UN member countries.[5] Spending five weeks in Palestine, the team set out to determine a solution to the Palestine question once and for all.

The committee submitted its report in August, which consisted of a majority report of seven nations (Australia abstained), and a minority report submitted by Iran, India, and Yugoslavia. The majority report suggested partition of Palestine into two states, Jewish and Arab, with Jerusalem existing as an international entity. All this was on the condition that each state signed a treaty establishing "the economic union of Palestine."[6] The minority report, on the other hand, proposed an "independent federal state" composed of an Arab state and a Jewish state. These states would have autonomy but would also be part of a federation creating "a single Palestinian nationality and citizenship."[7] The Arabs rejected the UNSCOP reports altogether. Historian Mark Tessler elucidates the Arab response:

> They adhered to their long-held position that Palestine was an integral part of the Arab world and that from the beginning its indigenous inhabitants has opposed the creation in their country of a Jewish national home. They also insisted that the United Nations, a body created and controlled by the United States and Europe, had no right to grant the Zionists any portion of their territory. In what was to become a familiar Arab charge, they insisted that the Western world was seeking to salve its conscience

for the atrocities of the war and was paying its own debt to the Jewish people with someone else's land.[8]

The Zionists cautiously approved the majority report and began a campaign to garner Truman's support for it. As one scholar put it: "The Palestine issue in the fall of 1947 was an Arab–Zionist contest within an Anglo-American controversy about to be drawn into the Soviet–American cold war."[9] Yet, in late September, Great Britain unilaterally (acting by itself) decided to end its mandate and withdraw from Palestine. The UN General Assembly would now determine definitively the matter of partition and Palestine.

In the time before the General Assembly vote, lobbying on the issue was thick and fast. Truman, though supportive of Zionism, was not a guaranteed vote for partition. However, with Zionist pressure from both Palestine and within the US government, along with Soviet support for partition, Truman adopted a pro-partition stance. During this period of lobbying Truman expressed his feelings on the matter thus: "I do not think I ever had as much pressure and propaganda aimed at the White House as I had in this instance."[10] Moreover, on the eve of the vote, the necessary two-thirds majority was not in place (by a small margin), which resulted in the not-so-gentle American–Zionist persuasion of the countries that were planning on voting it down. Threats of aid termination and embargoes were generally the method of persuasion.[11] The vote for partition as proposed in the UNSCOP majority report was held on November 29, 1947, with 33 nations in favor, 13 against, and 10 abstentions, thus passing UN Resolution 181.[12] The US and the Soviet Union voted in favor, with Great Britain abstaining. The boundaries of the partition were modeled on the delineations in the UNSCOP report, but with slight modifications. The land allocated to the Zionists comprised 56 percent of Palestine – and then war broke out.

CIVIL WAR, ISRAELI STATEHOOD

The Arabs were outraged at the UN's vote. They could not abide what essentially amounted to Europe and the US giving 56

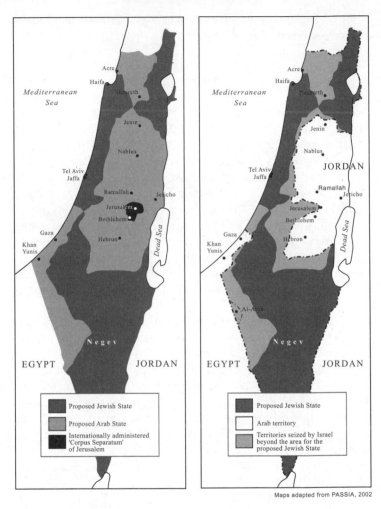

Maps adapted from PASSIA, 2002

Map 2   UNGA Partition Plan, 1947 (UN 181), and Armistice Lines, 1949

percent of Palestine to a foreign population that only made up slightly over 30 percent of the whole. (The population figures for 1946 are 1.3 million Arabs and 600,000 Jews, with 30,000 other.[13]) What followed was a year of war. The first phase (from the UN vote to May 14, 1948) was a civil war between Jews and Palestinian Arabs, all within Palestine. The second phase was an international war (from May 15, 1948 to the end of the year) between the new state of Israel and the surrounding Arab nations – Syria, Jordan, Egypt, Iraq, and to a lesser degree, Lebanon. By the end of the international war the map of what we've been calling Palestine assumed its present-day form.

Having attempted to create a solution in Palestine, the UN ended up making things worse. With questionable legal authority for the UN to impose partition, and no intervention of peacekeeping forces to implement such a plan, Palestine resorted to self-reliance in the form of violence. The UN and the international community kept their distance, both hesitant to enforce partition directly on a majority Arab population; in light of the UN's purpose of protecting *self-determination*, this was a sticky situation. The US, for its part, was cautious about an engagement where the Russians might become involved.

The civil war predominantly featured Palestinian Arabs and Jews locked in guerilla warfare. Less than a handful of Arab mercenaries and irregulars from the surrounding Arab countries came to assist the Palestinian Arabs, but their numbers were insignificant and their contribution to the cause even less so. The Zionist forces were comprised mainly of the Jewish defense force, Haganah, along with the LEHI and Irgun terrorist groups. The Zionists, on the whole, were far better trained and organized, and had a command structure that was part and parcel of their fairly developed political organization. The Palestinian Arabs, on the other hand, had remained practically leaderless since the Arab revolts of the 1930s. Though various members of leading Arab families assumed temporary roles here and there, they were usually corrupt, self-serving, and ineffective. All the same, for six months, bombs and ambushes raged throughout Palestine, assuming a provocation–reprisal pattern of violence, bloodshed, and terrorism. Women, children, and the elderly were frequently fair game, and both sides plumbed the depths of brutality. For the first half of the civil war the Arabs fought offensively, ambushing Jewish settlements and convoys, etc. The Zionists fought defensively, holding their UN-designated territory intact. In April 1948 the Haganah, along with LEHI and Irgun forces, went on the offensive, ushering in the period of the civil war featuring the worst violence. The most atrocious and notorious Zionist attack, and also a watershed in the civil war (one that still reverberates), was the attack at Deir Yassin.

Lying five miles west of Jerusalem, the village of Deir Yassin was attacked on April 9 by joint Irgun–LEHI forces, and a smaller number of Haganah troops. Though the village had agreed to a non-aggression pact with Haganah and its Jewish neighbors to avoid such violence, 254 men, women, and children were killed; the bodies of many were mutilated and thrown down wells.[14] Some survivors of the village were then put in the back of trucks and paraded in the streets as showpieces. The point in examining one Zionist attack is not for the sake of emphasizing Zionist terrorism; Arab fighters, too, carried out appalling attacks on defenseless civilians during this period. But, aside from being an instance of savage atrocity, both the severity of Deir Yassin and its promulgation and propaganda by Arabs and Zionists alike created vast Arab panic. This terror and flight affected the demographics of the UN-designated territories along with the outcome of the war. As Arab radio stations broadcast news of Deir Yassin, Zionists forces in trucks with loudspeakers further terrorized Arab peasants and villagers with threats of similar violence. By the end of the civil phase of the war in 1948, 300,000 Arabs had fled their homes for other areas in Palestine, or entered surrounding Arab states.[15] This was the start of a Palestinian refugee problem that changed the course of Palestinian–Israeli history and has yet to be resolved.

By April, Haganah troops were well in control, and by May the Palestinian guerilla effort was in tatters. On May 14, 1948, the last of the British departed at the port of Haifa, bringing to an end three decades of Great Britain's colonial presence. That same day, at 4:00 p.m. in the Tel Aviv Museum, the Jewish leadership listened in person while the world did so by radio as Ben-Gurion declared the "establishment of the Jewish State in Palestine, to be called *Medinath Yisrael* (the State of Israel)."[16]

With trust in the Rock of Israel, we set our hands on this declaration at this session of the Provisional State Council in the city of Tel Aviv, on this Sabbath Eve, the fifth day of Iyar, in the year five thousand seven hundred and eight.[17]

David Ben-Gurion
May 14, 1948

The declaration of independence starts with a brief description of Jewish history, and then sets forth its principles – a hand extended in peace to its neighbors, cooperation with the UN, etc. – against a backdrop of justification for the state to exist. As historian Howard M. Sachar describes:

[The declaration] notified the world that the Land of Israel was the historic birthplace of the Jewish people, that the Zionist movement was testimony to the role Palestine had fulfilled in Jewish history and religion, that the Balfour Declaration, the United Nations Partition Resolution, the sacrifice of the Zionist pioneers, and the torment suffered by Jews in recent years – all laid the moral and legal foundations for the new state.[18]

The first country to acknowledge Israel was the United States, which it did that day, the Russians quickly following suit. Zionism had become a reality.

INTERNATIONAL WAR AND THE BIRTH OF THE ARAB–ISRAELI CONFLICT

The allegory commonly used when describing the international phase of the 1948 war is that of David and Goliath. The Old Testament story (1 Samuel 17:1–58) describes an Israelite peasant boy doing battle with a mighty Philistine warrior named Goliath. David kills Goliath with a slingshot and goes on to become the king of Israel. This is tempting imagery, and on paper all of the Arab Middle East did attack 650,000 Jews, with Israel emerging the victor. But the reality of the 1948 war was something altogether different; the Israeli Defense Forces (IDF; Haganah's successor) were certainly a formidable, well-trained, and organized fighting force to be sure, but no one is *that* good. In reality the invading countries – Egypt, Jordan,

Iraq, Syria, and a handful of soldiers from Saudi Arabia and Lebanon – sent approximately 23,000 troops into Palestine, and were met by 30,000–40,000 IDF troops.[19] These numbers would increase throughout the war, with Israeli increases being far more significant. In summary, all the Arab Middle East invaded Israel, and was not only outnumbered, but roundly defeated as well. So what does all this mean? A look through the lens of Arab politics provides the needed clarity.

Before the Zionists announced statehood, the previous two months were spent with the US and the UN motivating the Jews and the Arabs to sign a truce. The hope was to put an official end to the civil war and prevent an international upheaval involving the surrounding Arab countries. The US had cooled on the idea of partition in early 1948 and was kicking around the idea of a trusteeship for Palestine that would place all of it in the direct care of the UN. When the US-led initiative was met with dismay, it scrapped the trusteeship idea and focused on a truce. In mid-April the UN Security Council voted on a truce plan, with Egypt in favor. The truce was rigidly rejected by David Ben-Gurion and King Abdullah of Transjordan: Ben-Gurion would not postpone declaration of statehood and wanted to avoid precise UN-defined boundaries in the case of a truce, and Abdullah's plans of annexing Palestine for himself didn't fit within these parameters either. With Zionists aware of their military superiority – and Abdullah's willing compliance – the Zionists declared statehood.[20]

Note: The UN is an international body composed of many organizations and agencies that work in concert, as stated in the UN Charter,

> to save succeeding generations from the scourge of war,... to reaffirm faith in fundamental human rights,... to establish conditions under which justice and respect for the obligations arising from treaties and other sources of international law can be maintained, and to promote social progress and better standards of life in larger freedom.[21]

Two of the UN's main bodies, which will receive frequent mentioning from here onwards, are the General Assembly and the Security Council. The General Assembly is the collective membership of the UN. When the UN was first established there were 51 member states; there are now 191. Among its duties are to discuss issues and make suggestions through resolutions. The Assembly's resolutions are not legally binding and have no power of enforcement. The Security Council, on the other hand, is mandated to "promote the establishment and maintenance of international peace and security." It is composed of 15 members – 5 permanent, and 10 rotating (originally 6). The permanent members are the US, Great Britain, Russia, France, and China. Security Council resolutions are legally binding and enforceable. During a vote, any of the permanent members have the power to veto a resolution by simply voting against it. (More information can be found on their website, www.un.org.)

Though the populations of the Middle East seethed with anger at the fate of the Palestinians – partition, defeat, and displacement – the governments were less than interested in war with Israel. They were locked in rivalries of power and preeminence with one another, and gave war with Israel hardly a serious thought. Aside from crumbling economies, domestic political instability, and competition for the position of leading Arab nation (especially between Transjordan and Egypt), Transjordan played a key role in international hesitancy to invade Israel. With an interest in annexing what was left of Palestine for itself, a secret non-aggression pact between Transjordan's King Abdullah and Israel was made one week before the UN partition. In the pact, Abdullah promised Israel noninterference, and in return Israel granted Transjordan's annexation of UN-designated Palestine. Abdullah's plotted course was a step toward his plans for a "Greater Syria," which were neither secret nor popular with his Arab neighbors. It is also important to keep in mind that Transjordan was very much a British client state, whose military was commanded by a British officer, Sir John Bagot Glubb. Any plans Abdullah had of expanding his holdings were viewed as not only an obvious threat to the other Arabs states, but also included

British benefit with London's possible reinvolvement in the region. Transjordan had one ally in the region (Israel) and was surrounded by countries (its Arab neighbors) hostile to its plans for cooperation with the Zionists, its plans for territorial expansion at their expense, and its British servitude.[22] So the Arab states were torn with concerns of (1) maintaining forces at home to keep order among unstable populations; (2) saving face in front of their domestic populations and thus invading on the *pretense* of fighting for Palestine's honor; and (3) invading Israel just to keep Transjordan from walking away with Palestine. With the truces tossed out, overwhelming public support on both sides, Ben-Gurion's defiance, as well as Abdullah's determination to occupy UN-designated Palestine, the Arab countries invaded, initiating what Glubb later referred to as "a curious imitation of a war."[23]

As one might predict, with a lack of cohesion, no plans, and insufficient troops, the Arab countries did not fare well in the conflict. (None of the Arab armies had fought a war before.) The fighting that lasted from mid-May to July, with a flare-up in October after a three-month truce, produced a victorious Israel and a humiliated and limping Arab Middle East. Israel had suffered the death of approximately one percent of its population, about 6,000 people; a majority of the military deaths resulted from offensive maneuvers.[24] When the dust settled the 56 percent of Palestine that the UN had allotted to the Zionists expanded to 78 percent. The 44 percent allotted to Palestine was cut in half, leaving 22 percent to the Palestinians (see map 2, p. 92).

During the first half of 1949 Egypt, Lebanon, Transjordan, and Syria signed armistices with Israel (all except for Iraq). In separate agreements, the remaining 22 percent of Palestine was divided up between Egypt and Transjordan. Egypt would assume control of Gaza, and Transjordan would be handed the part of UN-designated Palestine that lay along the west bank of the Jordan River. After the armistice, this portion of land would become known as the "West Bank," designating it as a mere extension of Transjordan, or what would become the Hashemite Kingdom of Jordan, or Jordan for short. Abdullah actually went so far as to issue a decree banning the word "Palestine" from all official documents.[25]

Note: The boundary of the 1949 Armistice, distinguishing the West Bank and Gaza from Israel proper, has become known as the "Green Line." This designation is the internationally recognized border that remains today.

The defeat of 1947–48 and allocation of Palestine to Egypt and Jordan marked the abandonment of the UN partition plan and the collapse of the independence Palestinians so desired. To this day Palestinians refer to 1947–48 as *al-Naqba* (the Catastrophe, or Disaster). As the armistice agreements were being signed, the situation was this: Israel was a fixed and permanent reality, Palestinian sovereignty was a dream lying in ruin, and a state of no war–no peace took hold of the entire Middle East.

A NOTE ABOUT THE PALESTINIAN REFUGEES

Note: This section functions essentially as a large note. The subject of the refugee problem, created between 1947 and 1949, has brought disagreements in the historical literature. Below is a discussion of the facts and figures, and where scholars disagree as to the causes of these data.

A long-disputed issue has been the dispossession of hundreds of thousands of Palestinians from their homes during the civil and international phases of the 1947–48 war. Over the last two decades documents have been made available and serious research has been carried out and published on this subject revealing a great deal of new information.[26] Over the course of the war approximately 700,000 Palestinians fled or were forced from their homes and into Arab-held Palestine or the surrounding Arab countries. The remaining Arab population was distributed between Israel (150,000), the West Bank (400,000), and Gaza (60,000).[27] What remains in dispute to a degree are the causal elements that created the refugee problem. Historian Benny Morris suggests from his research that there was no explicit Zionist policy or master plan of expulsion before or during the war. Instead he maintains that, "while military attacks or expulsions were the major precipitant to flight, the exodus was, overall, the result of a cumulative process and a set of causes."[28] Morris arrives at this assessment via studies of declassified documents and an appraisal of the two poles of the argument, establishing his own position somewhere between the two.

According to Morris, "Arab and pro-Arab commentators" maintain that the refugee problem was the result of a "Zionist 'master-plan' of expulsion,'" while "old-school Zionist commentators and historians" assert that the "sporadic talk among Zionist leaders of 'transfer' was mere pipe-dreaming and was never undertaken systematically or seriously." Morris's view is that talk of transfer among Zionists in the 1930s and early 1940s "was not tantamount to pre-planning and did not issue in the production of a policy or master-plan of expulsion." However, he does maintain that "... transfer was inevitable and inbuilt into Zionism – because it sought to transform a land which was 'Arab' into a 'Jewish' state and a Jewish state could not have arisen without a major displacement of Arab population ..."[29]

Nevertheless, some scholars maintain that Morris hasn't gone far enough in how he judges the data, and suggest a higher degree of Zionist intent and premeditation.[30] The general criticism is that Morris's research provides proof for the existence of premeditated intent, and that his findings undermine his conclusions. Unfortunately, we are unable to fully address the ins-and-outs of the various arguments here. It is important, however, to note a few contours of the problem.

In the early moments of the war some Jews tried to prevent flight, though upper- and middle-class Arabs having the resources to leave did so, and with the intention of returning when the violence subsided. This set a precedent for the peasant classes to emulate, as well as reducing personnel in schools, businesses, etc., thus creating more incentive for peasants to leave. Yet, by April 1948, attacks like Deir Yassin were occurring and exodus was then as much due to fear as forced expulsion. Later, towns like Lydda and Ramleh were forcibly expelled in their entirety, rendering 50,000–60,000 people homeless in one fell swoop.[31] Moreover, it is important to note that the notion of expelling the Palestinians was not a remote or recent consideration, especially at the elite level.

The issue of population transfer appears in the diaries, memoirs, and correspondence of top-level leadership throughout early Zionist history.[32] From Zionism's earliest beginnings the problem of a native population in Palestine demanded a solution, as even Theodor Herzl commented in his diaries:

> We must expropriate [confiscate] gently ... We shall try to spirit the penniless population across the border by procuring employment for it in the transit countries, while denying it any employment in our country ... Both the process of expropriation and the removal of the poor must be carried out discretely and circumspectly.[33]

David Ben-Gurion shared an identical logic in a speech to the Twentieth Zionist Congress in 1937:

> Transfer is what will make possible a comprehensive settlement programme. Thankfully, the Arab people have vast empty areas. Jewish power, which grows steadily, will also increase our possibilities to carry out the transfer on a large scale.[34]

Given Zionism's goal of forging a Jewish state in an Arab country, a solid Jewish majority was an obvious necessity, and standing in the way was a large Arab population and potential "fifth column" (subversive element). What evolved throughout the war was an increased realization of the benefits, and relative ease, of such methods. The war offered a bridge between theory and practice. As Morris summarizes:

> By 1948, transfer was in the air. The transfer thinking that preceded the war contributed to the denouement [outcome] by conditioning the Jewish population, political parties, military organisations and military and

civilian leaderships for what transpired. Thinking about the possibilities
of transfer in the 1930s and the 1940s had prepared and conditioned
hearts and minds for its implementation in the course of 1948 so that,
as it occurred, few voiced protest or doubt; it was accepted as inevitable
and natural by the bulk of the Jewish population.[35]

Further evidence of this mindset is the policies preventing
and denying the right of return for refugee populations. In
1948, once a village was emptied, it became common to loot
and destroy it – or leave it intact depending on its quality, in
order to make it available for Jewish immigrants. Refugees
were and still are refused return, a position Israel continues
to stand firm on, and a problem that still contributes to the
current impasse.

THE ARAB–ISRAELI CONFLICT

*Note: Now is as good a time as any to clarify this. When browsing
books on the subject, you'll notice that this conflict gets called all
sorts of things: the Palestinian–Israeli conflict, the Zionist–Arab
conflict, the Arab–Israeli conflict, and on and on. Though not a
critical issue, the wording can be confusing. The conflict within
Israel and Palestine is the Palestine–Israel conflict, though other
variations are acceptable, e.g., Israeli–Palestinian conflict, etc. The
conflict that developed between Israel and the rest of the surrounding
Arab countries (Egypt, Jordan, Syria, Lebanon, as well as Saudi
Arabia and Iraq) is known as the Arab–Israeli conflict. This book
could just as easily have been titled,* The Arab–Israeli Conflict:
A Basic Introduction, *but I chose to focus on the conflict within,
it being first and giving rise to the greater Arab–Israeli conflict.
The label "Arab–Israeli conflict" can also detract from the actual
issue; the larger, more general conflict tends to replace and obscure
the conflict with the Palestinians. As we see in this section, the
Palestinians are almost forgotten in the wake of the conflict between
Israel and the rest of the Arab states.*

The backdrop to this section (1949–56) is the Cold War. US and
British interest in containing Soviet expansion into the Middle

East played a key role in how these two nations dealt with the no war–no peace Middle East situation after 1947–48. In the foreground of this period, however, were Arab resentment and rivalry (which was typical), and Israeli militancy (which was becoming typical).

As noted, the Arab nations were not domestically stable before the war, and defeat by Israel didn't help matters. For the younger generation this humiliation clearly indicated a lack of leadership. The attendant dismay at both the elite and popular levels resulted in severe instability, and finally revolution. Syria's leadership was overturned with one coup after another in the postwar period; King Abdullah of Jordan continuously attempted to establish a relationship with Israel, which resulted in his assassination by a Palestinian nationalist in 1951; and Egypt's King Faruq was deposed in a bloodless coup that brought to power the young Colonel Gamal Abdul Nasser, the first leader of native Egyptian lineage to take sustained control in 2,000 years. Postwar Arab attention was focused primarily on domestic concerns, and secondarily on competition with one another – Israel and Palestine were, at this point, something of an afterthought, though for saving face before the Arab populations a posture of anti-Israeli belligerency was generally struck.

Israel, on the other hand, was aglow with confidence and defiance. But despite its recent military success, there still lingered the doubt over Arab desire to destroy Israel, and a general sense of vulnerability and isolation, creating a hyper-defensive mindset among the populace, and an assumed stance of aggressive defense, or "activism," at the top levels of government. Charles D. Smith explains:

> Israel's attitude toward the Arabs and its relations with the outside world were predicated on the Jewish experience in Europe, the Holocaust, and the Arab hostility it encountered in the Middle East. Whereas Jews had previously been subject to the will of non-Jews, Israel, as the Jewish state, would never submit to constraints imposed by others. In Ben-Gurion's view, Israel alone was responsible for its existence. Though it might rely on outside help, economically and militarily, that would not

signify its willingness to limit its independence in any way. For Ben-Gurion and those allied with him in the Israeli government, the opinions of the outside world meant little, regardless of the aid other countries might give. He made a nearly absolute distinction between Israel and world Jewry on the one hand, and the *goyim*, or non-Jews, on the other. If the latter did not fulfill their perceived obligations to Israel, they would be at best ignored, at worst be fought.[36]

To this psychological make-up of the Middle East must be added Cold War politics.

There was a pronounced Anglo-American interest in establishing alliances that would serve as buffers to obstruct potential Soviet involvement in the region. Moreover, there was a fear that the instability of the Arab states would make them vulnerable to Soviet influence. One such alliance was called the Baghdad Pact (February 1955), which consisted of Great Britain, unofficial US sponsorship, Iraq, and the countries that seal the Soviet Union off from the Middle East, or the "northern tier" countries – Turkey, Iran, and Pakistan. Iraq was the only Arab country to belong to the alliance, for which it was severely criticized by Egypt's Nasser. In the Anglo-American effort to establish a Cold War Middle East bulwark, one country that was unwilling to cooperate was Egypt. Nasser opposed such pacts, interpreting them as further attempts to sustain Western control over the Middle East. His objective was pan-Arab independence, as he loathed British imperialism, which still maintained its presence in Egypt. With his support of Algeria's resistance to French occupation, contempt for Israel as an instance of Western colonialism, suspicion of US intervention, as well as hatred for Britain and imperialism in general, Nasser was needless to say unpopular in the West.

Just before the Baghdad Pact, Nasser made an agreement with London (July 1954, signed in October) for Britain to withdraw its military from bases in the Suez Canal Zone. The canal was a vital international route in ferrying freight in and out of the Mediterranean and had been under the military control of the British since 1882. Certain Israeli leaders viewed this agreement as a potential threat and attempted to discourage Britain's withdrawal. In response Israeli military intelligence launched an operation involving a spy ring in Cairo, which would set off bombs at American and British embassies there and centers frequented by Westerners. The idea was to cause panic and doubt over Nasser's control of security and thus led to the termination of the Anglo-Egyptian agreement. The operation (July 1954) never got off the ground. One of the agent's bombs ignited prematurely, ruining the plot and exposing the entire network. This incident became known as the "Lavon Affair," named after Israel's defense minister, Pinhas Lavon.

The Lavon Affair had been planned and executed without the knowledge of the prime minister, Moshe Sharett, whose methods tended toward moderation and diplomacy compared to the activist elites around him. Sharett became prime minister in 1953 when Ben-Gurion went into retirement, but in early 1955 Ben-Gurion returned to government, replacing Lavon as defense minister. Eleven days after Ben-Gurion's return Israeli paratroopers raided Egyptian military bases in Gaza. The rationale Israel gave for the raid was as a reprisal for infiltrations and attacks coming from Egyptian-controlled Gaza into Israel. Though tension and violence existed on Israel's borders (as will be discussed in the next section) Israeli documents reflect a period of relative calm, making the raid into Gaza seem suspicious.[37] The source of the Gaza raid most likely came from both discord between Ben-Gurion and Sharett, and the desire to send Egypt a message and possibly provoke Nasser into response. As Sharett stated in his diaries shortly after the Gaza raid:

> The army spokesman, on instructions from the Minister of Defense, delivered a false version to the press: a unit of ours, after having been attacked supposedly inside our territory, returned the fire and engaged a battle which later developed as it did. Who will believe us?

He then goes on to say:

> Who would be foolish enough to believe that such a complicated operation could 'develop' from a casual and sudden attack on an Israeli army unit by an Egyptian unit?[38]

Secret contacts and attempts at diplomacy had been made between Sharett and Nasser, both of whom were interested in pursuing a level of agreement.[39] Nevertheless, the developments and resultant tension led to Nasser's increased hostility toward Israel and an arms race that ultimately brought with it war.

Nasser sought arms from the US but the Americans placed stipulations that he deemed unacceptable and thus rejected what was offered. In turn, Nasser successfully secured an arms deal from Russia. At the same time, the Egyptian leader was embarking on a dam-building project on the Nile at Aswan, for which he needed financing. The US, in an attempt to reestablish relations with Egypt, offered to provide economic assistance for the project. Though the offer was made, the US was losing patience with Egypt's nationalism and independent attitude; Eisenhower's secretary of state, John Foster Dulles, steered US policy in the Middle East at the time, and Nasser's noncompliance elicited Dulles's irritation. When Nasser proclaimed recognition of Communist China in May 1956, it was all the secretary could take. Shortly thereafter, the US withdrew support for the Aswan Dam project in an attempt to reprimand Cairo. The response was unexpected: Nasser decided to nationalize the Suez Canal. The canal was owned by an Anglo-French company, but Nasser was within his rights according to pertinent treaties and laws. The shareholders of the canal were promised compensation for their holdings, and the canal's traffic went unhindered, and in some cases even improved.[40] On top of this Nasser had closed the Strait of Tiran at the tip of the Sinai Peninsula, denying transit of ships heading for Israel. The fuse had been lit.

SUEZ CANAL CRISIS (1956)

The Suez War went something like this: Britain and France believed that control of the Suez Canal could be regained, and Nasser toppled, with the practical use of force. Israel joined the plan to teach Nasser a permanent lesson, and planning began for a British–French–Israeli invasion of Egypt. The scheduled attack revolved around favorable weather conditions, along with the two world superpowers being distracted – by an upcoming election (America's distraction), and rebellion in Hungary and Poland (Russia's distraction). The plan was for Israel to invade Egypt via the Sinai Peninsula, and upon reaching the canal London and Paris would issue an ultimatum for Israel and Egypt to withdraw their forces ten miles from the canal. Knowing that Nasser would hardly comply with such a demand, the two European forces would then descend upon the Suez Canal to "separate" the two Middle Eastern forces.

On October 29, 1956, Israeli paratroopers landed near the canal while other battalions under the command of Ariel Sharon made their way through Sinai and arrived at the Suez. Egypt engaged its troops; the ultimatum was issued from Britain and France; Egypt said no; Britain and France advanced their forces, bombing Egyptian airfields and landing at Port Said on the canal. On November 2, the UN General Assembly passed a resolution with near unanimity for a cease-fire and withdrawal of all invading forces. With harsh UN, US, and Russian condemnation, France and Great Britain agreed to the resolution days later. Israel dismissed the resolution until it completed its entire capture of the Sinai Peninsula, after which it agreed to the cease-fire.

Nasser, though trounced, emerged a hero and a figure of Arab nationalism, while the invasion only hardened the Arab view of Israel as an agent of Western imperialism. Egypt also secured increased backing from Russia, including support for the Aswan Dam. Israel, though condemned as an aggressor by the US and the UN – and forced by both to withdraw from Gaza and Sinai – elevated its reputation as a formidable force on the international stage. UN Emergency Forces (UNEF) were placed in Gaza and the southern tip of Sinai to prevent border clashes, a presence that Egypt reserved the right to terminate. The Egyptian–Israeli border would remain quiet for the next decade. The relative ten-year calm that also fell over the Middle East as a whole was of the kind that precedes violent weather.

THE JUNE 1967 WAR (THE SIX-DAY WAR)

The years between 1957 and 1967 were relatively quiet in the Arab–Israeli arena, but general tumult and rivalry carried on as usual between the Arab countries, on Israel's border, and amongst the Israeli leadership. Over the course of the John F. Kennedy and Lyndon B. Johnson presidencies US–Israeli relations warmed considerably, including intelligence cooperation between the US's Central Intelligence Agency (CIA) and Israel's Mossad (its foreign intelligence agency, something like the CIA). The Cold War remained a factor, playing a role in increased American support for Israel. (Johnson's personal feelings on the matter, along with the sympathy of the American people, also played a significant part.) US economic aid to Egypt increased at first but deteriorated over the course of the 1960s. While US support of Israel increased, so too did Soviet support of Egypt, Syria, and Iraq. Yet, Israel's military superiority never wavered, and in addition to its arms acquisitions it began a program for developing nuclear weapons over the course of the 1950s and 1960s with the aid of France, and eventually the US.

Among the Palestinians the seeds of rebellion were sown with the formation of the Palestinian Liberation Organization (PLO) as well as a smaller, more militant group called al-Fatah, the leaders of which included a young nationalist named Yasser Arafat. The PLO, which formed in May 1964, was mainly under the control of Nasser and was an organization lacking teeth and autonomy. The goal of alleviating the situation of the Palestinian refugees made for powerful speech-making, but the Arab countries were less than interested in acting on those sentiments. Fatah, on the other hand, operated with far greater ideological resolve. Though founded in 1958, it wasn't until 1964 that Fatah started infiltrating into Israel in earnest to plant explosives. It was influenced by Algeria's uprising against the French and felt violence and militancy should precede diplomacy and politics.

Guerilla infiltrations into Israel in general increased during the 1960s, especially along the borders of Jordan and Syria; the UN presence along the Egyptian border continued to discourage such activity. The Israeli–Syrian border in particular became a hotbed of fighting, escalating to the use of artillery and fighter planes. Raids from Syria eventually led to a major, and curious, Israeli reprisal on the southern West Bank town of Samu (November 1966), where homes and public buildings were destroyed, with 18 people killed and 54 wounded.[41] The attack was condemned by the UN and US. Unlike Syria, the Jordanian government, which controlled the West Bank, instigated no guerilla activity, though aggression still came from the Jordanian border. Yet the attack and subsequent condemnation for his inaction embarrassed Jordan's King Hussein (Abdullah's grandson), as well as Nasser, the face of Arab unity, for not defending an Arab state. Aside from the strategic value of contributing to intra-Arab rivalry, the attack on the Jordanian-controlled West Bank begged the question, even by supporters of Israel, about its rationale for doing so. Nevertheless, clashes continued on the Syria–Israel border, inching the region in the direction of another war.

Reports began to emanate from Damascus that the Israelis were massing troops in heavy concentration along the Syrian border, poised for imminent attack. Russia "confirmed" these reports, which escalated the tension and placed Nasser on high alert; Egypt and Syria, at Russian behest, signed a defense pact that would help protect Soviet objectives in the region. The reports of massing Israeli troops, however, were false. Later Syrian reconnaissance flights provided conclusive photos that revealed no such troop concentrations, and UN observers, too, confirmed the falsity of the claim. Though reasoning behind Russian behavior here is speculative, most assume that it feared an Israeli attack on Syria and thought a potential Egyptian response might encourage Israeli hesitation. Whether Nasser knew of the intelligence being bogus or not, he began assembling troops in Sinai. Nasser's response is also an occasion for speculation, but the intent of polishing up his image probably wasn't far from his mind. And then he took it the extra step. To the shock of just about everyone, Nasser requested UNEF to withdraw from the Egyptian border and Sinai, as was his legal right according to the agreement after the Suez Crisis.

Then, to an even greater shock – probably including Nasser's – UN Secretary General U Thant granted the request without question and pulled the UNEF troops from the region. Nasser immediately further militarized Sinai and closed once again the Strait of Tiran (May 22) to ships heading for or belonging to Israel. Syria, Jordan, and Iraq all began to mobilize in the event of hostility; Jordan's Hussein even flew to Cairo (May 30) to sign a defense agreement with Egypt. The stage was set: Arab troops mobilized; Israeli troops also mobilized; belligerent speeches were made by Nasser; Israel's terrified population feared a second Holocaust; and Israel's IDF leadership was champing at the bit for war, though Prime Minister Levi Eshkol was much less so, at first. Israel invaded Egypt on the morning of June 5, 1967, and five days later it was all over – though some would say in *three hours* it was all over.

The June 1967 War, or the "Six-Day War" as the victors preferred to call it, has been written about at great length,[42] however, a quick synopsis here will serve our purposes: At 7:45 a.m. on that Monday, Israeli planes flying low and under the radar destroyed Egypt's air force while it was still on the ground. Within three hours Israel had already maimed Egypt's greatest threat. The rest was a clean-up. While Israeli troops took Gaza and eventually the entirety of Sinai over the next couple of days, it managed to destroy the air forces of Jordan and Syria. Israel offered Jordan a cease-fire during the first day on the condition that Jordan hold its reins and not engage in the conflict. King Hussein, who had already entered into a pact with Egypt, and whose country housed the bulk of the Palestinian refugees, had little choice but to attack and began shelling Israel. The IDF responded in full force. Over the course of June 6 and 7 (days two and three), Hussein sought a cease-fire. The UN responded with a Security Council resolution (233), but Israel continued its drive toward the Jordan River, dismissing the resolution, and by the end of June 7 had taken all of the West Bank along with all of Jerusalem. Then only did Israel acknowledge the cease-fire. On June 8, Egypt also accepted the cease-fire, along with Syria, whose involvement in the war had been insignificant. Israel decided to wait for its attack on Syria.

The Israelis were worried that the US would try to prevent an attack on Syria. America was focused on the war in Vietnam, as well as mindful of potential Soviet involvement in the Middle East owing to the war, and an Israeli attack on Syria was too sensitive for US interests. Meanwhile, a US intelligence-gathering ship called the USS *Liberty* was stationed in the Mediterranean off the Sinai coast, monitoring the communications of the war. On June 8 (day four) unmarked planes, later identified as Israeli, rocketed and strafed the ship, along with dropping napalm canisters and destroying lifeboats, even after they had been deployed. Shortly after the air attack, Israeli torpedo boats torpedoed the ship's hull. The *Liberty* somehow did not sink through all of this, though in the course of two hours the ship had been utterly devastated. Thirty-four members of its crew were killed and over one hundred wounded. Israel extended its apologies, claiming it was a case of mistaken identity. The Johnson administration accepted Israel's apologies, keeping the story quiet at home.[43] As a result of the *Liberty* attack, American surveillance of Israeli plans in Syria, who had agreed to the UN cease-fire, was no longer an issue. On the same day Israel initiated the air and artillery phase of its attack. The day after (June 9, day five) Israel began a full invasion of Syria in violation of another UN cease-fire to which it had agreed. By June 10 Israel ended its attack, having acquired the Golan Heights, a portion of southwestern Syria off the Israeli border. The war was over and Israel was in control of Sinai, Gaza, the West Bank (including all of Jerusalem), and the Golan Heights. Egypt, Jordan, and Syria had been pulverized. Israel had tripled its size.

In the acquisition of Gaza and the West Bank, Israel came in control of 1.1 million Palestinians: 600,000 in the West Bank, 70,000 in East Jerusalem, and 350,000 in Gaza. (200,000 West Bank Palestinians had become refugees and fled or were expelled into Jordan.[44]) Homes and villages of fleeing Palestinians were frequently demolished. In the Maghrabi Quarter facing the Western Wall in the Old City of Jerusalem, in one example,

135 homes were bulldozed and 650 people were evicted from the area to make way for a plaza for Jewish prayer in front of the wall. This type of action became routine throughout the occupied territories.[45]

Ian J. Bickerton and Carla L. Klausner's summary of the June 1967 war is worth quoting in full:

> The long-range causes of the 1967 war were the continued inability of the Arabs to recognize and accept the political sovereignty of the Jews in Israel; the antagonism and desire for revenge that had been fueled by defeats and humiliation in the previous wars, as well as by Israel's excessive retaliations; Arab fear of Israeli aggressiveness and expansionism; and Israeli "hawkishness" and the determination to maintain military superiority. The inability to find a solution for the plight of the Palestinian refugees, because of intransigence on both sides, provided the *raison d'être* [reason for being] and rallying point for the Arab crusade against Israel. The short-term and more proximate causes were the arms build-up on both sides in the previous decade; superpower interference and especially Soviet meddling; the volatile situation in Syria; Nasser's brinkmanship; the defense pacts that linked together Egypt, Syria, and Jordan; and the failure of the international community to prevent war through diplomacy. All sides thus must share the blame for the outbreak of hostilities and for the consequences that followed.[46]

RESOLUTION 242

The end of the Six-Day War found Israel confident, reputed as a formidable power, and three times its previous size. As for the Arab countries, they had been flattened, militarily and morally. The immediate concern of everyone involved, including the region's sponsors in Washington and Moscow, was how to proceed with negotiations and peace settlements. The Israelis were willing to engage in direct negotiations (Arab–Israeli talks with no outside involvement) and relinquish their newly acquired land for peace and Arab recognition of them as a state, though this view would slightly cool off with increased interest in retaining most of the territory. The Arabs wanted Israeli withdrawal to the pre-June 5 borders (Green Line), and to proceed with indirect third party negotiations involving the UN. In August–September 1967 the Arabs held a summit in the Sudan capital of Khartoum. The summit sent a mixed signal, one of diplomacy and militancy, as well as arriving at the so-called "Three No's": "no peace with Israel, no recognition of Israel, [and] no negotiations with it...."[47] Along with this rhetoric was included the contradictory mention of uniting "political efforts at the international and diplomatic level" to ensure Israeli withdrawal. The ambiguities of Khartoum allowed for the accommodation of divergent positions – those in support of inflexibility and militancy (Syria and the Palestinians), and those eager to negotiate a withdrawal (Egypt and Jordan). The need for ambiguity was also the order of the day at the UN.

After months of deliberation and revisions, the UN Security Council, on November 22, 1967, passed Resolution 242 (see p. 115). The gist of 242 is land-for-peace, or peace-for-land – the order wasn't established. What is called for is a "termination of all claims or states of belligerency and acknowledgement of the sovereignty, territorial integrity and political independence of every state in the area...." Also stated is the "inadmissibility of the acquisition of territory by war," calling for the "[w]ithdrawal of Israeli armed forces from territories occupied in the recent conflict." In an earlier version of the resolution Israel was called upon to withdraw "from *the* territories occupied" but this was changed in response to Israel's concerns about what it deemed the specificity of the word "the." The wording was then changed to withdrawal "from territories occupied." The Israelis viewed their obligations as withdrawal from *some* of the territories, thus protecting their "right to live in peace within secure and recognized boundaries," which was also addressed in the resolution. The Arab interpretation was withdrawal from *all* territories, period.

Differences in interpretation aside, Egypt, Jordan, and Israel signed the resolution, which became the basis for all peace efforts, and remains so today. For implementation of the resolution, the UN assigned the Swedish UN diplomat Gunnar Jarring the unenviable task of bringing the involved parties

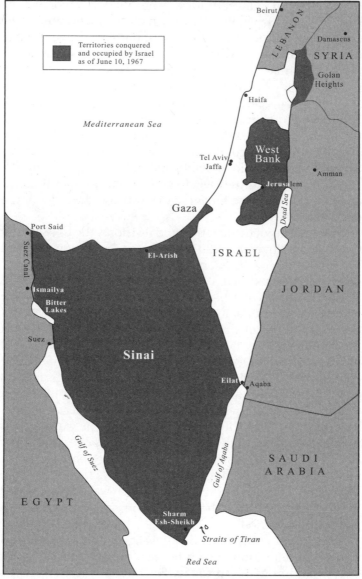

Territories conquered
and occupied by Israel
as of June 10, 1967

Beirut

LEBANON

Damascus

SYRIA

Golan
Heights

Haifa

Mediterranean Sea

West
Bank

Tel Aviv
Jaffa

Amman

Jerusalem

Gaza

Dead Sea

Port Said

Suez Canal

El-Arish

ISRAEL

JORDAN

Ismailya

Bitter
Lakes

Suez

Sinai

Eilat   Aqaba

Gulf of Suez

Gulf of Aqaba

SAUDI
ARABIA

EGYPT

Sharm
Esh-Sheikh

Straits of Tiran

Red Sea

Map adapted from PASSIA, 2002

Map 3   Post-June 1967 War: Territories occupied by Israel

to the table. As for the Palestinians, the only mention in 242 regarding their concerns is the urging of a "just settlement of the refugee problem." Being relegated to a mere human rights issue, some Palestinians felt theirs was a political issue involving statehood and sovereignty, and now being subject to oppressive Israeli military occupation was all they could bear.

Note: UN 242 says what now? As historian Arthur Goldschmidt remarks, Resolution 242 "joined the Hussein–McMahon Correspondence and the Balfour Declaration in that gallery of ambiguous documents complicating the Arab-Israeli conflict."[48] In essence the UN Security Council, under the influence of the US and the USSR, came up with a document that was loose enough in its wording to make everyone happy (more or less). The Arabs are asked to recognize and get along with Israel, and Israel in turn is supposed to give back "territories occupied." For Israel that meant some of the land, for the Arabs that meant all of the land, for the Security Council that meant all of the land, and for the US that meant pretty much most of the land. The cornerstone of 242, however, is the "inadmissibility of the acquisition of territory by war," which is fairly cut and dry. The Palestinians, in 242, are reduced to a "refugee problem."

With the exception of Israel occupying the Sinai Peninsula, where we have just now left off is where the conflict remains, for all intents and purposes, to this very day.

UN 242[49]

The Security Council,

Expressing its continuing concern with the grave situation in the Middle East,

Emphasizing the inadmissibility of the acquisition of territory by war and the need to work for a just and lasting peace in which every State in the area can live in security,

Emphasizing further that all Member States in their acceptance of the Charter of the United Nations have undertaken a commitment to act in accordance with Article 2 of the Charter,

1. *Affirms* that the fulfillment of Charter principles requires the establishment of a just and lasting peace in the Middle East which should include the application of both the following principles:

▶

    (i) Withdrawal of Israeli armed forces from territories occupied in the recent conflict;

    (ii) Termination of all claims or states of belligerency and respect for and acknowledgement of the sovereignty, territorial integrity and political independence of every State in the area and their right to live in peace within secure and recognized boundaries free from threats or acts of force;

2. *Affirms further* the necessity

    (a) For guaranteeing freedom of navigation through international waterways in the area;

    (b) For achieving a just settlement of the refugee problem;

    (c) For guaranteeing the territorial inviolability and political independence of every State in the area, through measures including the establishment of demilitarized zones;

3. *Requests* the Secretary General to designate a Special Representative to proceed to the Middle East to establish and maintain contacts with the States concerned in order to promote agreement and assist efforts to achieve a peaceful and accepted settlement in accordance with the provisions and principles in this resolution;

4. *Requests* the Secretary-General to report to the Security Council on the progress of the efforts of the Special Representative as soon as possible.

8

The 1970s to Lebanon 1982
The Continuation of the Arab–Israeli Conflict

Note: Once again, a state of no war–no peace existed in the Middle East. With Resolution 242 floating in space, and no real agreement between Israel and its Arab neighbors holding anything together (even as a mere formality), things were tense and undefined. Israel was in the power position, and with its newly acquired territories and a healthy stream of support coming from the US, it was content with the new status quo. The Arab countries, especially Egypt, were smoldering with defeat and humiliation and, refusing to negotiate from the weaker position, sought further Soviet armaments. As for superpower relations, things thawed slightly between the US and the USSR. Though arms flowed into the Middle East, and interests in the region remained constant, their focus on the Arab–Israeli conflict did back off to a degree. All the same, the subtitle of the present chapter gives it away, and over the course of six years we add 1969 and 1973 to the list of 1948, 1956 (Suez), and 1967 (Six-Day War).

THE PLO AND PALESTINIAN NATIONALISM

The Palestinians were coming into viewing themselves as a political entity in the modern sense, quickly leaving behind the notion of being only part of a larger Arab whole. By "Palestinians" we include here not only the roughly one million people living in the West Bank and Gaza under Israeli occupation, but also the refugee population living in camps along Israel's borders. Coming under Israeli control after the Six-Day War, the Palestinians had an increased sense of identity.

While living under Jordan and Egypt in the West Bank and Gaza was far from a perfect situation, it was still Arab rule and was not likely to change. With Israeli occupation (far worse than prior Arab control), however, came the possibility of *not* being under Israeli occupation. Given Israel's withdrawal, called for in Resolution 242, Palestinians could evolve into what had been promised them under both the British mandate and the 1947 UN partition.

Not long after the June 1967 war, the Palestine Liberation Organization (PLO) started to evolve into a serious and unified front. Its puppet leadership, hand-picked by Egypt's Gamal Abdul Nasser, resigned under pressure (December 1967) and was supplanted by a guerilla organization that wished to garner international attention and engage the situation in commando-style fashion. The PLO and the resistance movement in general quickly built up both a reputation and a following. In March 1968 Israel heavily attacked the Jordanian town of Karameh, a Palestinian camp and guerilla headquarters for Fatah, in response to an Israeli bus that had been blown up by a mine. Though Fatah was ultimately defeated, it put up an intense fight, with Israel sustaining relatively high casualties and loss of equipment. The battle at Karameh became an instant legend among Arabs, and thousands of young Arab nationalists flocked to Fatah and the resistance movement, wanting to join the ranks of the commandos, or *fedayeen* ("those who sacrifice themselves"). Fatah and the PLO began to grow, and with growth came increased independence. In its host countries, especially Jordan, the PLO became what is commonly described as a state-within-a-state.

Four months after Karameh, the governing body of the PLO, the Palestine National Council (PNC), convened in Cairo and amended their original charter. The revised charter of July 1968 stated clearly the PLO's intent for full-fledged revolution: "Armed struggle is the only way to liberate Palestine." "Commando action constitutes the nucleus of the Palestinian popular liberation war." Some other excerpts from the charter:

- Palestine, with the boundaries it had during the British Mandate, is an indivisible territorial unit.

- The Palestinians are those Arab nationals who, until 1947, normally resided in Palestine regardless of whether they were evicted from it or have stayed there. Anyone born, after that date, of a Palestinian father – whether inside Palestine or outside – is also a Palestinian.

- The Jews who had normally resided in Palestine until the beginning of the Zionist invasion will be considered Palestinians.

- The partition of Palestine in 1947 and the establishment of the state of Israel are entirely illegal, regardless of the passage of time, because they were contrary to the will of the Palestinian people....

- [Zionism] is racist and fanatic in its nature, aggressive, expansionist, and colonial in its aims, and fascist in its methods.[1]

Though the language of the charter is at times ambiguous about the ultimate goal the PLO had for Palestine, it states without doubt its aim to "destroy the Zionist and imperialist presence." Other statements made on this matter attempted to soften this stance over the following decade, suggesting that Israelis could stay as Palestinian citizens once they rejected Zionism.[2] The different organizations and factions within the PLO made it difficult to produce a straightforward manifesto of precise intentions.[3]

The next year (1969), Yasser Arafat, the leader of Fatah, was elected chairman of the PLO and remained in that position until his death on November 11, 2004. Fatah at this point was the preeminent PLO guerilla organization, in size and status. But, along with Fatah, there were a number of other groups such as the Popular Front for the Liberation of Palestine (PFLP) and the Popular Democratic Front for the Liberation of Palestine (PDFLP). These groups, unlike Fatah, preferred to address revolution in the Arab world as a whole, not just in Palestine. The PFLP and the PDFLP, among others, hijacked airplanes and committed acts of terrorism in an effort to further their cause and bring the Palestine question to international attention. This militancy would eventually result in an Arab–Arab confrontation.

The PLO soon began to wear out its welcome in Jordan. Attacks inside the occupied territories and Israel proper brought stiff Israeli reprisals, something King Hussein wanted to avoid. Between the Israeli–Jordanian border becoming hot with attacks and counter-attacks, and the resultant pressure on Hussein, violence erupted between the Jordanian army and PLO members, mostly the PFLP. The clashes escalated and the PFLP hijacked three Western commercial aircraft (September 1970), landed them in Amman, and after emptying them of hostages blew the aircraft up as a final slap in the face to Hussein. What resulted was a small-scale war in Jordan. During the course of that month, Syrian battalions approached Jordan to aid the *fedayeen*. In a strange twist of developments, the US urged Israel to intervene in defense of Jordan in order to discourage Syrian advance. Upon Israel's movement in that direction, Syria stopped in its tracks. The Jordanian army finished the war, ending with the PLO forces taking a severe beating, and the civilians in the camps a worse one. With thousands dead (most of whom were civilians), a cease-fire not worth the paper it was printed on was negotiated by Nasser and signed by the PLO and Jordan. The "Cairo Agreement," as it was called, drew hostilities to an official close on September 27. (Nasser died of a heart attack the next day.) The civil war in Jordan would be remembered as "Black September."

Though skirmishes continued over the next few months, in less than a year Hussein finally pushed the PLO out of Jordan. The next base of operation for the Palestinians was Lebanon, which would contribute to the breakdown of that already unstable country, as we will see later in the chapter.

THE WAR OF ATTRITION (1968–70), DIPLOMACY

Note: Though we just ended with the events of 1970, we need to go back for a moment and look at what's been going on in the Arab–Israeli conflict, in particular Egypt, Israel, and their respective sponsors, the Soviet Union and the US.

At the end of the 1967 war Israel occupied, among other territories, the east bank of the Suez Canal, in Sinai. With Israel on the right side of the channel and Egypt on the left, the situation was potentially volatile. Israel stood inflexibly on its position and resisted Gunnar Jarring's peace mission to the region. The UN sent Jarring as a mediator to facilitate a diplomatic settlement, where he encountered Egyptian and Jordanian openness to talks. Egypt, recovering from the war and receiving heavy shipments of Russian weaponry, wanted Sinai and Gaza back and knew that by force it could either bring about a political solution, or successfully regain the territory militarily. Nasser chose not to mince words: "What was taken by force must be restored by force."[4] In October 1968, Egypt shelled Israeli positions across the canal, sent commandos on raids, and sank an Israeli destroyer off the Sinai coast. Israel reciprocated by shelling the Egyptian side of the canal, with the Israeli Defense Forces (IDF) sending air raids deep into Egyptian territory. These ongoing tit-for-tat hostilities became known as the "War of Attrition." Heavy artillery bombardments, commando raids, and eventual aerial warfare continued, with months turning into years. As the conflict grew in intensity, Nasser flew to Moscow (January 1970) and secured not only more armaments, but Soviet pilots to fly the Soviet-supplied aircraft; the Israeli Air Force thus became involved in dogfights with Soviet pilots. All the necessary ingredients for the development of a full-scale war were certainly in place, but the Israelis, the Russians, and the Americans all knowing this, made attempts to prevent it.

Richard Nixon entered the White House in January 1969, and his secretary of state, William Rogers, proposed the "Rogers Plan" (December 1969) during US–Soviet talks in 1969 over concerns about the War of Attrition. The Rogers Plan was based on Resolution 242, with mention of Israeli withdrawal, mutual recognition, solving the refugee problem, and a resumption of Jarring's diplomatic efforts. Though the Soviets at first rejected the plan, as did the Israelis who were particularly dismayed, agreement was achieved from all the parties. The plan was signed by Egypt and Israel (July 1970), and a 90-day cease-fire began the following month. Israel did so hesitantly, only after the US confirmed that it would not be subjected to American pressure regarding UN 242.[5] Not long after the signing, Egypt began to move Soviet-supplied surface-to-air missiles (SAMs) to the Canal Zone, in violation of the cease-fire; the Israelis in return refused involvement in the Jarring talks.

In the War of Attrition Egypt took the worse beating by far, but interpreted its performance as successful having fought a continued fight with Israel.[6] At the same time, the Israelis, despite a superior performance against larger numbers and increasing Soviet support for Egypt, felt a lull in morale and made every effort to downplay back home the stiff competition it had met. Yet, irrespective of interpretation, thousands were dead, severe financial costs had been incurred, and, after Nasser's death on September 28, 1970, the Arab–Israeli conflict found itself pretty much right back where it started after June 1967.

THE 1973 WAR

Nasser's death ushered in the era of his vice-president, Anwar Sadat, who succeeded him as president. Egypt's economy was in tatters, and the incurred difficulties of 1967 and the expenses of the War of Attrition – casualties, destruction, and financial strains – didn't help matters in the least. Though less focused on issues of pan-Arab nationalism than Nasser had been, Sadat was no less interested than his predecessor in negotiating a peace settlement and regaining the territory lost to Israel. Under US pressure from Secretary Rogers and the State Department, Gunnar Jarring resumed his diplomatic efforts at trying to facilitate a peace settlement. In 1971 Jarring began his renewed endeavor, to which Egypt and Jordan had responded favorably, both willing to sign peace treaties with Israel based on withdrawal and UN 242. In addition to Jarring's mission, Sadat, in February 1971, extended a peace initiative of his own in Israel's direction, based on security, recognition, and withdrawal. In response to the Jarring mission as well as Sadat's peace offer, Israel (under its then prime minister, Golda Meir) held its reins in rejectionist silence.[7] Even at US and UN urging, Israel would not budge on the issue of withdrawal. A senior member of the US State Department would express what probably reflected the international consensus: "Israel will be considered responsible for the rejection of the best opportunity to achieve peace since the establishment of the state."[8] It should be noted that US diplomatic efforts in 1971 worked against opposition emanating from the Nixon White House. Nixon's then national security adviser, Henry Kissinger (who became secretary of state in 1973), encouraged Israeli resistance to Jarring and Sadat in hopes of stalling matters and getting Sadat to reduce his interests. Kissinger hoped it would encourage Sadat to abandon Russian sponsorship and in turn give the US greater control of the region.[9] However, it must also be noted that the USSR served as no obstacle to peace, as historian Avi Shlaim summarizes:

> Although the Soviet Union was allied to the Arab radical regimes, it never questioned Israel's right to exist and indeed offered to guarantee Israel within the pre-1967 borders. Like America, the Soviet Union took Resolution 242 to mean an Israeli withdrawal to the old borders with only minor modifications. Unlike America, the Soviet Union strictly rationed the supply of arms to its allies in the region. In fact, the Soviets' refusal to give Egypt a military option against Israel led Sadat to expel all Soviet advisers in 1972. All the available evidence suggests that following Sadat's rise to power there was opportunity for a negotiated settlement. The chance was missed not because of the Soviet stand but as a result of Israeli intransigence backed by global strategists in the White House.[10]

The year 1971, which Sadat declared the "year of decision," came and went, and by 1972 the deadlock remained. For Sadat, the decision to exercise his military option began to replace attempts at diplomacy – he would break the deadlock one way or another.

At first Sadat met with a lukewarm Soviet response to his requests for newer hi-tech weaponry. After a number of trips to Moscow and meeting with no success – late shipments, wrong supplies – Sadat retaliated by ejecting Russian advisors from Egypt (July 1972), to the surprise of the Soviets, the US, and

Israel. Sadat was sending Russia a sort of wake-up call, as well as giving the US and Israel the impression that Egypt was looking to change its diplomatic course. His gamble worked, and as the US stepped up shipments of fighter-bombers to Israel Moscow began sending Egypt fighter jets, SAMs, tanks, etc. Russia did not want to lose its client. In the US, presidential elections were nearing, and the White House was soon to become distracted by scandal (Nixon and Watergate). Throughout all of this, Kissinger, who by 1973 was more or less running the United States, felt the stalemate in the Middle East would hold out longer. It did not.

Over the spring of 1973 Sadat got to work, bringing Syria on board, a very willing partner in this endeavor, and one that had not signed 242. On October 6, Egypt and Syria attacked Israeli forces in Sinai and the Golan Heights, respectively. The ensuing war would become known as the Yom Kippur War, as the attack took place on the Jewish Day of Atonement, the holiest day on the Jewish calendar. For the Arabs it was Ramadan (the Muslim month of fasting). The day of attack also coincided with the anniversary of Muhammad's first military victory, at the Battle of Badr (624 CE). However, it should remain clear that this war had nothing to do with religion for those pulling the strings, and rarely does it ever.

Self-assure from its 1967 victory and viewing the Arabs as incompetent and unlikely to risk another war, Israel dismissed the warning signs. Though Israeli intelligence had pieced together the likelihood of what was to come, it wasn't until the midnight prior to the attacks that agents phoned in the fact that war was imminent. Israel's leadership finally took seriously what it had until now ridiculed, albeit somewhat late. That morning (October 6) Golda Meir and Defense Minister Moshe Dayan discussed the options and decided that it was best not to launch a preemptive attack. Not wanting to risk losing American aid, they feared the Arabs might claim self-defense when they invaded the occupied territory. Syria and Egypt attacked that afternoon. At 2:00 p.m. "Operation Badr" was unleashed.

With fierce fighting that overwhelmed the Israelis, Egypt crossed the Suez Canal while Syria entered the Golan Heights. Over the first week the Arabs were coordinated, well-planned, and focused; the Israelis had never seen such intense fighting. Though overrun at first, the IDF eventually got its footing and turned the tide. A contributing factor to how the war played out was superpower involvement. In the first week Israel suffered significant equipment loss and turned to the US for more supplies. Kissinger hesitated at first. He worried about provoking an Arab oil embargo (a prohibition of commerce), as well as provoking the Russians.[11] However, it was a massive Soviet rearmament of Egypt that spurred the US to respond with unprecedented airlifts to Israel. In turn, the Arab oil-producing countries countered the US airlifts (which included a $2.2 billion aid package given to Israel) with an oil embargo against the Americans and any European nations aiding Israel and the US. The shipments to Israel continued regardless. By the end of the war Israel pushed Syria back, claiming more of the Golan Heights than it started with. At the canal the Egyptians suffered Israeli penetration of their offense resulting in the IDF crossing over to the canal's west bank and entering mainland Egypt.

The combatants rejected early attempts at a cease-fire, until the US and the USSR threatened direct involvement. Moscow contacted Kissinger to negotiate cease-fire terms on October 21. The two came to an agreement, and the following day the Security Council passed Resolution 338 in a unanimous vote, with China abstaining:

The Security Council

1. *Calls upon* all parties to the present fighting to cease all firing and terminate all military activity immediately, no later than 12 hours after the moment of the adoption of this decision, in the positions they now occupy;

2. *Calls upon* the parties concerned to start immediately after the cease-fire the implementation of resolution 242 (1967) in all of its parts;

3. *Decides* that, immediately and concurrently with the cease-fire, negotiations shall start between the parties concerned under appropriate auspices aimed at establishing a just and durable peace in the Middle East.[12]

Sidestepping the UN and the USSR, Kissinger engaged in "shuttle diplomacy," negotiating directly with the various leaders in Cairo (Sadat); Jerusalem (Meir); Damascus (Hafiz al-Assad); Riyadh, Saudi Arabia (King Faisal); and Amman, Jordan (Hussein). Over 1974 and 1975 the secretary managed to secure partial land-for-peace agreements between the three involved countries; Israel made limited withdrawals from Sinai and the Golan in exchange for Arab pledges of non-belligerency. The two accords – Sinai I and Sinai II – were achieved in October 1974 and January 1975. The diplomatic momentum stopped here, and wouldn't resume until 1977.

Israel emerged the victor, for what it was worth. Losses were heavy all around, and though Israel scored a technical military victory (though not by much) the shock of the war was significant. Previously held assumptions were called into question, with popular resentment and anger soaring to unprecedented levels in Israel's history. After an internal commission of inquiry – the Agranat Commission – a number of senior officials in the military and intelligence departments were dismissed. In the spring of 1974 Golda Meir and Moshe Dayan announced their resignations. Egypt, on the other hand, had scored a psychological and political victory. Sadat's plan to bring his territorial concerns to international attention had worked, and though this cost him a military defeat, he returned a sense of satisfaction to his country as well as adding a feather to his own cap. The US ended up the sole power-player in the region, having secured a newfound relationship with Egypt, Russia's primary client in the Middle East.

THE CAMP DAVID ACCORDS (1978)

Note: From the end of the previous section until now there's been a turnover in leadership. After Golda Meir resigned, Yitzhak Rabin held the position of prime minister until 1977. Rabin was then succeeded by Menachem Begin, the former leader of the Irgun terror squad. Gerald Ford replaced Richard Nixon in August 1974 after Nixon resigned under what was imminent impeachment for the Watergate scandal. The 1976 elections ushered in the Jimmy Carter Administration. But as of the same year Egypt was still under Anwar Sadat's charge. That all said, our key players in this section are: President Jimmy Carter of the United States, Prime Minister Menachem Begin of Israel, and President Anwar Sadat of Egypt.

With new leadership came new philosophies and approaches that would end up redefining the Arab–Israeli conflict. Carter brought to the White House the hope of settling the conflict with sit-down multilateral (group) negotiations to work toward a comprehensive settlement – a sharp departure from Kissinger's method of step-by-step diplomacy. Sadat, as we've discussed, was consistently and primarily interested in Egypt's economic woes and the return of Sinai, and was eager to recommence with negotiations. The changes in Israel saw a sharp turn toward hard-line conservative thinking. Begin and his Likud party emphasized their intention to retain the West Bank and Gaza, referring to the West Bank as "Judea and Samaria" and proclaiming it an integral part of Eretz-Israel, or biblical Israel – "... between the Sea and the Jordan [River] there will only be Israeli sovereignty."[13] Though colonial settlements had been developed in the occupied territories since 1967 under previous Labor party governments, Likud made settlements a focal point. Over the first two years under Likud the number of settlers doubled, from under 5,000 to 10,000.[14] Despite their differences of perspective and concern, the two Middle Eastern leaders entered round-table talks facilitated by the American president, after his efforts for comprehensive settlement had failed.

Note: The issue of Israeli settlements in the occupied territories will continue to crop up throughout the rest of the book. Settlements are simply housing and land developments where civilians from the "occupying power" take up residence in the occupied territories.

Transfer of a civilian population into occupied territory is a contravention of international law. The UN upholds the following two documents in its assertion that settlement of an occupied state or territory is illegal: (1) the Geneva Convention Relative to the Protection of Civilian Persons in Time of War (August 12, 1949); and (2) the Hague Convention IV of 1907.[15]

Carter convened a multilateral meeting of the US, USSR, Israel, Jordan, and Egypt. At first he indicated a wish to include the PLO and made mention of a Palestinian "homeland," though he maintained the PLO would have to acknowledge UN 242, something the Palestinians refused to do owing to its lack of any mention of Palestinian independence and sovereignty. After intense Israeli and domestic pressure, Carter backed off.[16] What then followed was a US–Soviet joint communiqué (October 1, 1977) to set the groundwork for a comprehensive peace conference. The communiqué was patterned in substance and style after 242, calling for settlement of the conflict, a resolution of the Palestine question that ensured the "legitimate rights of the Palestinian people," and Israeli withdrawal from "territories occupied" in the June 1967 war. Though Sadat and the Arabs were unenthusiastic – there was no mention of the PLO, and the wording was obviously constrained – they agreed to it. Israel rejected it outright. After a meeting between Carter's people and Israeli foreign minister Moshe Dayan (former defense minister), a separate US–Israeli joint communiqué was issued stating: "Acceptance of the Joint US–USSR Statement of October 1, 1977, by the parties is not a prerequisite for the reconvening and conduct of the Geneva Convention."[17] With things off to a slightly ludicrous start, Sadat decided that if he wanted peace and the Sinai back, and in a reasonable timeframe so as to attend to Egypt's failing economy, he had to go it alone.

    In a speech to the Egyptian National Assembly on November 9, Sadat announced, with Yasser Arafat in the audience, that he was willing to go to Jerusalem and discuss the matter with Begin in the Israeli parliament (the Knesset) itself. The Egyptian president arrived in Jerusalem ten days later as Begin's invited guest. The talks and meetings led to nothing conclusive or tangible, and eventually back to the same impasse. Sadat pressed for withdrawal from the occupied territories, including Sinai, and self-determination and statehood for the Palestinians, essentially reiterating his 1971 offer. Begin offered partial withdrawal from Sinai and total inflexibility regarding the West Bank and Gaza. The talks eventually ground to a standstill. Sadat's trip did help to readjust the atmosphere between the two countries, with Begin also traveling to Egypt in return. If any harm came of these meetings it was by way of Arab anger (mainly from Syria and the PLO) directed against Sadat for "selling out" by moving in the direction of a separate peace. In July 1978 Carter invited Begin and Sadat to the Camp David presidential retreat in Maryland.

The turbulent Camp David talks spanned just under two weeks (September 5–17), ending with the signing of two accords, or "frameworks," on the last day. The first addressed the issue of the West Bank and Gaza, calling upon Egypt, Israel, Jordan, and "representatives of the Palestinian people" to negotiate the resolution of the "Palestinian problem in all its aspects." A five-year transitional period was established for determining the "final status" of these territories with a self-governing authority established to oversee administration during the transitional period. The second accord was a draft proposal for a treaty between Egypt and Israel to be signed within three months. This accord established the "withdrawal of Israeli armed forces from the Sinai," and the "right of free passage by ships of Israel through the Gulf of Suez and the Suez Canal...."[18] After continued difficulties regarding particulars and semantics, the treaty's ceremonial signing took place at the White House on March 26, 1979.[19]

The Camp David Accords brought peace between Egypt and Israel. However, beyond this bilateral peace, the Arab–Israeli conflict continued. The West Bank and Gaza were left to final status determination; the PLO received no mention; the issue of East Jerusalem being occupied and annexed by Israel was not addressed, nor was the Golan Heights issue. This lack of a comprehensive peace settlement brought with it Arab condemnation of Sadat as a fraud. Israel agreed to withdraw from Sinai, in exchange for peace (as well as continued occupation of the remaining territories); Begin interpreted "autonomy" for Palestinians, called for in the frameworks, as applying to the *people* and not the *land*. But as the region continued to degenerate, as we will soon see, the Egyptian–Israeli peace agreements held together, and still do to this day.

THE PLO AND PALESTINIAN NATIONALISM, PART II

Throughout the 1970s the PLO grew in reputation and recognition. Though still fractured and heterogeneous, Arafat attempted to steer the organization toward moderation and unity. Regardless of his efforts, the PLO was plagued with internal disputes among its divergent factions, as well as the violence and terrorism that it became notorious for in northern Israel and on the international level. Arafat did make diplomatic strides, and by 1974 the PLO was recognized at the Arab summit in Rabat, Morocco in October of that year. The "Rabat Declaration" affirmed the right of the Palestinian people to "establish an independent national authority" under the PLO, which was to be their "sole legitimate representative."[20] A month later, Arafat was invited to New York to speak in front of the UN General Assembly.

On November 13, Chairman Arafat addressed the assembly with a review of Palestinian history, condemning Zionism as colonial and racist, and speaking about the hope of Jews and Arabs one day living in the "framework of a just peace in our democratic Palestine." He closed his speech with a now-famous admonition: "Today I have come bearing an olive branch and a freedom-fighter's gun. Do not let the olive branch fall from my hand."[21] (His holster was empty, but the point was made.) A little over a week after Arafat's address the General Assembly passed two resolutions, 3236 and 3237. The first affirmed the Palestinian "right to self-determination without external interference" and "the right to national independence and sovereignty." It also stated the "right of the Palestinians to return to their homes and property from which they have been displaced and uprooted...." The second resolution conferred "observer status" (within the UN) upon the PLO.[22] Needless to say, Israel and its supporters were furious. The General Assembly the next year passed Resolution 3379 (November 1975). This resolution determined that "zionism is a form of racism and racial discrimination," equating it with *apartheid* South Africa, the legally sanctioned policy of racial segregation in force in that country from the 1950s to the 1990s.[23] The resolution was repealed in 1991.

The PLO's achievements in the realm of international diplomacy reflected both its movement toward a more moderate stance and a changing international consensus. The resolutions passed in the General Assembly in 1974–75 indicated a larger UN, one more globally composed and not confined to looking through a predominantly European prism, though Western Europe started to change its stance as well. And while the PLO garnered its newfound attention, so too did the West Bank and Gaza. As Israel's occupation and settlement policy continued, political consciousness in the territories grew by leaps and bounds, the vast majority of its citizens desiring independent statehood. A 1982 poll taken in *Time* magazine revealed that 98 percent of the people in the occupied territories wanted a state, while 86 percent thought the PLO should govern that state.[24] But as noted, by the mid-1970s the PLO had pitched camp in Lebanon after being expelled from Jordan, joining the more than 250,000 Palestinian refugees already there, and eventually running the refugee camps.[25] Not long after, the PLO found itself involved in the civil war there, the violence of which was merely an overture for the massive destruction that was to come.

THE INVASION OF LEBANON (1982)

Note: The outset of the 1980s saw, again, a turnover in leadership. The 1980 US elections brought the defeat of Jimmy Carter and the inauguration of the Ronald Reagan Administration, along with a new secretary of state, Alexander Haig. The 1981 elections in

Israel resulted in the re-election of the Menachem Begin government, which brought with it Ariel Sharon to the position of minister of defense. That year also witnessed the assassination of Anwar Sadat by Egyptian extremists who were displeased with their president's domestic and foreign policies. Sadat's vice-president, Hosni Mubarak, replaced the assassinated leader and remains in power today.

This section involves the culmination of certain issues, namely: (1) the increasing tension in the West Bank and Gaza owing to Israeli occupation and the continued policy of settlement construction in the territories; (2) a civil war in Lebanon, the origin of which goes back to the late 1950s and came to a head in the mid-1970s; and (3) the PLO's rise to prominence and global recognition. To summarize, the PLO established its headquarters in Lebanon, making Israel's north border a site of hostility and frequent attacks. Israel, wishing to retain control of the occupied territories, had no desire to deal with the PLO at all, as Arafat and company represented the idea of Palestinian statehood. Lebanon, boiling with domestic instability, was under the leadership of a minority group, the Maronite Christians, who desperately wanted to hold on to power. Israel and the Maronites struck a deal. Israel would help push the PLO and occupying Syrian forces out of Lebanon and guarantee Maronite authority. In return, Lebanon would enter into a peace treaty with Israel and essentially become a client state. In Begin's perspective, this action would achieve the destruction of the PLO and therefore the Palestinian desire for statehood, while also creating a secure northern border. This isn't how it would play out, as we will now see when we add 1982 to our 1948–1956–1967–1969–1973 list: on average, a war every six years.

Lebanon's multiethnic political fabric began to rend in 1975. The Maronite Christians met rising dissent from the majority Muslim population who felt the disproportionate makeup of the government should be adjusted. This opposition was called the Lebanese National Movement (LNM), which was a patchwork of different political and ethnic groups. Though it is tempting to see the lines drawn according to religion it is important to keep in mind that Lebanon's unrest was borne of political and economic concerns. Though the LNM was largely Muslim there were Christian members, and likewise the ruling elite, mostly Christian, also had Muslim elements. In April 1975 civil war broke out and lasted until October 1976. The LNM sympathized with the PLO, and the Palestinians soon joined the fight against the Maronites. While the civil war raged on, each side received foreign support. The LNM–PLO had the backing of Syria, and Israel provided aid to the Maronites. However, the successes of the LNM–PLO alliance against the Maronites began to concern Syria; with the potential overthrow of the Maronite government, the Israelis would undoubtedly become directly involved. So the Syrians shifted loyalties and began to support the Maronites. (Yes, Israel and Syria were *both* supporting the same side.) Maronite forces eventually regained their losses and the fighting continued until October 1976, when a cease-fire was formalized in Riyadh, Saudi Arabia. Syria, as part of the accord, sustained the presence of its military occupation force in Lebanon, and reshifted its loyalty *back* to the LNM–PLO opposition. The civil war was vicious, resulting in tens of thousands dead, mostly civilians including women, children, and the elderly.[26] Nothing was resolved; indeed things were only made worse, while political divisions drew deeper and wider.

Israel remained focused on the obliteration of the PLO, whose popularity was growing in the West Bank, and who might eventually emerge as a force to be reckoned with in the diplomatic arena. The policies of the Begin government were crystal clear in terms of its intentions in the territories – annexation, and suppression of nationalism. Going after the PLO was, for Begin and Sharon, the next logical step. PLO attacks on targets just over the northern border of Israel continued (1977–81), as they had throughout the 1970s. It was also at this time that Israel entered into agreements with the Maronite leadership regarding even more direct involvement in Lebanon. The Israelis developed a proxy (substitute) army in South Lebanon, comprised mostly of Christians and led by Saad Haddad. This militia, the South Lebanese Army (SLA), would battle the PLO in place of the IDF.

In March 1978, PLO commandos hijacked a bus near Haifa. A shootout occurred, resulting in the deaths of six Palestinians and 34 Israelis.[27] Israel's response was a full-scale invasion of South Lebanon. Its first direct military venture in Lebanon – "Operation Litani" – began on March 15, and spanned a week of bombing and shelling, claiming mostly civilian lives and causing 100,000 people to flee their homes.[28] Following the invasion, Israel occupied South Lebanon for three months. The UN Security Council passed a resolution (425) calling for Israel's withdrawal, and deployed a peacekeeping force, the United Nations Interim Force in Lebanon (UNIFIL), to form a security buffer between Lebanon and Israel. UNIFIL's presence notwithstanding, clashes and attacks continued between the Israelis and the PLO. In the spring of 1981 Israel initiated heavy aerial bombing of South Lebanon. With a lull in the attacks following the diplomatic efforts of US Ambassador Philip Habib, elections in Israel, and the light resistance of the PLO owing to fear of an Israeli ground invasion, Israel stepped up its bombing raids again in early July. In this renewed phase of what became known as the "Two-Week War," Israel, in addition to attacking South Lebanon, bombed Lebanon's capital, Beirut. The PLO responded with heavy rocket and artillery attacks into northern Israel. The hostilities continued to escalate until Habib worked out a cease-fire that both sides signed. The agreement would last for eleven months.

Shortly after the cease-fire, Ariel Sharon got to work developing a full-scale and final invasion to settle the PLO issue once and for all. Bashir Gemayel was the next up-and-coming leader of the Maronite Christians and head of the dominant Christian militia, the Phalange (founded by his father, Pierre). Gemayel had been in contact with the Israeli leadership since the end of the civil war, and it was he they were to assist in becoming president. But, establishing a new political order in Lebanon was just one item of business in the Begin–Sharon objective. Split up into two plans – "Small Pines" and "Big Pines" – the smaller initiative entailed an invasion up to the Litani River in the south, and the larger, more ambitious invasion involving a full-scale attack on Beirut.

Knowing the Knesset would not be terribly eager to siege an Arab capital, Small Pines was emphasized in cabinet meetings.[29] Yet, Big Pines addressed Begin and Sharon's ultimate goals, which ran parallel with Gemayel's – the destruction of the PLO infrastructure, the expulsion of Syrian forces, and the installation of Gemayel and the Phalange.

> The essentials of his [Sharon's] grand strategy were never deliberated by the Cabinet – or the General Staff, for that matter – either before the war or once it was in progress. Basically, they determined that the PLO must be driven entirely out of Lebanon, and to prevent the Palestinian organizations from making a comeback Bashir Gemayel must be sworn in as the country's next president. Meanwhile, to prevent any interference from the Syrians, their army too must be evicted from Lebanon. ... Then, following the wholesale expulsion of the PLO – particularly from Beirut, where its constituent organizations had their headquarters – Israel would be able to manage its conflict with the Palestinians to its own liking.[30]

The only order of business before execution of the operation called "Peace for Galilee" was to secure a reasonably sufficient amount of permission from the United States. Sharon met with Reagan's secretary of state, Alexander Haig. The secretary stressed that only a flagrant violation on the part the PLO would justify a substantial response of the kind Sharon had planned. In the dialogue between Sharon and Haig, "one side spoke in veiled language and allusive gestures that made it possible for the other to understand exactly what it wanted to."[31] Sharon returned to Israel with what he felt was permission enough. Pulling the trigger was all that remained.

On June 3, an anti-Arafat splinter group by the name of Abu Nidal attempted to assassinate the Israeli ambassador, Shlomo Argov, in London. Though Israeli intelligence knew and reported who the perpetrating organization was, the incident was justification enough for Sharon. Regardless of the PLO's compliance with the July 1981 cease-fire, events had already been set in motion. The next day Israeli fighter jets hit PLO targets in Beirut and South Lebanon, prompting the PLO "violation" that would provide the desired pretext for attack. Begin's cabinet was notified of a limited 25-mile invasion, and once their approval was secured, *Big* Pines was set in motion.

On June 6, 80,000 Israeli ground troops entered Lebanon. Though that night the Security Council passed a resolution (509) demanding immediate Israeli withdrawal from Lebanon, Israel exhibited the same defiance as the IDF had when moving past the UNIFIL security zone at the border. The ground divisions moved through South Lebanon with tanks, artillery and air support, and in the matter of a few days accomplished (and surpassed) the goals of Little Pines. In the first week thousands of Palestinians and Lebanese had been killed, the vast majority of whom were civilians.[32] By the end of the first week Israel had overwhelmed the hesitant Syrian troops, and with American pressure, entered into a cease-fire with Syria; the PLO offered to join the agreement but was dismissed. With the Palestinians displaced in the south and Syria out of the picture, Lebanon's capital lay wide open. The IDF then sealed off and shelled West Beirut for the next two months.

By the beginning of August Arafat's only option was withdrawal, which was simultaneously being called for by the Israelis. The US sent Philip Habib to arrange a final settlement, and by August 11 a plan was forged and agreed upon by all parties. An international peacekeeping force was deployed – French, Italian and US troops – to ensure safe passage of the PLO out of Beirut as well as protection for remaining non-combatant Palestinians in the refugee camps. Sharon, who didn't share the cabinet's agreement with the Habib plan, gave the order for a renewed attack on Beirut, which featured a solid day of saturation bombing and causing an estimated 300 dead.[33] The Americans and the Israeli cabinet were outraged with Sharon, the latter suspending his power to order attacks. By September 1 the last of the PLO left Beirut via boat with the international force pulling out over the next two weeks.

Bashir Gemayel was elected president on August 23. In a moment typical of international affairs, Gemayel, upon being reminded by Begin and Sharon of the discussed peace treaty between the two countries (as well as the president-elect's indebtedness) the Maronite leader wasn't forthcoming. His newfound power had expanded his horizons. Nevertheless, Sharon and Gemayel shared the same concern, that of the remaining Palestinians, an element both men wanted to see rooted out and expelled from Lebanon.[34] Things changed course (or at least timing) when a bomb set off by a Syrian extremist killed Gemayel while he was delivering a lecture in East Beirut (September 14). Sharon immediately sent IDF forces into West Beirut to secure the two Palestinian refugee camps of Sabra and Shatila. He asserted that approximately 2,000 terrorists remained in the area, and once secured by the IDF, transported 150 Phalangists to the camps. The Phalangists were brimming with hatred for the opposition, and the Israeli chief of staff notified Sharon that, "They're thirsting for revenge and there could be torrents of blood."[35] Sharon dismissed the warning. The fighters entered Sabra and Shatila on the evening of September 16 and emerged the morning of September 19. When it was all over the massacre left behind between 800 and 2,000 dead men, women, and children, all of whom had been unarmed civilians.[36] Reports surfaced of accounts of rape, serial execution, and mutilation; the bodies of children and women littered the camps. The numbers were strategically curious: Sending in 150 Phalangists to do battle with 2,000 armed PLO remnants started to raise questions, however late.[37]

After the Sabra–Shatila incident the multinational forces, who had originally been there to protect non-combatants, returned to Beirut. The American military presence along with the Reagan Administration's negotiations with, and apparent support of, the ruling Maronites brought the US into direct involvement. Non-Christian militias began attacking US Marines. The American embassy was bombed with a truckload of explosives in April 1983, killing 60. After US naval bombardments of opposition targets, another truck bomb killed 241 US service personnel at a Marine barracks outside Beirut. Despite Reagan's desire to stay and fight terrorism and prevent what he perceived as a Soviet threat, the US pulled out of Lebanon in February 1984.[38] Israel would withdraw from South Lebanon, barring a strip of land at the southern border, in June 1985. The civil war in Lebanon continued on and would do so into the early 1990s. Israel's goal of extinguishing Palestinian nationalism did not achieve the desired effect. In fact, it achieved the exact opposite.

POSTSCRIPT TO LEBANON

The bloodshed and destruction wrought in Lebanon in the early 1980s was punctuated by diplomatic initiatives. In the space of two weeks the autumn of 1982 saw three different peace proposals placed on the table. President Reagan's administration created the "Reagan Plan" (September 1), calling for Palestinian autonomy and federation of the West Bank and Gaza with Jordan, but no statehood; a freeze on construction of Israeli settlements in the occupied territories; Israeli withdrawal in return for Arab peace; and a determination of the status of Jerusalem through negotiations. Reagan also sent a separate note to Begin promising that no settlements would be dismantled. Israel rejected the plan outright while Arafat and King Hussein remained open to the possibilities. One week later, at an Arab summit in Fez, Morocco, the "Fez Plan" was produced.[39] This plan called for: full Israeli withdrawal (in accordance with Arab interpretation of UN 242); a Palestinian state under the PLO; compensation for refugees; peace and security for regional states; and the dismantling of Israeli settlements in Israel. And a week after that the Soviet Union, looking to inject its influence into the matter, followed up the Fez Plan with the "Brezhnev Plan", named after Russia's prime minister. The Russians, who supported the Fez Plan while judging the Reagan Plan a "farce,"[40] echoed what was outlined at the Arab summit, except the Russian plan referred to Israel by name; the Fez Plan makes only implicit mention. In addition to the Reagan Plan, Israel rejected the subsequent two programs. This inflexibility regarding the occupied territories would survive another change of leadership.

In addition to growing protests over the war in Lebanon, the issue of lost Israeli lives became a foreground issue, which in turn increased protests. Of the 600 IDF personnel who died in the war, roughly half had died in the sustained occupation after the PLO had been evacuated.[41] Coming on top of a list of failed achievements – no treaty with Lebanon, increased Palestinian nationalism, etc. – Menachem Begin resigned from his premiership early and retired into obscurity (August 1983). The new prime minister, Yitzhak Shamir, would only hold the post exclusively for a year, until elections (July 1984) where the two main political parties, Likud and Labor, ended up splitting the vote, thus indicating a polarized public. The two parties would combine to form a coalition government, the leaders of which would each spend two years as prime minister: Shamir for Likud, and Shimon Peres for Labor.

After the PLO left Beirut, Arafat set up a new headquarters (the third) in Tunisia's capital city of Tunis. He also faced deep divisions within sections of the PLO, especially his own branch, Fatah. This internal instability was the result of the defeat under the Israeli invasion, the Sabra–Shatila massacre, and Arafat's continued diplomatic efforts along with his moderate involvement with the various peace plans – Reagan, Fez, and Brezhnev. Though condemned by Israel as a terrorist enemy of the Jewish state, certain factions of Arafat's organization condemned him with equal ferocity for being a diplomatic moderate with pro-Western leanings. In the spring of 1983 fighting broke out in Syria-controlled northern Lebanon between Arafat loyalists and Fatah rebels with the help of Syrian forces. Arafat returned to Lebanon in September to resolve the matter, hoping to bring political and international pressure on the opposition and Syria. By November the loyalists had suffered significant setbacks, and by December a cease-fire was declared with Saudi Arabia forging an agreement with Syria. Arafat, for a second time, was forced out of Lebanon.

However, the PLO chairman would continue along his diplomatic path, eventually working out a joint agreement with Jordan that was announced in February 1985. The items of the agreement included total Israeli withdrawal, Palestinian self-determination in the context of the "confederated Arab States of Jordan and Palestine," and negotiations conducted by an international conference involving the UN Security Council.[42] Israel and the US rejected the communiqué, both refusing to conduct negotiations with the PLO, as well as refusing to work within an international conference.

The diplomatic process was interrupted when on September 25, 1985 three Israeli tourists were murdered in Cyprus by PLO extremists.[43] In response Israel bombed the PLO headquarters in Tunis on October 1. A cycle of violence naturally ensued. Among other acts of terrorism, extremist Palestinians, a week after the attack on Tunis, hijacked an Italian cruise ship, the *Achille Lauro*, on which a disabled Jewish-American man was murdered and cast overboard. This most recent diplomatic cycle dissolved like its predecessors. Yet, if one element in the total Palestinian–Arab–Israeli conflict remained uninterrupted, it was the ever-increasing tension in the West Bank and Gaza, and the popular support in those territories of the PLO, its chairman, and statehood.

9

The Intifada and the Peace Process

Note: Our focus now returns to the Palestine–Israel conflict. As the Arab-Israeli conflict continued to play out like a perpetual ballet of violence, failed diplomacy, and rejection, things in the occupied territories of the West Bank and Gaza were undergoing steady transformation. Where we start out in this chapter, in the latter half of the 1980s, the people born during the Six-Day War were now turning twenty. A whole new generation had grown up only knowing Israeli control of what remained of Palestine. For Palestinian youth this meant growing up under harsh military occupation, and for the young Israeli generation it meant never knowing the occupied territories to belong to anyone else. What happened next placed the West Bank and Gaza at center stage in the evolving conflict, to the surprise of Israel, the Arab world, the international community, and even the PLO.

THE INTIFADA (1987–91)

On December 8, 1987 an IDF vehicle crashed into a truck in Gaza carrying Palestinian laborers home from work. In the accident four were killed, along with seven wounded. Rumors spread alleging that the accident was an act of vengeance for an Israeli who had been stabbed to death the previous week. The turnout for the funerals of the deceased workers numbered in the thousands and immediately evolved into angry protest. The IDF, viewing the disturbance as a routine demonstration, emerged to disperse the crowd with tear gas and live ammunition, killing twenty-year-old Hatem al-Sisi, who became the first martyr of the uprising. Israeli occupation troops at the scene had met with an atypical level of resistance among the Palestinians. What had officially begun was the *Intifada*, an Arabic term meaning "shaking off."

As is common with major conflicts – political as well as personal – what sets off the explosion is usually remarkably small. That a fatal traffic accident could ignite the anger and hatred of over 1.5 million people indicates the level of cumulative and collective frustration that existed in the occupied territories. As noted, the Israelis viewed the funeral demonstrations as commonplace, at first. Since the 1967 war Palestinians had chafed under occupation, with protests and resistance being a daily affair. Life in the territories featured "stone throwing, Molotov cocktails, strikes, demonstrations, [and] refusal to pay taxes," while enduring "large-scale arrests, imprisonment without trial, deportations, punitive destruction of homes and property, beating, and the use of tear gas and live ammunition against crowds."[1] From 1968 to 1975 the IDF counted 350 incidents of rebellion a year, or about one a day. From the mid-1970s to the early-1980s the number doubled, and then into the 1980s it reached 3,000 incidents a year, roughly eight a day. In the first six months of the Intifada, however, 42,355 incidents were recorded.[2] The ever increasing urge to rebel that eventually led to the Intifada was in direct response to not only the occupation, but also a sense of political isolation. The Arab world, which had done little or nothing in the way of aiding the Palestinians, left those in the territories with a sense of abandonment; the PLO's ultimate inability to make serious headway regarding Palestinian sovereignty and statehood was also another major factor. Though Palestinians still supported the PLO as the symbol of national unity, West Bankers and Gazans alike began to see the necessity of taking matters into their own hands: "We support the PLO because we are the PLO."[3]

The conditions in the occupied territories were the primary concern and cause of Palestinian unrest. Though the 1970s saw an increase in wages and living standards, especially in the West Bank when compared to the times of Jordanian rule, the 1980s saw a sharp economic decline in Israel. The resultant drop in value of the shekel (Israeli monetary unit), to which the Palestinian economy was tethered, directly affected the territories. Nevertheless, economic fluctuations merely offered varying degrees of distraction; life under occupation, as the constant and growing number of incidents of unrest indicated, was increasingly intolerable.

As mentioned in the previous chapter, settlement activity rose significantly. With the rise to power of Menachem Begin and his Likud party in 1977 came a focused and aggressive effort to colonize as much of the West Bank and Gaza as possible. The average annual number of settlers moving to the occupied territories from 1967 to 1977 was 770, whereas the average in the period of 1978–87 leapt to 5,690 annually.[4] Moreover, with settlement obviously came requisition of land and resources. From the Six-Day War to the Intifada – the first twenty years of occupation – Israel had requisitioned half of the West Bank and a third of Gaza.[5] The burgeoning numbers of Israeli settlers in the West Bank alone – 20,000 in 1982 to 60,000 in 1986 – amid the native population of 800,000 created a sense of emergency and fear.[6] Israel's drive into that territory ultimately achieved virtual annexation. The loss of land to an encroaching colonial population rested on top of day-to-day conditions that the Palestinians found unbearable.

Permanent fixtures of life under occupation included checkpoints, searches, curfews, and school closures. In response came anti-occupation methods such as strikes, demonstrations, boycotts, and clashes. What ensued was an upward spiral: the pressure of the IDF's rule over the territories inspired protest, which in turn increased IDF pressure. While the levels of oppression and resistance increased, the older generations, too, began to move toward a less passive course of action. The concept of *sumud*, or steadfastness, had generally been the approach to life under occupation. In a sustained act of passive resistance the Palestinians in the territories remained on the land and refused to budge, all the while creating their own organizations and services to make occupation life easier. But the people of the occupied territories began to resist more actively, taking matters of leadership into their own hands, creating what one political scientist referred to as the "new *sumud*."[7] Yet despite these sorts of developments, when things came to a head in December 1987, it was the younger generation who started and carried out the beginning of the Intifada.

For young Palestinians, the concept of *sumud*, old or new, was lost on them. The older generations had known better times and were more or less willing to suffer through and wait it out, hoping for the return of some kind of normalcy. The young, on the other hand, grew up angry and less tolerant of the constant searches, curfews, and periodic shutting down of their schools. Kids ranging in age from seven through the teenage years organized, divided up responsibilities, tied *khaffiyas* (checkered headscarves) around their heads like masks, and met head-on with the IDF's occupation troops. Roads were barricaded, tires set on fire, and stones and iron bars were hurled. The leaders of the revolt were in their late teens and early twenties, delegating authority down through the ranks that were composed by age. While the smaller children lit fires and set up roadblocks, the older youth handled direct confrontation and organizational responsibilities. The spontaneous grassroots uprising quickly evolved into a unified front.

While the "children of the stones" carried on in the streets, Palestinian society followed suit.[8] Leaflets were distributed weekly with various instructions to maintain organization. Strikes, boycotts on Israeli goods, food distribution to communities locked in by curfew, and daycare for children were all concerns that were addressed by the various grassroots committees. Women's groups, labor unions, professional associations, and the average citizen were all now involved in a revolution. "Family gardens became a symbol of resistance to Israeli authorities, who at times arrested Arabs for growing their own food, as happened in the village of Bayt Sahur."[9] The lines of society began to dissipate in the heat of organization:

> The occupation had substantially weakened what ordinarily would have been the most prominent and influential social class – that of the landowners and merchants. While certainly not eclipsing all the differences between rich and poor, the new institutional activities, led

by the university and high school graduates and aided by the general antipathy to Israeli occupation, served as meeting grounds for diverse groups of Palestinians. The occupation thus resulted in the first steps toward a political levelling of the society and in bases for association across formerly unbroachable sexual and class lines – key elements in the spontaneous outbreak of the Intifada.[10]

The various groups and task forces would eventually coalesce into a larger framework. The Unified National Leadership of the Uprising (UNLU) formed an underground coordinating hub that issued directives, printed leaflets, and maintained the political trajectory of the Intifada: statehood. With the PLO on the sidelines in Tunis, a partnership formed between the two groups, though the primacy of the exiled leadership was willfully recognized. Also beginning to sprout up were Muslim organizations, signaling an Islamic revival.

The Egypt-based Muslim Brotherhood was an organization that focused more on religious education and less on politics and revolution. However, groups that splintered off the Brotherhood adopted militant philosophies during the Intifada. One group was Islamic Jihad, which formed in Gaza over the course of the first half of the 1980s and remained a smaller movement. From the Brotherhood also emerged, in January 1988, a new group called Hamas (Islamic Resistance Movement).[11] Unlike the UNLU–PLO connection, which desired a secular state in the West Bank and Gaza brought about by civil resistance, the Muslim organizations desired an Islamic state in all of former Palestine, to be achieved by armed and violent means. From the fundamentalist perspective, *jihad*, or holy war, was the only mechanism by which a religious state could be wrested from the Zionists. Hamas gained significant support, especially in Gaza, and became the second largest organized effort in the territories next to the UNLU. All the same, for most of the Intifada Hamas avoided confrontation with the PLO. Though ideologically divergent from the secular leadership, it aimed to cooperate with the UNLU–PLO structure and maintain the integrity of the Intifada. The friction of divergence would increase over time, however.

At its outset, Hamas organized the building of schools, mosques, and clinics, in addition to honing its political agenda. Israel, viewing the religious groups as an alternative to the PLO, and possibly a competitor, supported Hamas's endeavors along with providing the group with financial assistance.[12] This changed once the group's militant intentions were brought to light in its official charter (August 1988). The document, anti-Semitic and anti-Zionist in nature, made clear the organization's interpretation of the struggle as a religious one. Some excerpts from the Hamas Charter:

- The Islamic Resistance Movement is a distinguished Palestinian movement, whose allegiance is to Allah, and whose way of life is Islam. It strives to raise the banner of Allah over every inch of Palestine, for under the wing of Islam followers of all religions can coexist in security and safety where their lives, possessions and rights are concerned. In the absence of Islam, strife will be rife, oppression spreads, evil prevails and schisms and wars will break out.
- There is no solution for the Palestinian question except through Jihad. Initiatives, proposals and international conferences are all a waste of time and vain endeavors. The Palestinian people know better than to consent to having their future, rights and fate toyed with.
- The day that enemies usurp part of Moslem land, Jihad becomes the individual duty of every Moslem. In face of the Jews' usurpation of Palestine, it is compulsory that the banner of Jihad be raised.[13]

But irrespective of the various emerging factions and organizations, secular and religious, the engine of the Intifada was the effort in the street: kids throwing stones and confronting well-armed and trained troops.

Israeli policies in the West Bank and Gaza went from harsh and restrictive to worse with the advent of the Intifada. What became known as an "iron fist" policy was a severe procedural response to the threat posed by organized rebellion among the indigenous Arabs. Though the IDF's stated method of "might, power, and beatings" was presented as a *less* severe policy – made in response to strong domestic and international criticism of military brutality – the degree of violent suppression persisted.[14] Pre-Intifada measures now seemed mild compared to Israel's heightened reaction to the uprising. Human rights organizations issued reports and made cases at the UN regarding gross violations of international law. In late 1988 the UN General Assembly passed a resolution (43/21) criticizing Israel's "persistent policies and practices against the Palestinian people":

> [The United Nations] Condemns Israel's persistent policies and practices violating the human rights of the Palestinian people in the occupied Palestinian territories, including Jerusalem, and, in particular, such acts as the opening of fire by the Israeli army and settlers that result in the killing and wounding of defenceless Palestinian civilians, the beating and breaking of bones, the deportation of Palestinian civilians, the imposition of restrictive economic measures, the demolition of houses, collective punishment and detentions, as well as denial of access to the media.[15]

The only two nations to vote against the resolution were the United States and Israel. Despite the international consensus, the IDF's tactics continued. In the case of house demolition, by mid-1990 300 homes had been razed.[16] The act of levelling homes was usually carried out in response to stone throwing, and based on the suspicion that the perpetrator lived there.

By 1991 the Intifada began to lose momentum, though skirmishes and uprisings of lesser intensity continued into 1993. By the end of 1992 over 100 Israelis (civilian and non-civilian) had died. By the end of 1993 over 1,000 Palestinians were dead, roughly 20 percent of whom were under sixteen years of age; the wounded numbered in the tens of thousands.[17] Four years of resistance and protest had not only withstood severe suppression but was further unified by it. However, the focus of the Intifada was slowly replaced with an increase in fighting among Palestinians in cases of suspected traitors. Militant religious fundamentalism was also on the rise in the territories, and brought with it acts of armed terrorism instead of stone throwing. As for the "external" leadership (the PLO in Tunis), their eyes turned to the international arena with the intent of securing a settlement through politics and diplomacy, instead of rebellion and confrontation. Though the Intifada had been sustained, nothing decisive had come of it. The PLO had to parlay what had been achieved, namely, world attention and a new focus on the issue of Palestinian statehood, into a further, more concrete political achievement.

Note: So far in this section we've covered just the street-level aspect of the Intifada. While this was certainly the essence of the uprising, we should also take a glance at what was churning politically in the background. A brief description follows.

A meeting of the PLO's parliamentary body, the Palestinian National Council (PNC), was held in Algiers in November 1988. At the meeting Chairman Yasser Arafat announced the State of Palestine in a formal declaration of independence.[18] Along with proclaiming statehood and a two-state solution, the PNC issued a resolution calling for an international peace conference, one based on Resolutions 242 and 338, and addressing "the issue of the Middle East and its core, the question of Palestine."[19] Though acceptance of the PLO's announcement of statehood garnered significant acceptance, with over one hundred countries recognizing the declaration, the US was less enthused, claiming the Palestinian leadership was involved in terrorism – regardless of the US State Department's findings to the contrary. The Americans refused the chairman a travel visa to speak in New York before the forthcoming UN meeting. The General Assembly moved the session to Geneva, Switzerland, where Arafat spoke in December. After two speeches emphatically renouncing terrorism and clarifying his peace proposal in a more acceptable way to the US, Washington agreed to enter into dialogue with Arafat and the PLO. With the PLO meeting US demands and the resultant dialogue Israel began to feel pressured into producing a response.

Prime Minister Yitzhak Shamir (1986–92) proposed in May 1989 that elections be held in "Judea, Samaria and Gaza." Reminiscent of the Camp David Accords in 1978, the territories would be allowed "self-rule" during an interim period while "permanent solution" decisions were made. But the Shamir plan rejected negotiations with the PLO and opposed "the establishment of an additional Palestinian state in the Gaza district and in the area between Israel and Jordan."[20] The PLO rejected the plan, the US looked on it with favor, the Arabs in general viewed it as a hoax and a ploy to stall the matter, and Shamir's own party members felt he was giving away too much. Ultimately the plan went nowhere and died shortly after it was issued. Further proposals made by the US and Egypt in autumn 1989 met with Israeli rejection, bringing the phase of diplomacy to a standstill. In the spring of 1990 a small faction within the PLO made an unsuccessful attack on the coast of Tel Aviv. The US demanded condemnation of the act, and discipline of the perpetrators, but Arafat made only a general and limited response emphasizing his lack of involvement in the affair. As a result the US discontinued its dialogue with the PLO. With a renewed sense of abandonment, and frustration with the growing lack of direction of the Intifada, the Palestinians looked in the direction of Iraq and its leader, Saddam Hussein.

THE GULF CRISIS (1990–91)

From 1980 to 1988, Iraq and Iran were locked in a long and vicious war, which resulted in nothing more than a stalemate and massive casualties on both sides. While still in possession of the fourth most powerful military in the world, Baghdad was in economic straits. It was in debt to Kuwait for financial support during the war, all the while accusing the tiny oil-rich monarchy of depressing oil prices (by exceeding production quotas) and stealing from an oil field that straddled the border between the two countries. Kuwait's response to Hussein's demands for compensation and debt relief was total refusal, which infuriated the Iraqi dictator. On August 2, 1990, Baghdad poured 100,000 troops over the border and, literally overnight, surrounded Kuwait City, eventually annexing the entire country. The Security Council passed Resolution 678, giving Hussein an evacuation deadline (January 15) and authorizing "all means necessary" in the event of failure to comply. A US-led coalition commenced "Operation Desert Storm" on January 16, 1991. In five weeks Iraq was expelled from Kuwait and Baghdad lay in ruins. Though we can't go into a thorough review of the Gulf War here, it should be noted that during the operation Iraq launched 39 Scud missiles (ground-to-ground) into Israel's largest city, Tel Aviv. Though the physical damage was severe, the attacks accounted for only a couple of fatalities. At US request, however, Israel made no response to Iraq's aggression.

Over the course of the conflict in the Persian Gulf the PLO and Palestinians on the popular level looked to Hussein as a source of support. The rationale was this: As the Intifada dwindled and lost direction, Palestinians were frustrated by lack of progress, lack of PLO achievement, lack of Arab-world support, and lack of the world community's application of international law (UN 242). Hussein, with his fiery anti-Western rhetoric and pro-Palestinian sentiments, gave the appearance of hope to those in the occupied territories. Perhaps with Iraq's powerful military a revolution might be raised within the Arab world, and present a military solution to Israeli occupation. The PLO pledged support for Hussein, and though Arafat initially presented a peace plan for Iraqi withdrawal from Kuwait, he too vowed support for Saddam. PLO–Palestinian support for Baghdad would prove both fruitless and ill chosen: (1) opinion of Palestine, inside the Middle East and out, turned negative; (2) the oil-rich Gulf states, especially Saudi Arabia, which served as a source of financial assistance for the West Bank and Gaza, were outraged and withdrew aid; and (3) Israel's view of, and refusal to negotiate with, the PLO was only further cemented. Nevertheless, by the end of the Gulf War the US was left looking at the Arab–Israeli conflict. The Soviet Union collapsed over the course of 1991, which sounded the death knell for the Cold War. With the removal of the USSR as a factor in Middle East politics, the list of external controls in the Middle East – Ottoman, European, and Superpower – was increased by one, and one that remains today: American.

THE PEACE PROCESS: MADRID AND OSLO I & II

The US in January 1989 saw George H. W. Bush enter the White House. It was under this administration in 1991 that the US found itself in this new and unique position regarding the Middle East: (1) it was the sole power player in the region; (2) it had garnered a list of Arab countries that were willing to cooperate, and did so in the American-led coalition in the Gulf War; (3) the former Soviet clients, such as Syria, Iraq, and Libya, were now without a backer; and (4) the idea of Israel as a strategic asset for the US was now under reconsideration, especially given its lack of tactical value against Iraq. On top of all this, immediate American response to Kuwait's occupation began to confound some as to why the US would not tolerate one occupation (Iraq in Kuwait), but tolerated another (Israel in Palestine). President Bush and his secretary of state, James Baker, were looking for a political victory to add to their military victory in Iraq. They also saw an open opportunity to get Israel and the Arab world around the negotiating table in an attempt to smooth out the Arab–Israeli conflict and establish stable US control of the Middle East. That table was located in Madrid, Spain.

The Madrid Conference (1991–93)

Bush and Baker managed to gather together into the same room Egypt, Israel, Lebanon, Syria, and a joint Jordanian–Palestinian delegation. When they assembled on October 31, 1991, in the Royal Palace in Madrid, each country was willing (for the most part) to engage in negotiations. The meetings were co-chaired directly by the Bush–Baker team as well as Mikhail Gorbachev, the leader of the USSR. (Bear in mind the Soviet Union was very soon to become the Russian Federation (still called Russia), and regardless of the projected image of partnership, Gorbachev was there as a hopeful recipient of American aid just as much as anybody else.) Serving as a basis for the conference were UN Resolutions 242 and 338, along with the concept of land-for-peace. As you can probably predict by now, Israel's position was "autonomy" for the Palestinians as well as continued settlement construction, whereas the Palestinians were looking for statehood. Their respective commitments were fixed, as they had been for decades, and this wouldn't change throughout the talks.

Prime Minister Shamir headed Israel's delegation. But demands made by Israel and followed by the US kept the PLO from being admitted or involved in the Madrid Conference. What was assembled instead was a small group of intellectuals from the occupied territories to represent the Palestinian leadership. Among them were Haidar Abdul Shafi, a physician from Gaza; Hanan Ashrawi, a professor of English literature, who was educated in the United States; and Faisal al-Husseini, a political activist and a leader of the Intifada. During the conference's opening addresses, Shafi delivered the speech for the Palestinian delegation, an eloquent address that still garners comments by scholars. Historian Avi Shlaim humorously notes: "As Abdu Shafi delivered his speech, Israel's stony-faced prime minister passed a note to a colleague. A joke going around the conference hall was that the note read, 'We made a big mistake. We should have let the PLO come.'"[21]

Multilateral and bilateral talks went on through 1992 and into the first half of 1993, taking place in a number of cities, including Washington, DC. The panels frequently bogged down, as American guidance was minimal and distant at best. Leaving the sharply divided delegations to sort it out for themselves created a hopeless situation. In 1992, elections in Israel saw the fall of the Shamir government and Yitzhak Rabin's rise to the seat of prime minister. On the American side, Bush fell in defeat to William Jefferson Clinton, who entered the White House in January 1993. Though Rabin presented himself as being more resilient and willing to negotiate than Yitzhak Shamir, his cabinet stayed the established course. Bill Clinton's administration, however, was far more supportive of Israel than the Bush administration. In addition to the lack of American involvement in the Madrid panel discussions under Bush–Baker, Clinton and Secretary of State Warren Christopher's concern for Israel meant certain death for the talks. (Regardless of Clinton's increased interest in Israel, it must be noted that aid for Israel, even through Bush's term, stayed high and constant at $3 billion a year, and remains at that level today.[22])

The symbolic significance of the Madrid conference far outweighed its accomplishments, which were thin indeed. However, a precedent had been set and it was the first time these countries had been gathered face-to-face. It was also the first time Israel and the Palestinians met in open dialogue. As Madrid was withering from Bush–Baker's neglect and Clinton–Christopher's decided position, another set of secret talks were going on in Oslo, Norway.

The Oslo Accord (September 1993)

Undisclosed talks had begun in January 1993 between the Israelis and the PLO at the invitation of the Norwegian government. These meetings were conducted over an eight-month period, and produced what became known as the "Oslo Accord." These clandestine ("back channel") discussions were conducted while the Madrid Conference sputtered into limbo. Aside from the two parties involved, the rest of the world knew nothing about the discussions being hosted by the Norwegians. Even the US, which knew *about* them, was not familiar with the substance of the meetings. On August 20, 1993, the accord was announced in Oslo. On September 13, it was signed on the White House lawn with Bill Clinton as master of ceremonies – irrespective of total lack of American involvement. Featuring a somewhat awkward handshake between Israeli Prime Minister Yitzhak Rabin and Chairman Yasser Arafat, a breakthrough of major historic significance had been achieved. The image of the Rabin–Arafat handshake, with Clinton as overseer, would become an icon of the twentieth century.

It is important to remember that the Oslo Accord is *not* a peace treaty or a final settlement of any kind – far from it. It is an agenda or interim agreement to negotiate such things. The accord is composed of two parts: The first is mutual recognition of the other, which came in the form of letters that were exchanged by the two leaders. The second component is the Declaration of Principles (DOP), spelling out initial responsibilities (which were few), and a timetable for negotiating various outstanding issues (which were many). The agenda that the accord lays out calls for: Israeli withdrawal from Gaza and the "Jericho area" (a town in the West Bank); establishment of a Palestinian police force for internal security affairs; elections for a "Palestinian Interim Self-Government Authority" or Palestinian Council; and transfer of authority to the Palestinians regarding "education and culture, health, social welfare, direct taxation, and tourism."[23] Permanent status negotiations would begin in two years and a final settlement be achieved within five years. This is about as detailed as the document gets. Everything else is left up to the established timelines and agendas, and the mutual promise to see things through. Historian Avi Shlaim comments:

> The shape of the permanent settlement is not specified in the DOP but is left to negotiations between the two parties during the second stage. The DOP is completely silent on vital issues such as the right of return of the 1948 refugees, the borders of the Palestinian entity, the future of the Jewish settlements in the West Bank and Gaza, and the status of Jerusalem. The reason for this silence is not hard to understand: if these issues had been addressed, there would have been no accord.[24]

Oslo marked a momentous occasion where Israel and the PLO had managed not only to engage one another directly, but also produce a framework that both agreed upon; and all this accomplished without external influence or guidance. Yet, much was left undone. The extremely general and ambiguous language of the accord allowed both parties to bestow upon it whatever interpretation suited their actual desires and/or needs. The PLO saw a path toward statehood, and Israel viewed it as retention of the territories without the burden of having to administer them. Both Arafat and Rabin came under harsh condemnation for what each leader's detractors viewed as a sacrifice of core philosophy. For the Israelis this meant the goal of Greater Israel from the Jordan River to the Mediterranean Sea. For the Palestinians it was statehood inside the pre-1967 Green Line. Historian Charles D. Smith notes:

From a Palestinian rejectionist viewpoint, Arafat had done what they had always feared, recognized Israel's existence without gaining mutual acknowledgment of a Palestinian right to self-determination. Conversely, from an Israeli rejectionist standpoint, the very fact that the existence of a Palestinian people had been acknowledged, let alone the PLO, was anathema and the prelude to a Palestinian state in areas they were determined to retain for Israel.[25]

Regardless of the criticism, popular sentiment on both sides was generally favorable to the accord. Polls by Gallup, CNN, and French Television revealed 65 percent approval ratings among both Israelis and Palestinians.[26]

In July 1994, Arafat returned from exile and took up residence in Gaza, where he established a police force and the Palestinian Council. Israel began its withdrawal from the Jericho area and Gaza. In December, Arafat, Rabin, and Israeli Foreign Minister Shimon Peres all received Nobel Peace Prizes.

Oslo II (September 1995)

On September 24, 1995, at the Egyptian Red Sea resort of Taba, the Interim Agreement established in the Oslo Accord's DOP (Article VII) was negotiated and signed. Four days later a ceremony at the White House with Rabin, Peres, and Arafat made official what became known as Oslo II, or the Taba Accord (also known as the "Second Phase," or the "Interim Agreement"). For our purposes here we'll use "Oslo II" to distinguish the Taba Accord from the original Oslo accord. Just know that Oslo II was one of the "things to do" in Oslo I.

The nucleus of the Oslo II Accord – all 300-plus pages of it – is the establishment of zones of control in the West Bank for the Palestinians and the Israelis. There are three zones, A, B, and C, designating the civil and administrative spheres of Palestinian jurisdiction:

- **Zone A:** 3 percent of the West Bank; under Palestinian control; and containing the six main cities of Bethlehem, Jenin, Nablus, Qalqilya, Ramallah, and Tulkarm. (Jericho

is included, but was already under Palestinian control,
and Hebron was to be handled separately and later, which
we'll discuss.)

- **Zone B**: 24 percent of the West Bank; under joint
  Palestinian–Israeli control; and containing 450 small
  towns and villages.
- **Zone C**: 74 percent of the West Bank; under Israeli
  control (pending "permanent status negotiations"); and
  containing Jewish settlements, Jerusalem, military bases,
  state lands, and external borders.

Again, vague language allowed for broad interpretation.
Obviously, the sticking point between the two parties was
going to be Zone C, the lion's share of the West Bank. The
actual wording in the accord is as follows:

> "Area C" means areas of the West Bank outside Areas A and B, which,
> *except for the issues that will be negotiated in the permanent status negotiations,*
> will be gradually transferred to Palestinian jurisdiction in accordance with
> this agreement.[27] [Emphasis added]

Arafat maintained that most of Zone C was soon to be
Palestinian. Israel's view was different: "In attempting to
reassure Israelis, Foreign Minister Peres noted that under the
accord, Israel would maintain control of 73 percent of the
land, 80 percent of the water, and 97 percent of the security
arrangements – a statement that only intensified Palestinian
anxiety."[28] Regardless of how the two perspectives differed, the
situation caused concern on both sides, not the least of which
came from religious extremists.

Hamas was livid that Arafat had negotiated away Palestinian
land, while various Jewish settler groups and fundamentalist
rabbis saw Oslo II as a desecration of biblical Israel.
Condemnation of Rabin also came from the Knesset itself,
including members of the Likud party. Acts of terrorism were
perpetrated from both sides in expression of this anger. But
Arabs killing Jews and Jews killing Arabs were not the only
acts of violence to punctuate this period. On November 4,

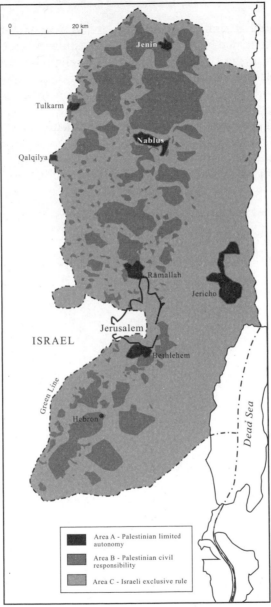

Map adapted from PASSIA, 2002

Map 4   Oslo II, 1995

1995, after attending a peace rally in Tel Aviv, Yitzhak Rabin was assassinated by a young Jewish law student. Shooting the prime minister twice in the back, the religious zealot, Yigal Amir, claimed divine guidance in his act to, as he viewed it, save Israel and Jewish lives from Rabin's concession of land to the Palestinians. Shimon Peres assumed the position of prime minister and continued with the developments of Oslo II. But a new era was descending upon Israel and the occupied territories, where the ambiguities of the Oslo Accords, occupation, and terrorism would become the status quo, and still are.

10

Current History
Camp David II to the Road Map

AFTER OSLO (1996–99)

After the assassination of Yitzhak Rabin, Prime Minister Shimon Peres took to implementing the terms of Oslo II, withdrawing from six Zone A cities and 400 Zone B villages. On the Palestinian side, elections took place in January 1996 for what became the Palestinian Authority (PA). PLO leader Yasser Arafat was elected president, taking 88 percent of the vote with high voter turnout in Gaza and the West Bank; turnout in occupied East Jerusalem was much lower owing to Israeli security measures and intimidation.[1] In addition to the presidency, an 88-seat legislature was established, making the PA complete. The image of a Palestinian state was taking shape, at least on paper. However, popular sentiment in the territories went from caution to suspicion as the various zoning established under Oslo II was implemented. Freedom of passage between towns and villages was replaced with checkpoints and territorial closures. Despite autonomy or self-administration, it quickly became apparent that less freedom was offered under the Oslo agreements than the previous form of occupation. Zone A and B territories were reduced to islands of Palestinian autonomy surrounded by Israeli control in terms of who went in and out. In addition to checkpoints and roadblocks, Jewish settlements were connected to one another via bypass roads allowing settlers free mobility throughout the territories, between one settlement and another and Israel proper. Aside from hemming in the Palestinian areas, the construction of such roads necessitated the utilization of Zone C land. What some members of the Palestinian negotiating team had warned Arafat about was becoming a reality.[2]

Beyond the nature of Oslo, and what it meant and boded for the future of those involved, things were moving along somewhat smoothly. However, the calm was soon disturbed by Peres's early January 1996 order for the assassination of Yahya Ayyash, an expert bomb-maker for Hamas ("The Engineer"). Though there had been no terrorist acts since August 1995, Ayyash's cell phone exploded in his ear later that month. This came on the heels of Israel's October 1995 assassination of a prominent leader of Islamic Jihad. In response, from late February to early March 1996, a wave of suicide bombings was unleashed against Israel. Anti-Israeli violence also erupted in the Israeli-occupied "security zone" in South Lebanon, established at the end of the invasion in 1982 – and not withdrawn from until 2000.

Another extremist organization emerging in the 1980s was Hizballah (Party of God). Begun by Shiite clerics in Lebanon, Hizballah's goal was to drive Israel from the South Lebanon security zone. In the weeks following the Hamas suicide bombings, Hizballah stepped up attacks against the IDF in South Lebanon, including a suicide bombing. The attacks by the Lebanese guerillas escalated to the firing of Katyusha rockets into Israel proper, causing injuries but no deaths. Peres, in response, launched "Operation Grapes of Wrath." In the period April 11–27, Israel sent F-16 fighter jets and helicopter gunships to bomb Hizballah centers as well as Lebanese infrastructure such as roads and power stations. The bombing reached as far as Beirut. Hizballah counterattacked, raining hundreds of Katyusha rockets down on northern Israel. During the invasion over 400,000 Lebanese fled their homes, with casualties reaching 200 dead and hundreds wounded.[3] On April 27, a US-brokered agreement was signed between Lebanon and Israel that brought the violence to an end. Not only had the disproportionate IDF response brought international criticism and condemnation from friend and foe alike, Shimon Peres inspired little domestic confidence in his actions throughout the spring of 1996. Israeli elections in May saw the Likud party regain power with the thin (1 percent) victory of Benjamin Netanyahu.

The new prime minister began his tenure by securing in place the status quo. Closure of the territories after the spring Hamas attacks remained in place, and no further progress or movement was initiated regarding Oslo. In the "Basic Guidelines" issued by the new government no mention was made of Oslo, while emphasis was placed on the settlement program:

> Settlement in the Negev, the Galilee, the Golan Heights, the Jordan Valley, and in Judea, Samaria [West Bank] and Gaza is of national importance, to Israel's defense and an expression of Zionist fulfillment. The Government will alter the settlement policy, act to consolidate and develop the settlement enterprise in these areas, and allocate the resources necessary for this.[4]

On top of ending the four-year freeze on settlements and placing the peace process on hold, Netanyahu struck a provocative pose in East Jerusalem.

On September 24, Netanyahu ordered the opening of a second entrance to the Hasmonean Tunnel, an archaeological site that runs the western perimeter of the Temple Mount. Though intended for tourists, previous prime ministers had delayed opening the tunnel in recognition of the potential upheaval that it might ignite. Fearful that Israel was undermining the al-Aqsa Mosque and the Dome of the Rock, and with encouragement from Arafat, Palestinians poured out in protest. Regardless of the tunnel posing no actual threat of damage to the Muslim holy sites, the act accomplished what many knew it would. Demonstrations and stone throwing met with IDF rubber bullets, and eventually gunfire exchanged between both sides. As the situation degenerated into the IDF deploying tanks and helicopter gunships in the territories, Clinton called Arafat and Netanyahu to Washington where the conflict was put to rest and Oslo matters were resumed. The Hasmonean Tunnel incident claimed the lives of 60–80 Palestinians and 15 IDF troops.[5]

The Hebron Agreement (1997)

On January 15, 1997, Israel and the Palestinian Authority signed an accord addressing the outstanding matters tabled in Oslo II regarding Hebron.[6] The Hebron Agreement divided the West Bank city, apportioning 20 percent to its 450 Jewish settlers (designated as H2), and 80 percent to its 160,000 Palestinians (H1). Israeli troops withdrew ("redeployed") from H1, but would remain in H2 as a security force to protect the settlers as well as handle conflicts between the settlers and the 20,000–30,000 Palestinians living in that sector. Palestinian authority in H1 would be the same as other Zone A cities, while exercising Zone B control over H2 where Arab matters were concerned. Appended to the Hebron Agreement was a "Note for the Record" in which both leaders "reaffirmed their commitment to implement the Interim Agreement [Oslo II] on the basis of reciprocity."[7] Israeli responsibilities included further withdrawal from the West Bank (undetermined), a safe-passage route between the West Bank and Gaza, and the opening of the Gaza airport. Among the Palestinians' responsibilities were fighting terror, security cooperation, and prevention of "incitement and hostile propaganda." After the signing of the accord, Netanyahu proposed a withdrawal from 9 percent of the West Bank, but met with rejection from Arafat who maintained that the amount was insufficient. At the same time of this proposal Netanyahu announced plans to develop settlements on what the Jews call Har Homa (known to the Arabs as Jabal Abu Ghneim), a hill overlooking East Jerusalem. The plan to construct a 6,500-unit housing facility caused uproar around the world. Aside from protest and riots among Palestinians, the UN General Assembly passed resolutions with an overwhelming majority, emphasizing the illegality of settlement construction.[8] The vote went to the Security Council where only the US voted against it, thus vetoing the resolution. Punctuating the violence and upheaval was a Hamas suicide bombing that killed three people in Tel Aviv three days after the Har Homa settlement construction began. Netanyahu blamed Arafat for the attack, suspended the

Oslo progress, and proceeded with plans for new settlement expansion in the West Bank.

The rest of 1997 saw no movement on Oslo II or the Hebron Agreement. Efforts on the part of Clinton, Secretary of State Madeleine Albright, and special envoy Dennis Ross, to reinvigorate negotiations yielded little in the way of progress initially. It wasn't until 1998 that Clinton, Albright, and Ross had garnered agreement from Netanyahu and Arafat to enter talks once again.

The Wye River Accord (1998)

At the Wye River Plantation in Maryland, on October 15, 1998, the two leaders met under US mediation, with Albright and CIA Director George Tenet conducting the summit. On October 23 the Wye River Memorandum was signed in a ceremony at the White House; another footnote to Oslo had been forged. Again, responsibilities were assigned to the two parties.[9] The Palestinians were mainly given tasks regarding terrorism and security. Israel, in return, agreed to three redeployments, two detailed in the accord and another to be later addressed by a committee. The first two redeployments would transfer 1 percent from Zone C to Zone A, and 12 percent to Zone B; 3 percent of the 12 percent would be designated as "Green Areas and/or Nature Reserves" where construction was forbidden. Additionally, 14.2 percent of Zone B territory would become Zone A. Under these terms, the West Bank's new allocation (compared to Oslo) would break down as follows: Zone A: 18.2 percent, Zone B: 21.8 percent, and Zone C: 60 percent.

After delays and limited withdrawal from Zone C, Netanyahu's position was suffering; hard-line politicians criticized his giving land away to the PA, and the more moderate and left elements questioned his ability and/or willingness to see the peace process through. Netanyahu suspended the Wye agreements and voted with the Knesset to call early elections.

CAMP DAVID II (2000)

Israel's May 1999 elections brought the premiership of Ehud Barak, the country's most highly decorated veteran. After retiring from the military he became a political protégé of Yitzhak Rabin. Barak emerged as prime minister with determined talk of proceeding with Oslo and seeking a settlement with the Palestinians. Yet disagreement ensued almost immediately when Barak stated he wished to move on to final status talks with the Palestinians, as opposed to an incremental process as the various accords had been styled – a bit of land for a bit of peace. Amid meetings with Clinton–Albright, an agreement was reached and signed on September 4, 1999. The Sharm al-Sheikh Memorandum established a timeline spelling out how and when Israel and the PA would "commit themselves to full and mutual implementation" of all agreements since September 1993.[10]

Over the following two months talks took place in fits and starts. On final–status agreements the Palestinians and the Israelis were too far apart: The PA wanted a state in the West Bank and Gaza, with East Jerusalem as its capital, and the return of (or compensation of) the refugees. The Israelis refused to meet any of these points in full. Further, smaller disagreements regarding Israeli withdrawal from Zone C caused the breakdown of the Sharm al-Sheikh agenda. Ehud Barak then decided to abandon the process in exchange for talks with Syria. After three months of negotiations addressing predominantly the Golan Heights, which Israel had occupied since 1967, the Israeli–Syrian negotiations ended in futility. But by March 2000 the focus returned to the Israel–Palestine front.

Throughout the spring of 2000 preliminary talks and meetings took place between the US, Israel, and the PA. Clinton and Albright put out feelers to determine if the time was "ripe," as Albright put it, for a final summit between the Israelis and the Palestinian Authority. The situation had more to do with timing than anything else. Clinton was in the final hours of his second term in office, making him what is known as a "lame duck." Barak, too, was eager to convene a summit. He was under severe domestic pressure from within the government and was up against a crumbling coalition majority in the Knesset, no-confidence motions, and the imminent call for early elections. Arafat, on the other hand, was hesitant. He wanted more time to prepare for a final agreement, and felt wary of the impatient promptings on the part of Barak and Clinton. On July 5, 2000, President Clinton extended invitations to Arafat and Barak to a summit at the presidential retreat in Maryland's Catoctin Mountains where Carter, Begin, and Sadat had convened roughly twenty years before.

Note: As it's described in a new authoritative account of the proceedings, Camp David II, as it became known, was "one of the oddest episodes of the peace process."[11] So far in this chapter we've covered various agreements in the post-Oslo period – Hebron, Wye, and Sharm al-Sheikh – which are all connected to Oslo, while Camp David II stands somewhat on its own. For what was attempted, what happened, and the hotly contentious debates that it created (and still does), this "historic opportunity to reach an agreement on the permanent status," to quote Clinton,[12] produced drama, frustration, and ultimately, no results. Though it should be noted the accord was not bereft of small accomplishments and merits, Camp David II is seen, rightly or wrongly, as one of the chief pivotal points in the recent conflict.

The summit started on July 11 and lasted until July 25. Camp David II was and still is shrouded in a bit of mystery owing to the press "blackout," and the lack of any written records or maps being produced during the proceedings. Israeli proposals were made orally and then channeled through American mediators. Moreover, the distance between the two parties' fixed positions ("red lines") would remain, contributing to an already unpromising atmosphere. As in previous negotiations, the Palestinians wanted a state within the Green Line, and East Jerusalem as its capital. In May, during the various talks between Israeli and Palestinian negotiators, the Israelis had presented a map serving as an "illustration" of what might be a possibility for the West Bank. What was offered was between 66 and 76 percent of the West Bank that would belong to the PA, with that percentage broken into four disconnected enclaves, or cantons, none sharing a border with the Jordan River, or much of Israel proper.[13] The Palestinians rejected this map outright. Barak eventually was offering approximately 90 percent of the West Bank, with annexation of settlement blocks accommodating roughly 80 percent of the West Bank's Jewish settlers. Israel was also planning on holding the Jordan Valley along the Jordan River for twenty years. The percentages regarding the West Bank are approximate and difficult to assess given the lack of documentation or maps. The offer of 90 percent of the West Bank contained provisos regarding settlers, security zones, and bypass roads between settlements. A percentage in the high-sixties to low-eighties is probably closer to the actual amount the Palestinians stood to regain, and with those portions in the West Bank being noncontiguous.[14]

Beyond division of the West Bank and Gaza, the issues of Jerusalem and refugees were also extremely difficult points at the summit. The PA demanded East Jerusalem where the Israelis offered Abu Dis instead. This village, just outside East Jerusalem, would then become *al-Quds* (Arabic for Jerusalem). In this scenario Israel would retain all of Jerusalem (East and West) while the Palestinians would have their own "Jerusalem" outside the city. Needless to say, there was no movement on this issue – the red lines weren't about to budge. As for the right of return, held up by UN General Assembly Resolution 194,[15] the Palestinians were seeking return or compensation for all refugees. Israel, though refusing to acknowledge any legal or moral responsibility for the refugee problem, discussed accepting a limited number (never fully decided on) in a "family reunification" program, as well as an international compensation fund in which it would participate.[16]

Note: At the time of Camp David II the number of refugees, including their descendants, according to the UN Relief and Works Agency for Palestinian Refugees (UNRWA), was 3.7 million. Currently UNRWA calculates 4.1 million refugees.[17]

Again, distance and rigidity prevailed. Two weeks after the summit commenced, Clinton called the summit to a close.

As mentioned, Camp David II wasn't completely without accomplishment. The mere discussion of issues like Jerusalem

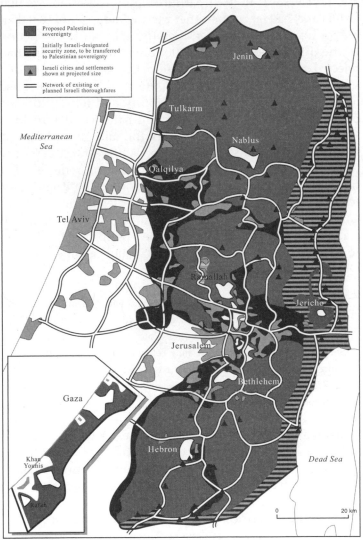

Map adapted from PASSIA / © Jan de Jong, 2001

Map 5   Projection of the West Bank Final Status Map presented by Israel, Camp David II, July 2000

and refugees was in itself pathbreaking. Also of note is that Ehud Barak had made offers that were far more substantial than any of his predecessors. Yet, his offers bore little distinction to the offers made in May 2000, ones the Palestinians had rejected out of hand. The fallout from Camp David II consisted of a good deal of finger pointing, most of which was aimed at Arafat in accusation of inflexibility and refusal to issue counterproposals. Both Clinton and Barak condemned the Palestinian leader for the failures of the summit – something Clinton had promised not to do. While Arafat certainly wasn't guilty of over-flexibility, his position reflected that of most people in the occupied territories. The Palestinians felt that losing all but 22 percent of Palestine in 1948 was compromise enough, and that regaining the West Bank and Gaza was a reasonable minimum. As political scientist and former US National Security Council staff member William Quandt summarizes,

> ... Arafat was widely suspected by his constituents of being too eager to become the first president of a Palestinian state. If the price [of Camp David II] were major territorial concessions to Israel or a relinquishment of rights in Jerusalem or concerning refugees, many Palestinians would oppose the deal. For most Palestinians, the acceptance of Israel within the 1967 lines was already a huge concession and should not be the starting point for further concessions.[18]

In a co-authored article published a year after the summit, Robert Malley, a member of the negotiating team at Camp David and close adviser to Clinton, and Hussein Agha, a scholar involved in Palestinian–Israeli affairs, observe:

> The war for the whole of Palestine was over because it had been lost. Oslo, as they saw it, was not about negotiating peace terms but terms of surrender. Bearing this perspective in mind explains the Palestinians' view that Oslo itself is the historic compromise – and agreement to concede 78 percent of mandatory Palestine to Israel.[19]

Nevertheless, Arafat's refusal to meet Barak's terms translated as his perceived lack of commitment to peace and compromise. And the PA being "more prone to caution that to creativity" was certainly a contributing element in Camp David II's lack of substantive gains.[20]

The leaders returned home empty-handed, but not entirely without profit. Arafat went home a hero for having not given up anything at the summit. Barak found his way into the good graces of Clinton and the US for having made groundbreaking concessions. His situation back home was less than solid, however. Certain concessions Barak was prepared to have made caused further instability on the hard-line side of his government, and his all-or-nothing handling of the negotiations provoked criticism from the left. As for Clinton, he didn't achieve the legacy agreement he was aiming for, but most viewed his effort favorably. However, as Quandt notes:

> If there were a criticism that seemed valid, it would be not so much that Clinton mishandled the negotiations at Camp David, but that so little of the preceding seven years had been used to lay the basis for the substantive discussion of the issues that finally came into focus at the summit.[21]

The Palestinians, regardless of how well received Arafat was upon arriving home, grew weary with the peace process. The situation in the territories hadn't improved and didn't look as though it would for the immediate, or not-so-immediate, future. Charges of corruption and betrayal against the PA were becoming recurrent. Autumn 2000 was starting to look a lot like autumn 1987.

THE SECOND INTIFADA (2000–3)

Note: We have now arrived at the current state of things in the Palestine–Israel conflict, as they exist during the writing of this and, most likely, your reading of this. As we've seen, the overall situation of the conflict changes in small increments, and generally for the worse. What became known as the "peace process" offered a period of relative calm and hope, but failed to transfigure the actual underpinnings of the conflict, namely, Israeli occupation and expansion, and Palestinian desire for legitimate statehood. Where we begin in this section is on the eve of another expression of the demoralization in the occupied territories.

On September 28, 2000, Ariel Sharon, the leader of the Likud Party, paid a dramatic and controversial visit to the Temple Mount / Haram al-Sharif in Jerusalem. Accompanied by approximately a thousand Israeli police officers and soldiers, Sharon made a number of symbolic gestures all at once. The day being the fifth anniversary of the signing of Oslo II was symbolic in itself. He was also asserting a posture that flew in the face of Barak and the concessions the prime minister was prepared to make at Camp David II. Sharon had been outspoken against transferring land to Palestinian control, and this highly publicized visit made it quite clear what his intentions and agenda would be if he took the position of prime minister. The Second Intifada, also known as the al-Aqsa Intifada, began the next day.

During Sharon's visit demonstrators assembled to block access to Muslim holy sites. The IDF responded by firing rubber-coated bullets and tear gas at the protesters. The following day, after Friday's prayers, Palestinian demonstrators poured out in protest, hurling stones at IDF forces and Jews praying at the Western Wall. IDF forces fired into the crowds, this time with live ammunition, killing four Palestinians.[22] Tension and violence of this proportion set the tone for what would define this second uprising. The UN Security Council passed a resolution (1322) on October 10 addressing the violence. The Council stated that it deplored "the provocation carried out at Al-Haram Al-Sharif in Jerusalem on 28 September 2000," and that it condemned Israel's "excessive use of force against Palestinians."[23] Human rights organizations also condemned the IDF's use of live ammunition and "lethal force" against unarmed demonstrators.[24] According to a US State Department document on human rights:

Deaths due to political violence increased significantly during the year due to the "al-Aqsa Intifada." At least 365 persons were killed between late September and the end of December in demonstrations, violent clashes, and military and civilian attacks, including 325 Palestinians, 36 Israelis, [and four internationals]. Additionally, at least 10,962 persons were injured during this period, including 10,600 Palestinians and 362 Israelis.[25]

As the Intifada picked up momentum it took on the features of all-out warfare, more than a "shaking off," as the term translates from Arabic.

Televised images of senseless brutality became imprinted icons that would characterize this chapter in the conflict's history. One scene caught on camera was 12-year-old Muhammad al-Durra and his father, both squatting against a wall in Gaza, hiding from the gunfire. The boy is fatally shot, falling limp against his father who is wounded soon after. In another image, the lifeless body of an Israeli reservist is thrown from a police station window in Ramallah, further beaten and paraded by the angry mob below; the reservist and a fellow soldier had both been murdered while hiding there. The Intifada of 2000 came on like an explosion compared to 1987. What started with the implements of the First Intifada – stones, bottles, and burning tires – very quickly escalated into the exchange of automatic-weapon fire between the IDF and Palestinians (police, and paramilitary groups more so). Palestinians employed the use of roadside bombs in addition to the traditional materials. The IDF deployed tanks and combat helicopters in Palestinian towns and villages, imposing dusk-to-dawn and 24-hour curfews and closures against the populations.

The violence raged, despite a number of feeble and ineffective attempts to establish truces, and statements by Barak and Arafat to quell the chaos. Two weeks after the uprising erupted Clinton convened a summit in Sharm al-Sheikh to attempt a truce. An unwritten arrangement was settled, with both sides agreeing to: (1) make statements calling an end to violence; (2) participate in an international fact-finding committee to determine the causes of the violence; and (3) promise to return to negotiations.[26] No implementation would follow. Further reluctant and ineffectual meetings took place between the Israelis and the PA, but to no avail. Arafat approached Russia's Vladimir Putin in Moscow, among other attempts to secure international involvement, but also with no success. With the approach of the new year came the approach of new leadership in the US, as well as Israel where elections were due in February 2001. The November 2000 elections in the US between Vice President Al Gore and Texas Governor George W. Bush, son of former-President George H. W. Bush, created a period of distraction in America. With Gore winning the popular vote, but the electoral vote hinging on Florida where a vote-counting controversy ensued, the Supreme Court settled the matter and declared George W. Bush the 43rd president of the United States. The two-month space between Bush's victory and his assumption of office, however, would feature a final diplomatic endeavor from the Clinton White House.

On December 23, 2000, Clinton assembled Barak and Arafat with their negotiators at the White House, a group closely resembling that of Camp David II. As was becoming customary for the peace process, the "Clinton Plan" was unwritten and, instead, presented in the form a speech delivered by the president.[27] Clinton essentially called for: (1) a Palestinian state consisting of Gaza and roughly 94 to 96 percent of the West Bank, allowing for "contiguity" and "80 percent of settlers in blocks"; (2) the principle that "Arab areas are Palestinian and Jewish ones are Israeli," and Jerusalem, with al-Quds (Abu Dis) would become the Palestinian capital; and (3) an undetermined but sketched-out plan to settle the refugee problem, focusing on the right of return to the Palestinian state (the West Bank and Gaza). In substance, what was proposed differed very little from what had been discussed before and during Camp David II. However, both sides cautiously, conditionally, and reluctantly accepted Clinton's parameters. What followed was a round of negotiations in Taba, Egypt (January 21–27), resulting in the Taba Statement.[28] Though merely a declaration of intent and an expression of the "spirit of hope and mutual achievement," for some Taba represented a high-water mark, especially amid the din of continuing violence and bloodshed.

BUSH, SHARON, AND THE INTIFADA

Whether the peace process was heading toward authentic peace, or just creating a pacifying illusion of progress, what has replaced it is deterioration with little hope of improvement. Upon taking office, George W. Bush's administration decided to put more distance between it and the conflict. The February 2001 elections in Israel saw the defeat of Ehud Barak and the election of Ariel Sharon as prime minister. The distance that the White House put between it and the conflict was commensurate with the distance Sharon put between his government and any continued negotiations. He has been outspoken for much of his career against transferring territory to the Palestinians, giving back any of Jerusalem, or the return of refugees. The reaction in the occupied territories was disbelief at his election, and anticipation of things getting worse, not better; the Palestinians were familiar with his career, especially his orchestration of the 1982 invasion of Lebanon. Bush, though removed from the situation, voiced his support for Sharon, identifying with his struggle against terrorism. Both leaders held Arafat responsible for the violence of the Intifada. Sharon has made many visits to the White House while Arafat was never invited for this very reason. The mantra recited continually to Arafat from both leaders was: Until the terror and violence cease, nothing.

Under these new circumstances, the violence of the Intifada grew worse. The trend of suicide bombings, which began at the end of Barak's term, dramatically increased under Sharon. Both religious (Hamas, Islamic Jihad) and secular Palestinian groups (Tanzim, al-Aqsa Martyrs Brigade) have engaged in acts of violence aimed almost exclusively at harming and killing Israeli civilians. Shopping malls, restaurants, and public buses have all been the sites of suicide attacks. Between November 2000 and mid-July 2003, the number of Israeli civilians killed by Palestinian civilians inside Israel was 317. Suicide bombings have become firmly integrated into the provocation–reprisal pattern characterizing the Second Intifada. Typical responses by the IDF have been "targeted killings" or assassinations of the various leaders and members of the organizations responsible for suicide bombing. From September 2000 to June 2004, 149 Palestinians were killed extra-judicially (outside court involvement) by Israel. In the course of these assassinations 100 other additional Palestinians were killed – generally bystanders. Another form of punishment employed by the Israeli military has been house demolitions. The residences of individuals suspected of involvement in terrorist activity are targeted for destruction, and most commonly bulldozed to rubble. Not a new policy, it was discontinued in 1997 and renewed in October 2001. Since 2001 Israel has demolished 578 homes in the occupied territories (as of June 2004). These policies of targeted killings and home demolition have brought condemnation of Israel from human rights organizations, the international community, and the UN.[29]

The relationship between Sharon and Bush developed further in the wake of an unprecedented attack on the United States on September 11, 2001. Terrorists hijacking four commercial aircraft flew two planes into the World Trade Center towers in New York City, one into the Pentagon in Washington DC, with the fourth crashing in a field in Pennsylvania. Nearly 3,000 people were killed. These terrorist acts were perpetrated by members of a network called al-Qaida ("The Base"). Al-Qaida operates under the inspiration and guidance of Osama bin Laden, the son of a wealthy Saudi businessman, and a sworn enemy of the West (mainly the US) and its intervention in the Middle East. With Bush's declared "war on terror," Sharon saw common cause with his own fight against Palestinian terror in Israel – referring to Arafat as "Israel's bin Laden"[30] – and increased the level of IDF response against the Intifada. To further carry out this initiative, the Sharon government reoccupied most of Zones A and B in spring 2002.

In an offensive maneuver called "Operation Defensive Shield," the IDF, over the course of late March to late April, reentered the territories they had withdrawn from after Oslo. In the process, the infrastructure of the Palestinian Authority in Ramallah was bombed and detonated. Buildings out of which the PA ran its civilian and security offices and agencies were leveled. Despite Security Council resolutions calling for an immediate end to the violence, Israel continued its reoccupation of major cities in the West Bank; the worst destruction and fighting occurring in Nablus and the Jenin refugee camp. The overall operation claimed the lives of 497 Palestinians. "Over 2,800 refugee housing units were damaged and 878 homes were demolished or destroyed ... leaving more than 17,000 people homeless or in need of shelter rehabilitation."[31] Sharon's next implemented plan to deal with terror is what is alternately referred to as a security fence, a separation barrier, and a wall.

Note: It might seem curious to some readers to make only limited mention of the September 11 attacks ("9/11"). This event and the ones that followed – US attacks on Afghanistan and Iraq – actually have no direct bearing on our subject. Al-Qaida's Osama bin Laden has made mention of Palestinian suffering under US support of Israel in his rhetoric condemning the US and the West. However, this invites analysis of bin Laden's history and a broader consideration of US foreign policy in the Middle East, something beyond our remit here.

THE WALL

Considered first as an option in the 1990s, Israel began construction of the barrier in June 2002. Starting at the north end of the West Bank, the barrier loosely traces the border as it heads south, mostly within the Palestinian boundary of the Green Line, and frequently snaking deep into the West Bank, claiming large portions of land. Its composition varies along its path, sometimes chain-link and razor wire, and sometimes a 25 feet-high concrete wall. Construction continues today with 87 of its projected 400 miles completed, as of July 2004. As stated by Israel's Ministry of Defense:

> The "Security Fence" is a manifestation of Israel's basic commitment to defend its citizens, and once completed, it will improve the ability of the IDF to prevent the infiltration of terrorists and criminal elements into

Israel for the purpose of carrying out terrorist attacks or the smuggling of arms and explosives.[32]

Israel has come under harsh condemnation from human rights organizations and the UN, all calling into question the legality of the fence being built inside the West Bank. The UN General Assembly passed two resolutions in 2003, stating that it was

> Gravely concerned at the commencement and continuation of construction by Israel, the occupying Power, of a wall in the Occupied Palestinian Territory, including in and around East Jerusalem, which is in departure from the Armistice Line of 1949 (Green Line) and which has involved the confiscation and destruction of Palestinian land and resources, the disruption of the lives of thousands of protected civilians and the de facto annexation of large areas of territory, and underlining the unanimous opposition by the international community to the construction of that wall.[33]

The International Court of Justice (ICJ; the UN's highest court) has also added to the international criticism of the barrier, stating in its July 2004 ruling that construction of the barrier is equivalent to annexation of West Bank land and that "the wall" is "contrary to international law."[34] The barrier remains a controversial subject and has become elemental in the conflict. Israelis generally support its construction, with approval ratings for it reaching as high as 80 percent.[35] Palestinians, especially ones directly affected by the wall, fear the long-term political ramifications, such as the wall creating a new Green Line, and resent the day-to-day consequences of being separated from schools, hospitals, farms, etc. Israel maintains the barrier is a temporary measure, but skepticism abounds in the occupied territories, pointing at its cost of roughly $4 million a mile.[36]

THE ROSE GARDEN AND THE ROAD MAP

As for diplomatic endeavors or resumption of the peace process, the Bush Administration has stepped lightly, with only a few statements and documents issuing from Washington.

Clinton's call for a fact-finding committee at Sharm al-Sheikh produced the Mitchell Committee (named after a senator on the committee), which submitted its report on April 30, 2001.[37] The Mitchell Report essentially asked of the Intifada: What happened? and Why did it happen? With headings in the document like "Resume Negotiations," "End the Violence," and "Rebuild Confidence," the report suggested they "find a path back to the peace process," and without placing blame on either of the parties. In its lists of suggestions, the report calls for Israel to "freeze all settlement activity." Though generally accepting the report's ideas, Sharon was not about to comply with a halt to settlement construction and expansion.[38] The Palestinians accepted the document. Much like the Sharm al-Sheikh meeting in October 2000 that inspired the commission, no implementation followed.

A year later, in June 2002, Bush gave a national address from the White House Rose Garden, calling for a change in Palestinian leadership:

> My vision is two states [Israel and Palestine], living side by side in peace and security. There is simply no way to achieve that peace until all parties fight terror. Yet, at this critical moment, if all parties will break with the past and set out on a new path, we can overcome the darkness with the light of hope. Peace requires a new and different Palestinian leadership, so that a Palestinian state can be born.[39]
>
> *George W. Bush*
> *White House Rose Garden, June 24, 2002*

Open discussion of, and plans for, a Palestinian state was new rhetoric for an American president, as was Bush's comment that "permanent occupation [of Palestine] threatens Israel's identity and democracy." Yet, Bush focused almost exclusively on Palestinian reform as a prerequisite for any movement on resolution of the conflict. (This view was shared by Israel's leadership, which released a statement from Ariel Sharon's office after the Bush address stating that advancement would not be possible until "the PA undertakes genuine reforms under new leadership so that there is a different authority."[40]) Though

Bush never mentioned Yasser Arafat by name, it was clear enough. The Palestinians praised the president's speech, and its discussion of the occupation: "... the Israeli occupation that began in 1967 will be ended through a settlement negotiated between the parties, based on UN Resolutions 242 and 338, with Israeli withdrawal to secure and recognize borders." (Bush was initially calling for Israeli withdrawal to the September 28 pre-Intifada positions.) However, regarding the president's call for leadership change, the PA was quick to point out that "Arafat was elected by the Palestinian people in a direct election" and that "President Bush must respect the choice of the Palestinian people."[41]

With the encouragement of British Prime Minister Tony Blair, Bush set out to formulate a new process to address the Palestine–Israel conflict. At this time the US was gearing up for its invasion of Iraq ("Operation Iraqi Freedom," March 2003–present) and the overthrow of its leader, Saddam Hussein, and Blair thought the declaration of a peace plan might illustrate the West's seriousness on the issue.[42] On April 30, 2003, the "Quartet" – the US, the European Union, the UN, and Russia – issued the "Road Map." The document established a three-phase "performance-based" plan for a "comprehensive settlement of the Israel-Palestinian conflict by 2005...."[43] The three phases featured the following headings:

- **Phase I**: "Ending Terror and Violence, Normalizing Palestinian Life, and Rebuilding Palestinian Institutions"
- **Phase II**: "Transition"
- **Phase III**: "Permanent Status Agreement and End of the Israeli–Palestinian Conflict."

The items and details called for "good faith efforts" from both parties for successful implementation. As part of Phase I, both sides were to cease all violence and incitement. The Palestinians were to begin reforming and rebuilding the Palestinian Authority including the appointment of a prime minister. The Israelis were to improve the humanitarian situation in the occupied territories, freeze all settlement activity (as called for in the Mitchell Report), and "dismantle settlement outposts erected since March 2001" (when Sharon took office). The contents of the Road Map were reasserted at the Aqaba Summit in Aqaba, Jordan in June 2003. Among those in attendance were Jordan's King Abdullah, George Bush, Ariel Sharon, and Mahmoud Abbas, who had recently been appointed prime minister of the Palestinian Authority, and who would function as a replacement for Arafat. Abbas resigned four months into his position, and was replaced by Ahmed Qurei. Bush, Sharon, and Abbas gave addresses expressing, in their own way, their support of the newly invigorated peace process, and their willingness to work "toward true peace."[44]

TODAY

The future of the conflict continues to hang in the balance. The US is currently mired in its intervention in Iraq, with the increasing insurgency in that country showing no sign of slowing. George W. Bush defeated his Democratic opposition, Senator John Kerry of Massachusetts, in November 2004 establishing a repeat administration. It remains to be seen if anything substantive will be attempted by the Bush White House regarding Palestine–Israel and the peace process. No movement has been seen on the Road Map, and political commentators of all stripes frequently speak of it in the past tense. Yet, Bush and Sharon's call for a change in Palestinian leadership, in their search for a "partner in peace," will have to be confronted with the passing of Yasser Arafat, and subsequent Palestinian elections.

Shortly after the US elections, four decades of Palestinian leadership under Arafat came to an end. He had spent the last of his few years holed up in his Muqata compound in Ramallah, being denied travel by Sharon's government to Gaza and Israel proper – or any international location, if he wished to return. However, in view of his failing health the Palestinian leader was granted travel to a hospital in Paris, France for medical attention. Going into a coma shortly after arriving, he died on November 11 at the age of 75. The effect of Arafat's departure from his place on the conflict's stage has yet to emerge, but the Palestinians forged ahead with presidential elections.

On January 9, 2005, ballots were cast throughout the West Bank, Gaza, and East Jerusalem for a new president of the Palestinian Authority. In a landslide victory, former Prime Minister Mahmoud Abbas won 62 percent of the vote, with his six challengers trailing behind him. Declaring his victory shortly after the election, Abbas announced to supporters: "Difficult and complicated missions face us – to establish a state with security and respect for our citizens, to give our prisoners freedom, to give our fugitives a dignified life and to reach our goal of a Palestinian state with Jerusalem as its capital."[45] President Bush announced his support for Abbas's victory, voicing optimism from Washington and noting the historical significance of the election. Ariel Sharon, too, phoned in congratulatory remarks to the president-elect. Both Abbas and Sharon agreed to meet in the future. Yet despite formalities, the prospects of diplomacy among the conflict's key players, as this book goes to press, remain wholly uncertain.

The last blip on the radar for diplomatic initiatives was the Geneva Accords. These were the product of secret negotiations between Israeli and Palestinian officials, conducted outside the authority of their respective governments. Released in October 2003, the accord bears resemblance to its predecessors, perhaps most closely to Camp David II, though without much said regarding the right of return for refugees. The senior leadership on both sides rejected the document outright. Upon publication both Israelis and Palestinians were evenly split in opinion polls.[46] Though merely a blueprint for formal negotiations, this represents the height of diplomacy in recent years.

In February 2004, Sharon announced a plan to withdraw, or "disengage," from the Gaza Strip. The disengagement would feature military withdrawal as well as the transfer of Gaza's 8,000 Jewish settlers (21 settlements in all). Also included in the initiative would be the removal of four settlements from the West Bank. The Disengagement Plan was passed in the Knesset in October, stating that Israel "will evacuate the Gaza Strip, including all existing Israeli towns and villages, and will redeploy outside the Strip." But regardless of withdrawal, "Israel will guard and monitor the external land perimeter of the Gaza Strip, will continue to maintain exclusive authority in Gaza air space, and will continue to exercise security activity in the sea off the coast of the Gaza Strip."[47] Some maintain that the plan still spells occupation for Gazans,[48] while Sharon faces fierce opposition for betraying the settlement cause from members of his own party, hard-line rabbis, and the settlers themselves. The stated timeline looks to the end of 2005 to finish the "process of evacuation," but this development in Israeli politics also remains an uncertainty.

The intensity of the Second Intifada has passed, yet what it expressed still reverberates. (It should be noted that the Intifada is still frequently discussed by a wide variety of sources in the present tense.) Palestinian hatred for the occupation remains at feverish levels to this day. Roadblocks, checkpoints, curfews, and closures imposed by the IDF have caused severe economic damage in the West Bank and Gaza, with malnutrition levels being compared to those in sub-Saharan Africa.[49] Likewise, Israelis and their economy have felt the toll taken by suicide bombings throughout Israel, where fear remains even with the dwindling of the Intifada. And while desire for statehood in the West Bank and Gaza has not changed, thoughts of broader possibilities have now entered the equation. Birth rates in the two groups are disproportionate: Israel's population growth is 1.29 percent, while it is 3.21 in the West Bank and 3.83 percent in Gaza.[50] Some predict that in the next fifteen or twenty years Palestinians in the occupied territories and Israeli Arabs will outnumber Israelis, calling into question the future dynamic of the conflict.

Lack of a peace process of any kind; a sustained occupation that even members of Israel's intelligence elite say bodes ill for the country's future;[51] US inaction; and worsening conditions in the occupied territories are elements signifying a potentially turbulent near-future – and are certainly key components to a painful past. From the beginning of the Intifada to November 2004, 3,040 Palestinians had been killed in the occupied territories by Israeli soldiers, 606 of them minors. Inside Israel,

429 Israeli civilians had been killed by Palestinians (residents of the occupied territories), 78 of them minors; while 210 Israeli civilians were killed inside the occupied territories, most being settlers.[52] These numbers indicate the typical costs brought to bear by this conflict, one that began not so long ago, and one that has been well documented. But in most of the televised news quantity has not brought clarity. Reportage is abundant, but insufficient. Media agencies seem unwilling or unable to provide coverage that educates instead of mystifies. Top-level leadership all around, historically has proven its difficulties or lack of commitment in bringing the conflict to resolution. And in the meantime, history is made – more of it every day. Though a modern conflict in all aspects, a single moment of it, for its victims, can seem like *thousands of years.*

Appendices

I

Chronology

1.4 million years ago – 8500 BCE Paleolithic: Stone Age
8500–4300 BCE Neolithic: New Stone Age
4300–3300 BCE Chalcolithic: Copper Age
3300–1150 BCE Bronze Age: Age of Canaanite Kingdoms
1150–900 BCE Iron Age: United Kingdom of Israel; in 925 splits into
  Israel (north) and Judah (south)
925–720 BCE Israel
925–586 BCE Judah
900–609 BCE Assyrian Empire
612–539 BCE Neo-Babylonian Empire
539–332 BCE Persian Empire
330–67 BCE Hellenistic / Greek Empires
166–37 BCE Hasmonean dynasty
67 BCE – 330 CE Roman Empire
330–1453 CE Byzantine Empire
570–632 Life of Muhammad
600s–1200s Arab Empire
1095–1291 Crusades
1227 Genghis Khan dies, grandson Hulegu moves Mongols west into
  the Middle East
1299–1922 Ottoman Empire (1516–1918 Ottoman control over
  Palestine)

SECTION II

1882 First Aliyah
1894 Dreyfus Affair
1896 Theodor Herzl's *The Jewish State* published
1897 World Zionist Organization founded at Basel, Switzerland

1904 Second Aliyah

Aug. 1914 World War I begins

May 1916 Sykes–Picot Agreement

Nov. 1917 Balfour Declaration

Nov. 1918 end of World War I

Aug. 1919 King–Crane Commission

July 1922 Mandate system ratified by League of Nations

1933 Adolf Hitler sworn in as chancellor of Germany

1936–39 Arab Revolt

1937 Peel Commission suggests partition of Palestine

Sept. 1939 – Aug. 1945 World War II

SECTION III

June–Aug. 1947 UNSCOP visits and suggests partition of Palestine

Nov. 1947 UN General Assembly partitions Palestine

Dec. 1947 – May 14, 1948 Civil phase of Arab–Zionist war

May 14, 1948 State of Israel declares independence

May 15, 1948 – end of 1948 International phase of Arab-Zionist war

1956 Suez Crisis

1964 PLO forms

June 1967 Six-Day War

Nov. 1967 UN Security Council passes Resolution 242

Nov. 1967 – Aug. 1970 War of Attrition

Oct. 1973 Yom Kippur War

Sept. 1978 Camp David I (Carter, Sadat, Begin)

1982 Israeli invasion of Lebanon

Dec. 1987–1991 First Intifada

1988 Hamas forms

Jan.–Feb. 1991 First Gulf War

Oct. 1991 Madrid talks begin

Sept. 1993 Oslo Accord signed

Sept. 1995 Oslo II signed

July 2000 Camp David II (Clinton, Barak, Arafat)

Sept. 2000–2003 Second Intifada

April 2003 "Road Map" issued

Oct. 2003 Geneva Accords

Nov. 11, 2004 Yasser Arafat dies

Jan. 9, 2005 Mahmoud Abbas elected president of Palestinian
    Authority

2

Israel's Prime Ministers

David Ben-Gurion (1948–54)
Moshe Sharett (1954–55)
David Ben-Gurion (1955–63)
Levi Eshkol (1963–69)
Golda Meir (1969–74)
Yitzhak Rabin (1974–77)
Menachem Begin (1977–83)
Yitzhak Shamir (1983–84)
Shimon Peres (1984–86)
Yitzhak Shamir (1986–92)
Yitzhak Rabin (1992–95)
Shimon Peres (1995–96)
Benjamin Netanyahu (1996–99)
Ehud Barak (1999–2001)
Ariel Sharon (2001–)

3

Israel, Palestine – Data

ISRAEL

Population: 6,116,533 (July 2002 est.)
Note: Includes about 187,000 Israeli settlers in the West Bank, about 20,000 in the Israeli-occupied Golan Heights, more than 5,000 in the Gaza Strip, and fewer than 177,000 in East Jerusalem (February 2003 est.) (July 2003 est.)

Languages: Hebrew (official), Arabic used officially for Arab minority, English most commonly used foreign language

Religions: Jewish 80.1%, Muslim 14.6% (mostly Sunni Muslim), Christian 2.1%, other 3.2% (1996 est.)

Area: 8,019 sq mi (20,770 sq km)

WEST BANK

Population: 2,237,194 (July 2002 est.)
Note: There are also about 187,000 Israeli settlers in the West Bank and fewer than 177,000 in East Jerusalem (February 2002 est.) (July 2003 est.)

Languages: Arabic, Hebrew (spoken by Israeli settlers and many Palestinians), English (widely understood)

Religions: Muslim 75% (predominantly Sunni), Jewish 17%, Christian and other 8%

Area: 2,263 sq mi (5,860 sq km)

GAZA (THE "GAZA STRIP")

Population: 1,274,868 (July 2002 est.)
Note: There are also more than 5,000 Israeli settlers in the Gaza Strip
(July 2003 est.)

Languages: Arabic, Hebrew (spoken by Israeli settlers and many
Palestinians), English (widely understood)

Religions: Muslim 98.7% (predominantly Sunni), Christian 0.7%,
Jewish 0.6%

Area: 139 sq mi (360 sq km)

Source: US Central Intelligence Agency: *The World Factbook*, http://
www.cia.gov/cia/publications/factbook

Notes to the Text

NOTES TO THE INTRODUCTION

1. *Encyclopaedia Britannica*, 15th edn, s.v. "Middle East."
2. Ibid., s.v. "Arab."
3. For all data regarding Islam I relied on Don Belt, "The World of Islam," *National Geographic*, January 2002, 76.
4. This number reflects mid-2003 estimates according to UN projections in 2002. See *The World Almanac and Book of Facts, 2004* (New York: World Almanac Books), 855.

NOTES TO CHAPTER I

1. All biblical passages used in this chapter can be found in any study Bible.
2. One could debate endlessly the proper term to use: Israel, the Holy Land, the Southern Levant, the Eastern Mediterranean, Eretz-Israel, etc. Many scholars have dealt with the issue; I think Keith W. Whitelam, *The Invention of Ancient Israel* (London, New York: Routledge, 1996) handles it best and, though I cannot really claim to follow him to the letter here, I recommend reading his Chapter 2 before reading anything in the various subjects dealing with the history of the region.
3. In fact, the term "Canaan" makes its first appearance in an eighteenth-century BCE text from the site of Mari in Syria. For more, see Jo Ann Hackett, "Canaan," *Oxford Encyclopedia of Archaeology in the Near East*, Eric M. Meyers, ed. (New York; Oxford: Oxford University Press, 1997), vol. I, 408.
4. For one of the greatest twentieth-century archaeologists, and a true forefather to Syro-Palestinian archaeology, read anything by Albright and you are bound to find discussion on the biblical patriarchs and the Middle Bronze Age. While many of his ideas are now outdated some remain very influential.

5. Niels Peter Lemche, "Hapiru," in Meyers, *Oxford Encyclopaedia*, vol. III, 7.

6. Mentioned in Deuteronomy 33:2, Judges 5:4, and Habakkuk 3:3.

7. William F. Albright and John Bright are the two biggest proponents of the Conquest Model. See anything by Albright, and see John Bright, *A History of Israel*, 2nd edn (London: SCM, 1972). For the Peaceful Infiltration Model, see Albrecht Alt, *Essays on Old Testament History and Religion* (New York: Doubleday, 1968), particularly the essays, "The Settlement of the Israelites in Palestine" and "The Formation of the Israelite State in Palestine."

8. One of the earliest articles by Mendenhall: George E. Mendenhall, "The Hebrew Conquest of Palestine," *Biblical Archaeologist*, no. 25 (September 3, 1962): 66–87. For Gottwald's version of events, see Norman K. Gottwald, *The Tribes of Yahweh: A Sociology of the Religion of Liberated Israel, 1250–1050 BCE* (Maryknoll, NY: Orbis Books, 1979).

9. 2 Kings 17–18. Also the "Annals of Sargon," *Ancient Near Eastern Texts: Relating to the Old Testament*, James B. Pritchard, ed. (Princeton, NY: Princeton University Press, 1969), 284–5.

10. "Annals of Sargon," ibid., 284–5.

11. The name Israel disappears as a political and geographical term from then on. See Gösta W. Ahlström, *The History of Ancient Palestine* (Minneapolis, MN: Fortress Press, 1993), 690. There is some debate about what peoples Israel was repopulated with, but Miller and Hays are pretty reliable. See J. Maxwell Miller and John H. Hays, *A History of Ancient Israel and Judah* (Philadelphia, PA: Westminster Press, 1986), 39.

12. 2 Kings 18–19. Also the "Oriental Institute Prism," in Pritchard, *Ancient Near Eastern Texts*, 287.

13. Ezra 1:3.

14. Ahlström, *History of Ancient Palestine*, 822–3.

15. They crowned themselves kings of their region: Antigonus 306, Ptolemy 305/4, and Seleucus 305/4.

NOTES TO CHAPTER 2

1. Philip K. Hitti, *History of the Arabs*, 10th edn (London: Macmillan & Co. Ltd, 1970), 8. For my research in this area I used Hitti's major

work, which I have cited here and throughout, but his shorter work, *The Arabs: A Short History* (1943; reprint, Washington, DC: Regnery Publishing, Inc., 1996), is very useful and features most of what I cover in this chapter.

2. Hitti, *History of the Arabs*, 21.
3. *Encyclopaedia Britannica*, 15th edn., s.v. "Arabia."
4. Hitti, *History of the Arabs*, 90.
5. Albert Hourani, *A History of the Arab Peoples* (New York: Warner Books, 1991), 13.
6. Arthur Goldschmidt Jr, *A Concise History of the Middle East*, 7th edn (Boulder, CO: Westview Press, 2002), 24.
7. Hitti, *History of the Arabs*, 93.
8. Ibid., 26.
9. Constantinople, as Emperor Constantine I called it, was located in modern-day Istanbul, Turkey. Before it was called Constantinople it was known as Byzantium. The Roman Empire would eventually split into East and West; and after Rome fell in 476, the Eastern Roman Empire carried on, and is referred to by historians as the Byzantine Empire.
10. The translation I have used is *The Koran*, translated by N. J. Dawood (1956; reprint, London: Penguin Classics, 1999). Also worth looking at is *The Koran Interpreted*, translated by A. J. Arberry (1955; reprint, New York: Touchstone, 1996).
11. W. Montgomery Watt, *Muhammad: Prophet and Statesman* (1961; reprint, Oxford: Oxford University Press, 1974), 52. I use Watt as one of my main sources for discussion of Muhammad. His work *Muhammad: Prophet and Statesman* is an abridgment of his two larger works, *Muhammad at Mecca* and *Muhammad at Medina*. Watt also prepared the entry in the *Encyclopaedia Britannica* (15th edn, s.v. "Islam") pertaining to the Prophet's life and works, to which I have also referred. In addition, I found helpful Maxime Rodinson, *Muhammad*, translated by Anne Carter (1971; reprint, New York: The New Press, 2002).
12. It is not known as to whether these Jews were Arabs who had adopted Judaism as their chosen faith, or whether they were descended from Jewish refugees. It is, however, safe to assume that these clans were, in their look, manner, and lifestyle, more or less identical to the other clans in Yathrib. See Watt, *Muhammad*, 6, 84–5.

13. Ibid., 228.
14. Goldschmidt, *Concise History*, 67. The term was coined by the historian Marshall Hodgson.
15. Hitti, *History of the Arabs*, 240. This quote is a classic in its own right and has been cited by a number of authors. Though I primarily used Goldschmidt and Hourani in this particular section, Hitti is very helpful with descriptions of what was going on culturally and intellectually during this period.
16. J. R. Hayes, ed., *The Genius of Arab Civilization: Source of Renaissance*, 2nd edn (Cambridge, MA: MIT Press, 1983), 6.

NOTES TO CHAPTER 3

1. Before their conversion to Islam, the Turks practiced a form of shamanism. The shaman, or mystic, was a medium between the natural and supernatural worlds, and practiced healing and divination.
2. Thomas H. Greer, *A Brief History of the Western World*, 5th edn (San Diego: Harcourt Brace Jovanovich, 1987), 235.
3. Arthur Goldschmidt Jr, *A Concise History of the Middle East*, 7th edn (Boulder, CO: Westview Press, 2002), 96. For a more detailed description of the Mongol invasions, and their subsequent empire, I found helpful and would suggest J. J. Saunders, *The History of the Mongol Conquests* (1971; reprint, Philadelphia: University of Pennsylvania Press, 2001). For more detail on what is covered in the Goldschmidt quote, look at chapter 4 in Saunders, *History*, 54–61.
4. William L. Cleveland, *A History of the Modern Middle East*, 2nd edn (Boulder, CO: Westview Press, 2000), 50.
5. For this chapter, in addition to the above authors, I relied on *Encyclopaedia Britannica*, 15th edn, s.v. "Crusades" and "Ottoman Empire."

NOTES TO CHAPTER 4

1. Theodor Herzl, *The Jewish State* (1946; reprint, New York: Dover Publications, Inc., 1988), 69.
2. David Vital, *The Origins of Zionism* (1975; reprint, Oxford: Oxford University Press, 2001), 3.

3. *Encyclopaedia Britannica*, 15th edn, s.v. "Declaration of the Rights of Man and of the Citizen."
4. Howard M. Sachar, *A History of Israel: From the Rise of Zionism to Our Time*, 2nd edn (New York: Alfred A. Knopf, 1996), 4.
5. Vital, *Origins of Zionism*, 37–40.
6. Sachar, *History of Israel*, 8.
7. Quoted in Vital, *Origins of Zionism*, 52–3.
8. Sachar, *History of Israel*, 13.
9. *Encyclopaedia Britannica*, 15th edn, s.v. "Zion."
10. The acronym comes from the Hebrew: *Beit Ya'akov lekhu ve-nelkha*.
11. Herzl was aware of his work not being entirely unprecedented, though he was not versed in a good deal of the literature. During his writing of *The Jewish State* he was unfamiliar with the works of Pinkser (*Autoemancipation*), which he read immediately after, and Hess (*Rome and Jerusalem*), which he read two years later. Quite taken with both, he maintained that had he been more familiar with the literature he might not have undertaken his project in the first place.
12. Herzl, *Jewish State*, 69.
13. Ibid., 77.
14. Walter Laqueur and Barry Rubin, eds, *The Israel–Arab Reader*, 6th edn (New York: Penguin Books, 2001), 9–10.
15. Quoted in Vital, *Origins of Zionism*, 369.

NOTES TO CHAPTER 5

1. *Encyclopaedia Britannica*, 15th edn, s.v. "Palestine."
2. Neville J. Mandel, *The Arabs and Zionism Before World War I* (Berkeley: University of California Press, 1976), xx.
3. Ibid., xxii.
4. Phrase used initially by Zionist leader and writer, Israel Zangwill, in 1901.
5. Justin McCarthy, *The Population of Palestine: Population Statistics of the Late Ottoman Period and the Mandate* (New York: Columbia University Press, 1990), 10.
6. The term "Sephardic" comes from the Hebrew *Sefarad*, meaning "Spain." These Jews are descendants of the Jews from Spain who were expelled in 1492. They settled in North Africa and parts of

the Ottoman Empire. The term "Ashkenazic" comes from the Hebrew *Ashkenaz*, meaning "Germany." This group lived in the Rhineland and France until they moved east to Russia and Eastern Europe after the Crusades. Some would eventually move west again during the seventeenth century. Eighty percent of Jews today are Ashkenazic.

7. Mandel, *Arabs and Zionism*, 29.
8. Quoted in Rashid Khalidi, *Palestinian Identity: The Construction of Modern National Consciousness* (New York: Columbia University Press, 1997), 101.
9. Howard M. Sachar, *A History of Israel: From the Rise of Zionism to Our Time*, 2nd edn (New York: Alfred A. Knopf, 1996), 73.
10. Mandel, *Arabs and Zionism*, 29. See also Benny Morris, *Righteous Victims: A History of the Zionist–Arab Conflict, 1881–2001* (New York: Vintage Books, 2001), 46.
11. From the Basel Declaration quoted in Chapter 4.
12. Quoted in Khalidi, *Palestinian Identity*, 102.
13. Morris, *Righteous Victims*, 38.
14. Quoted in ibid., 36.
15. McCarthy, *Population of Palestine*, 10, 23–4, 26.

NOTES TO CHAPTER 6

1. Benny Morris, *Righteous Victims: A History of the Zionist–Arab Conflict, 1881–2001* (New York: Vintage Books, 2001), 73.
2. Arthur Goldschmidt Jr, *A Concise History of the Middle East*, 7th edn (Boulder, CO: Westview Press, 2002), 202.
3. Walter Laqueur and Barry Rubin, eds, *The Israel–Arab Reader*, 6th edn (New York: Penguin Books, 2001), 11.
4. Ibid., 11.
5. Ibid., 16.
6. Quoted in Charles D. Smith, *Palestine and the Arab–Israeli Conflict*, 4th edn (Boston: Bedford / St Martin's, 2001), 75. See also Morris, *Righteous Victims*, 74.
7. Quoted in Baylis Thomas, *How Israel Was Won: A Concise History of the Arab–Israeli Conflict* (Lanham, MD: Lexington Books, 1999), 12.
8. Quoted in ibid., 10.
9. T. E. Lawrence is an interesting historical figure, and the film *Lawrence of Arabia* (directed by David Lean, and one of this

author's favorites) is certainly worth seeing if you haven't done so. Also, Lawrence's account of his experiences in the Middle East, *The Seven Pillars of Wisdom*, is an enjoyable read to be sure. However, caution is advised when looking at these two works as actual history.

10. Doreen Ingrams, *Palestine Papers, 1917–1922: Seeds of Conflict* (New York: George Braziller, 1973), 20. See also Smith, *Palestine*, 79.

11. *Encyclopaedia Britannica*, 15th edn, s.v. "Fourteen Points."

12. For the text of the Covenant of the League of Nations, see The Avalon Project at Yale Law School, http://www.yale.edu/lawweb/avalon/leagcov.htm.

13. Laqueur and Rubin, *Israel–Arab Reader*, 23–5.

14. Ingrams, *Palestine Papers*, 73.

15. For the text of the British Palestine Mandate, see The Avalon Project, http://www.yale.edu/lawweb/avalon/mideast/palmanda.htm.

16. For the text of the White Paper of 1922, see Laqueur and Rubin, *Israel–Arab Reader*, 25–9.

17. For text of the Peel Commission report, see the United Nations Information System on the Question of Palestine (UNISPAL), http://domino.un.org/unispal.nsf.

18. Laqueur and Rubin, *Israel–Arab Reader*, 43.

19. For the text for the White Paper of 1939, see The Avalon Project, http://www.yale.edu/lawweb/avalon/mideast/brwh1939.htm; Laqueur and Rubin, *Israel–Arab Reader*, 44–50.

20. A few titles on the subject one might find helpful, if interested in heading off in that direction, would include the following: Raul Hilberg's *The Destruction of the European Jews* (one-volume student edition) is an excellent history and is worth consulting; Hannah Arendt's *Eichmann in Jerusalem: A Report on the Banality of Evil* covers not just the trial of a Nazi officer, but the history and themes surrounding the Jews, the Holocaust, and totalitarianism; Arthur Morse's *While Six Million Died: A Chronicle of American Apathy* recounts the refusal of Franklin Roosevelt's administration to adjust its immigration quotas and allow Jewish refugees sanctuary in the United States – an indifference that cost thousands of Jewish lives; another good text covering the same appalling topic is Henry L. Feingold's *The Politics of Rescue: The Roosevelt*

Administration and the Holocaust (the Morse and Feingold texts are
out of print); Norman G. Finkelstein's *The Holocaust Industry* is a
devastating critique of how Jewish suffering under the Nazis has
been, and continues to be, exploited by members of the Jewish
financial and intellectual elite.

21. These groups were composed of individuals representing the
most extreme and ultranationalist stripe of Zionism. The Irgun
Zvai Leumi (Irgun, IZL, or Etzel for short), established in 1937,
was the military branch of the rightwing Revisionists, a Zionist
faction started by Vladimir Jabotinsky. Though also violently anti-
Arab, the Irgun concentrated on London's presence in Palestine,
using terrorism and assassinations as means to oust the British. In
1943–48 the group was under the leadership of Menachem Begin,
who would become prime minister of Israel in 1977. In 1946
the Irgun terrorists bombed a wing of the King David Hotel in
Jerusalem, killing 91 (British, Arab, and Jewish). In 1940, the Irgun
splinter faction LEHI (Hebrew acronym for the "Fighters for the
Freedom of Israel") emerged. Known early on as the Stern Gang
(named after their founder, Abraham Stern), LEHI was a smaller
group but even more extreme than Irgun. In 1944 members of
LEHI assassinated Lord Moyne, a British minister of state, and in
1948 murdered Count Folke Bernadotte, a Swedish UN mediator
working in Palestine.

22. Quoted in Smith, *Palestine*, 180.

NOTES TO CHAPTER 7

1. The countries involved in the Marshall Plan were: Austria, Belgium,
Denmark, France, Greece, Iceland, Ireland, Italy, Luxembourg, The
Netherlands, Norway, Portugal, Sweden, Switzerland, Turkey, the
United Kingdom, and West Germany.

2. Charles D. Smith, *Palestine and the Arab–Israeli Conflict*, 4th edn
(Boston: Bedford / St Martin's, 2001), 183.

3. Ibid., 190. See also Benny Morris, *Righteous Victims: A History of
the Zionist–Arab Conflict, 1881–2001* (New York: Vintage Books,
2001), 180–1.

4. Morris, *Righteous Victims*, 181.

5. The UNSCOP team was composed of: Australia, Canada, Czechoslovakia, Guatemala, India, Iran, the Netherlands, Peru, Sweden,
Uruguay, and Yugoslavia.

6. Walter Laqueur and Barry Rubin, eds, *The Israel–Arab Reader*, 6th edn (New York: Penguin Books, 2001), 67.

7. Ibid., 68.

8. Mark Tessler, *A History of the Israeli–Palestinian Conflict* (Bloomington, IN: Indiana University Press, 1994), 259.

9. J. C. Hurewitz, quoted in Christopher Sykes, *Crossroads to Israel* (Cleveland: The World Publishing Company, 1965), 325.

10. Quoted in Sykes, *Crossroads*, 346. See also Smith, *Palestine*, 194.

11. The six countries of China, Ethiopia, Greece, Haiti, Liberia, and the Philippines were recipients of this pressure. All except for Greece either voted in favor or abstained.

12. *In favor*: Australia, Belgium, Bolivia, Brazil, Byelorussian SSR [Belarus], Canada, Costa Rica, Czechoslovakia, Denmark, Dominican Republic, Ecuador, France, Guatemala, Haiti, Iceland, Liberia, Luxemburg, Netherlands, New Zealand, Nicaragua, Norway, Panama, Paraguay, Peru, Philippines, Poland, Sweden, Ukrainian SSR, Union of South Africa, USA, USSR, Uruguay, Venezuela. *Against*: Afghanistan, Cuba, Egypt, Greece, India, Iran, Iraq, Lebanon, Pakistan, Saudi Arabia, Syria, Turkey, and Yemen. *Abstained*: Argentina, Chile, China, Colombia, El Salvador, Ethiopia, Honduras, Mexico, United Kingdom, and Yugoslavia.

13. Justin McCarthy, *The Population of Palestine: Population Statistics of the Late Ottoman Period and the Mandate* (New York: Columbia University Press, 1990), 36.

14. Most accounts in the literature cite 254 dead. Cf. Morris, *Righteous Victims*, 209, who suggests that the number is closer to 100–110. For general discussions of Deir Yassin, see Morris, *Righteous Victims*, 207–9; Smith, *Palestine*, 198–9; Sykes, *Crossroads*, 351–4; and Tessler, *History*, 291–4. [Smith adjusts the number to 115 dead in his fifth edition: Charles D. Smith, *Palestine and the Arab–Israeli Conflict*, 5th edn (Boston: Bedford / St Martin's, 2004), 194, 204n67. His new edition was published during production of this book and is used in Chapters 9 and 10.]

15. Smith, *Palestine*, 199.

16. Laqueur and Rubin, *Israel–Arab Reader*, 80.

17. Quoted in Sykes, *Crossroads*, 365. See also Laqueur and Rubin, *Israel–Arab Reader*, 81–3.

18. Howard M. Sachar, *A History of Israel: From the Rise of Zionism to Our Time*, 2nd edn (New York: Alfred A. Knopf, 1996), 311.

19. Calculations of troop strengths vary slightly, but a comparison of various sources can provide a reasonably accurate picture. See Morris, *Righteous Victims*, 215–18, who gives a fairly complete rundown of the militaries involved; cf. Simha Flapan, *The Birth of Israel: Myths and Realities* (New York: Pantheon Books, 1987), 193–7; and Eugene L. Rogan and Avi Shlaim, eds, *The War for Palestine: Rewriting the History of 1948* (Cambridge: Cambridge University Press, 2001), 81. In Rogan and Shlaim, see Avi Shlaim's "Israel and the Arab coalition in 1948," 79–103.

20. For a thorough elucidation of the March–April 1948 truce negotiations that preceded Israel's statehood and the international war, see Flapan, *Birth of Israel*, 155–86.

21. The UN Charter is available on the International Court of Justice's site, http://www.icj-cij.org.

22. Good general descriptions of King Abdullah's involvement in the proceedings of 1947–48 can be found in Flapan, *Birth of Israel*, 126–30, 135–41; Sykes, *Crossroads*, 327–31; and Tessler, *History*, 275–8. The standard work on this subject, both detailed and scholarly, is Avi Shlaim's *Collusion Across the Jordan: King Abdullah, the Zionist Movement, and the Partition of Palestine* (New York: Columbia University Press, 1988).

23. Sir John Bagot Glubb, *A Soldier with the Arabs* (New York: Harper & Brothers, 1957), 89.

24. Flapan, *Birth of Israel*, 198–9.

25. Tessler, *History*, 276.

26. The scholar who has done the foremost research on the subject is Israeli historian Benny Morris. His *The Birth of the Palestinian Refugee Problem Revisited*, 2nd edn (Cambridge: Cambridge University Press, 2004), when it was originally published in 1988, laid to rest many disagreements and myths surrounding the refugee problem. Though this work is lengthy and a bit technical for the beginning reader, one might find useful both his concise discussion of the issue in his *Righteous Victims*, 252–8, and his chapter in Rogan and Shlaim, "Revisiting the Palestinian exodus of 1948," 37–59. Cf. Flapan, *Birth of Israel*, 81–118.

27. Morris, *Righteous Victims*, 252.

28. Ibid., 257.

29. Morris, *Birth*, 60.

30. For a critique of Benny Morris's conclusions, see Norman G. Finkelstein's third chapter, "'Born of War, Not by Design': Benny

Morris's 'Happy Median' Image," in his *Image and Reality of the Israel–Palestine onflict*, 2nd edn (London: Verso, 2003), 51–87. See also the *Journal of Palestine Studies*, XXI, no. 1 (Autumn 1991) for articles by Finkelstein, Palestinian scholar Nur Masalha, and Morris. Masalha's piece is available, along with another essay by Morris, in Ilan Pappé, ed., *The Israel / Palestine Question* (London: Routledge, 2002).

31. Flapan, *Birth of Israel*, 100; cf. Morris, *Righteous Victims*, 257.

32. With the declassification of Israeli state documents, and a wealth of diary material available, the issue of transferring the indigenous Palestinian population out of Palestine – as a conscious Zionist thought and intention – has become increasingly visible. Helpful examinations of this issue can be found in the following texts: In chapter 2 of *Birth*, "The Idea of 'Transfer' in Zionist Thinking," 39–64, Morris describes the discussion of the issue at the elite levels of Zionist leadership well before statehood; see also, Simha Flapan, *Zionism and the Palestinians* (New York: Barnes & Noble Books, 1979); and Nur Masalha, *Expulsion of the Palestinians: The Concept of "Transfer" in Zionist Political Thought, 1882–1948* (Washington, DC: Institute for Palestine Studies, 1992). In addition to Finkelstein's third chapter (cited in note 30), see chapter 4 in his *Image and Reality*, "Settlement, Not Conquest: Anita Shapira's 'Benign Intentions' Myth," for a critical analysis of Jewish/Zionist frames of mind and views toward Palestine.

33. Raphael Patai, ed., *The Complete Diaries of Theodor Herzl*, translated by Harry Zohn (New York: Herzl Press and Thomas Yoseloff, 1960), vol. 1, 88. Cited in Morris, *Birth*, 41.

34. Quoted in Morris, *Birth*, 48.

35. Ibid., 60.

36. Smith, *Palestine*, 230.

37. Ibid., 238, 252n34; cf. Tessler, *History*, 344–5.

38. Livia Rokach, *Israel's Sacred Terrorism*, 3rd edn (Belmont, MA: AAUG Press, 1986), 39–40.

39. Stephen Green, *Taking Sides: America's Secret Relations with a Militant Israel* (New York: William Morrow and Company, Inc., 1984), 100–4. See also Rokach, *Israel's Sacred Terrorism*, 38–41.

40. Green, *Taking Sides*, 132–3.

41. Donald Neff, *Warriors for Jerusalem: The Six Days That Changed the Middle East* (New York: Linden Press / Simon & Schuster, 1984), 40–6.

42. In the general histories, see Ian J. Bickerton and Carla L. Klausner, *A Concise History of the Arab–Israeli Conflict*, 4th edn (Upper Saddle River, NJ: Prentice Hall, 2001), 137–54; Morris, *Righteous Victims*, 302–46; Nadav Safran, *Israel: The Embattled Ally* (Cambridge, MA: The Belknap Press of Harvard University Press, 1978), 381–413; and Smith, *Palestine*, 281–90, 301–7. Some texts dedicated solely to June 1967 and worth consulting are: Randolph S. Churchill and Winston S. Churchill, *The Six Day War* (London: Heinemann, 1967), which is a good readable review of the war, but predates declassified documents that came out decades later; and Donald Neff's *Warriors*, cited above. See also pertinent chapters in Green, *Taking Sides*.

43. For the attack on the USS *Liberty* I have relied on Green, *Taking Sides*, 212–42, and Neff, *Warriors*, 248–60.

44. Morris, *Righteous Victims*, 336.

45. For descriptions of land clearing and eviction of Palestinians, see Morris, *Righteous Victims*, 336–43; and Neff, *Warriors*, 289–300.

46. Bickerton and Klausner, *Concise History*, 154.

47. Excerpts of the Khartoum Summit are provided in Bickerton and Klausner, *Concise History*, 158–9; the text in its entirety is provided at the Avalon Project at Yale Law School, http://www.yale.edu/lawweb/avalon/mideast/khartoum.htm. See also quote and discussion in Smith, *Palestine*, 304–5.

48. Arthur Goldschmidt Jr, *A Concise History of the Middle East*, 7th edn (Boulder, CO: Westview Press, 2002), 322.

49. Though printed in Laqueur and Rubin, *Israel–Arab Reader*, 116, see the United Nations Information System on the Question of Palestine (UNISPAL) site for a complete archive of UN activity regarding the Palestine–Israel conflict, http://domino.un.org/unispal.nsf.

NOTES TO CHAPTER 8

1. All excerpts and quotes are from the Palestine National Charter (July 1968), which is printed in Walter Laqueur and Barry Rubin, eds, *The Israel–Arab Reader*, 6th edn (New York: Penguin Books, 2001), 117–21.

2. See Mark Tessler, *A History of the Israeli–Palestinian Conflict* (Bloomington, IN: Indiana University Press, 1994), 437–44.

3. For charts of the PLO's organizational structure, see Ian J. Bickerton and Carla L. Klausner, *A Concise History of the Arab–Israeli Conflict*, 4th edn (Upper Saddle River, NJ: Prentice Hall, 2001), 164–6; and Tessler, *History*, 431–2. A standard and useful study of the PLO is Helena Cobban, *The Palestinian Liberation Organization* (Cambridge: Cambridge University Press, 1984).

4. Benny Morris, *Righteous Victims: A History of the Zionist–Arab Conflict, 1881–2001* (New York: Vintage Books, 2001), 347.

5. See Charles D. Smith, *Palestine and the Arab–Israeli Conflict*, 4th edn (Boston: Bedford / St Martin's, 2001), 313; and Tessler, *History*, 449.

6. 10,000 Egyptians killed (military and civilian) compared to fewer than 400 Israeli deaths (military) are figures cited in Morris, *Righteous Victims*, 362.

7. A concise and well-documented analysis of Jarring's 1971 mission can be found in Norman G. Finkelstein, *Image and Reality of the Israel–Palestine Conflict*, 2nd edn (London: Verso, 2003), 150–64. For discussion of the significance of Sadat's 1971 peace offer, see Noam Chomsky, *Fateful Triangle: The United States, Israel, and the Palestinians*, rev. edn (Cambridge, MA: South End Press, 1999), 64–6.

8. Assistant Secretary of State Joseph Sisco, quoted in Morris, *Righteous Victims*, 389.

9. See Chomsky, *Fateful Triangle*, 66–7; Finkelstein, *Image and Reality*, 163–4; and Smith, *Palestine*, 313–16, 320–1.

10. Avi Shlaim, *War and Peace in the Middle East* (New York: Penguin Books, 1995), 47.

11. Suggested rationales for Kissinger's hesitation vary slightly in the general histories. See Howard M. Sachar, *A History of Israel: From the Rise of Zionism to Our Time*, 2nd edn (New York: Alfred A. Knopf, 1996), 769; Nadav Safran, *Israel: The Embattled Ally* (Cambridge, MA: The Belknap Press of Harvard University Press, 1978), 481–3. Cf. Smith, *Palestine*, 325; and Bickerton and Klausner, *Concise History*, 174.

12. Laqueur and Rubin, *Israel–Arab Reader*, 152. See also United Nations Information System on the Question of Palestine (UNISPAL), http://domino.un.org/unispal.nsf.

13. For excerpts from Begin's electoral platform, see Laqueur and Rubin, *Israel–Arab Reader*, 206–7.

14. Tessler, *History*, 520–1, 824n115.

15. The Geneva Convention document is available online at the Office of the United Nations High Commissioner for Human Rights (OHCHR), http://www.ohchr.org. The Hague Convention text is provided by the Avalon Project at Yale Law School, http://www.yale.edu/lawweb/avalon/lawofwar/hague04.htm.

16. Smith, *Palestine*, 358.

17. Quotes from both communiqués came from Morris, *Righteous Victims*, 447–8.

18. All quotes are from the Camp David Frameworks, printed in Laqueur and Rubin, *Israel–Arab Reader*, 222–7.

19. Though I have relied on secondary sources for this section, it should be pointed out that most scholars refer heavily to the work of William B. Quandt, who was a staff member on the US National Security Council. For full treatment of the 1978 talks at Camp David, see William B. Quandt, *Camp David: Peacemaking and Politics* (Washington, DC: Brookings Institution, 1986). See also William B. Quandt, *Peace Process: American Diplomacy and the Arab–Israeli Conflict Since 1967*, rev. edn (Washington, DC: Brookings Institution / University of California, 2001).

20. The Declaration at Rabat (October 28, 1974) is printed in Bickerton and Klausner, *Concise History*, 181.

21. The full text of his speech can be found in Laqueur and Rubin, *Israel–Arab Reader*, 171–82, though the closing comment is not included; cf. T. G. Fraser, *The Middle East, 1914–1979* (New York: St Martin's Press, 1980), 136–40.

22. For text of UN General Assembly Resolutions 3236 (XXIX), and 3237 (XXIX), see UNISPAL, http://domino.un.org/unispal.nsf. Resolution 3236 is printed in Fraser, *Middle East*, 143–4.

23. The roll call was 72 in favor, 35 against, and 32 abstaining. For text of UN General Assembly Resolution 3379 (XXX), see UNISPAL, http://domino.un.org/unispal.nsf.

24. Tessler, *History*, 567.

25. Ibid., 493.

26. Tessler, ibid., 820n71, cites 60,000–80,000 dead.

27. Smith, *Palestine*, 356.

28. Figures on the number of refugees are fairly consistent, most ranging between 100,000 and 200,000. Data on the death toll, however, vary widely. Compare the following texts: Chomsky, *Fateful Triangle*, 99; Morris, *Righteous Victims*, 501, 723n45; Smith, *Palestine*, 356; Sachar, *History of Israel*, 899; and Baylis Thomas,

How Israel Was Won: A Concise History of the Arab–Israeli Conflict (Lanham, MD: Lexington Books, 1999), 219, 236n55.

29. For discussion of Israel's plans for Lebanon, and for meetings held between Begin, Sharon, and the cabinet, see Ze'ev Schiff and Ehud Ya'ari, *Israel's Lebanon War*, edited and translated by Ina Friedman (New York: Simon & Schuster, 1984), 38–44, 45–61. Shiff and Ya'ari's text is a standard work on the subject of the invasion of Lebanon. Being Israeli journalists, they were subjected to an Israeli military censor who excised portions of the manuscript before publication. Despite censorship, their text still provides the proper sense of atrocity. Another authoritative account can be found in Robert Fisk, *Pity the Nation: The Abduction of Lebanon*, 4th edn (New York: Thunder's Mouth Press / Nation Books, 2002).

30. Schiff and Ya'ari, *Israel's Lebanon War*, 43.

31. Ibid., 77.

32. See Chomsky, *Fateful Triangle*, 221–3; and Tessler, *History*, 576.

33. Schiff and Ya'ari, *Israel's Lebanon War*, 225.

34. See Morris, *Righteous Victims*, 540–2.

35. Schiff and Ya'ari, *Israel's Lebanon War*, 258.

36. The Israeli Kahan Commission cites 700–800 dead, while Lebanese estimates reach as high as 2,000. See Chomsky, *Fateful Triangle*, 369–70, 397–410; and Tessler, *History*, 591–2, 833n125.

37. For examinations of Sabra and Shatila, see Chomsky, *Fateful Triangle*, 362–70; Schiff and Ya'ari, *Israel's Lebanon War*, 50–85; and Tessler, *History*, 590–9. See also Morris, *Righteous Victims*, 541–7; and Sachar, *History of Israel*, 913–16.

38. For Reagan's concern about a Soviet threat, see Smith, *Palestine*, 383; Tessler, *History*, 629, 631.

39. Laqueur and Rubin, *Israel–Arab Reader*, 257–65.

40. Fred J. Khouri, *The Arab–Israeli Dilemma*, 3rd edn (Syracuse, NY: Syracuse University Press, 1985), 437.

41. Tessler, *History*, 584.

42. Laqueur and Rubin, *Israel–Arab Reader*, 298–9.

43. For events leading up to this round of violence, cf. Smith, *Palestine*, 410–11; and Tessler, *History*, 660–3.

NOTES TO CHAPTER 9

1. Don Peretz, *Intifada: The Palestinian Uprising* (Boulder, CO: Westview Press, 1990), 4.

2. Baruch Kimmerling and Joel S. Migdal, *The Palestinian People: A History* (Cambridge, MA: Harvard University Press, 2003), 297.

3. Mark Tessler, *A History of the Israeli–Palestinian Conflict* (Bloomington, IN: Indiana University Press, 1994), 692.

4. Charles D. Smith, *Palestine and the Arab–Israeli Conflict*, 5th edn (Boston: Bedford / St Martin's, 2004), 400–1.

5. Peretz, *Intifada*, 9.

6. Ibid., 27; Tessler, *History*, 71.

7. Peretz, *Intifada*, 33; Tessler, *History*, 684.

8. PLO Chairman Yasser Arafat used this phrase in praising, and identifying himself with, the youth carrying out the Intifada.

9. Smith, *Palestine*, 409. See also Noam Chomsky, *Fateful Triangle: The United States, Israel, and the Palestinians*, rev. edn (Cambridge, MA: South End Press, 1999), 483.

10. Kimmerling and Migdal, *Palestinian People*, 292–3.

11. Hamas's name comes from the Arabic acronym for *Harakat al-Muqawama al-Islamiyya*, or Islamic Resistance Movement. The word *hamas* in Arabic also means "zeal" or "bravery."

12. David K. Shipler, *Arab and Jew: Wounded Spirits in a Promised Land*, rev. edn (New York: Penguin Books, 2002), 155–6. Cited in Peretz, *Intifada*, 104.

13. Excerpts from the Hamas Charter are printed in Walter Laqueur and Barry Rubin, eds, *The Israel–Arab Reader*, 6th edn (New York: Penguin Books, 2001), 341–8. For the entire document, see The Avalon Project at Yale Law School, http://www.yale.edu/lawweb/avalon/mideast/hamas.htm.

14. This policy was announced by then Defense Minister Yitzhak Rabin. See Peretz, *Intifada*, 45; and Tessler, *History*, 697.

15. For text of UN General Assembly Resolution 43/21, see UN Information System on the Question of Palestine (UNISPAL), http://domino.un.org/unispal.nsf. See also UN Security Council Resolution 605, passed shortly after the beginning of the Intifada on December 22, 1987.

16. Ian J. Bickerton and Carla L. Klausner, *A Concise History of the Arab–Israeli Conflict*, 4th edn (Upper Saddle River, NJ: Prentice Hall, 2001), 231.

17. Benny Morris, *Righteous Victims: A History of the Zionist–Arab Conflict, 1881–2001* (New York: Vintage Books, 2001), 596. See

also, Bickerton and Klausner, *Concise History*, 231; and Tessler, *History*, 697–8, 701.

18. Laqueur and Rubin, *Israel–Arab Reader*, 354–8.
19. Ibid., 349–53.
20. Ibid., 359–62.
21. Avi Shlaim, *War and Peace in the Middle East* (New York: Penguin Books, 1995), 114.
22. See David R. Francis, "Economist tallies swelling cost of Israel to US," *Christian Science Monitor*, December 9, 2002, http://www.csmonitor.com/2002/1209/p16s01-wmgn.htm.
23. For text of the Oslo Declaration of Principles, see Laqueur and Rubin, *Israel–Arab Reader*, 413–22.
24. Avi Shlaim, "The Oslo Accord," *Journal of Palestine Studies*, XXIII, no. 3 (Spring 1994): 34.
25. Smith, *Palestine*, 438–9.
26. Cf. Shlaim, "The Oslo Accord," 34; and Tessler, *History*, 754.
27. Laqueur and Rubin, *Israel–Arab Reader*, 510.
28 Bickerton and Klausner, *Concise History*, 286. See also Smith, *Palestine*.

NOTES TO CHAPTER 10

1. Ian J. Bickerton and Carla L. Klausner, *A Concise History of the Arab–Israeli Conflict*, 4th edn (Upper Saddle River, NJ: Prentice Hall, 2001), 288.
2. Former Palestinian National Council member and professor of English literature, Edward W. Said (1935–2003) was a supporter of Palestinian rights and an outspoken critic of Oslo and Yasser Arafat, from whom he parted company during the accords. For his critique of Oslo, see Edward W. Said, *Peace and Its Discontents: Essays on Palestine in the Middle East Peace Process* (New York: Vintage Books, 1996). Madrid negotiators Hanan Ashrawi and Haidar Abdul Shafi also became outspoken critics. See interviews with Shafi in *Journal of Palestine Studies*, XXIII, no. 1 (Autumn 1993): 14; and XXXII, no. 1 (Autumn 2002): 28.
3. See Bickerton and Klausner, *Concise History*, 293; and Benny Morris, *Righteous Victims: A History of the Zionist–Arab Conflict, 1881–2001* (New York: Vintage Books, 2001), 639.

4. Quoted from the Guidelines of the Government of Israel, June 1996. See Israel Ministry of Foreign Affairs, http://www.mfa.gov.il.

5. Cf. Bickerton and Klausner, *Concise History*, 298; Morris, *Righteous Victims*, 642; and Charles D. Smith, *Palestine and the Arab–Israeli Conflict*, 5th edn (Boston: Bedford / St Martin's, 2004), 459.

6. The text of the Protocol Concerning the Redeployment in Hebron is available on the United Nations Information System on the Question of Palestine (UNISPAL) site, though it is a non-UN document: http://domino.un.org/unispal.nsf. It is also printed in the *Journal of Palestine Studies*, XXVI, no. 3 (Spring 1997): 131–9.

7. The text of the "Note for the Record" is printed in Walter Laqueur and Barry Rubin, eds, *The Israel–Arab Reader*, 6th edn (New York: Penguin Books, 2001), 522–3.

8. The General Assembly resolutions 51/223 (March 1997) and ES-10/2 (April 1997) appear on the UNISPAL site, http://domino.un.org/unispal.nsf. In both resolutions only the US and Israel voted against, with Micronesia joining the dissent in the April resolution. The votes went as follows: Res. 51/223 (Yes: 130; No: 2; Abstentions: 2; Non-Voting: 51); Res. ES-10/2 (Yes: 134; No: 3; Abstentions: 11; Non-Voting: 37).

9. The Wye River Memorandum is printed in Laqueur and Rubin, *Israel–Arab Reader*, 529–34.

10. The Sharm al-Sheikh Memorandum is available online at the Avalon Project at Yale Law School, http://www.yale.edu/lawweb/avalon/mideast/mid024.htm. It is also printed in Bickerton and Klausner, *Concise History*, 348–51.

11. Charles Enderlin, *Shattered Dreams: The Failure of the Peace Process in the Middle East, 1995–2002*, translated by Susan Fairfield (New York: Other Press, 2003), 177.

12. Ibid., 180.

13. The May 2000 map was produced again at Camp David, showing, according to Enderlin, 76 percent (ibid., 201–2). Cf. Enderlin, ibid., 148, 166; and Smith, *Palestine*, 494–5.

14. Regarding discussion of settlement blocks, see Enderlin, *Shattered Dreams*, 184, 188, and 213. For the division of the West Bank, see ibid., 166, 207–8, 226–7, and 249–50.

15. Resolution 194, passed on December 11, 1948, states that the UN "Resolves that the refugees wishing to return to their homes and

live at peace with their neighbours should be permitted to do so at the earliest practicable date, and that compensation should be paid for the property of those choosing not to return and for loss of or damage to property which, under principles of international law or in equity, should be made good by the Governments or authorities responsible." See UNISPAL, http://domino.un.org/unispal.nsf.

16. For discussion of the refugee issue, see Enderlin, *Shattered Dreams*, 196–9, 227–9.

17. UNRWA's publications are available at http://www.un.org/unrwa/publications/index.html.

18. William B. Quandt, *Peace Process: American Diplomacy and the Arab–Israeli Conflict Since 1967*, rev. edn (Washington, DC: Brookings Institution / University of California, 2001), 362–3.

19. Robert Malley and Hussein Agha, "Camp David: The Tragedy of Errors," *New York Review of Books*, August 9, 2001, http://www.nybooks.com/articles/14380. In the September 20, 2001 issue, special envoy and Camp David negotiator Dennis Ross responds to the Malley–Agha article, after which Malley and Agha respond in turn ("Camp David: An Exchange"), http://www.nybooks.com/articles/14529. See also the June 13, 2002 issue, which features Israeli historian Benny Morris's interview with Ehud Barak, and a response to the interview by Malley and Agha ("Camp David and After: An Exchange"). Both are available online at http://www.nybooks.com/articles/15501 and http://www.nybooks.com/articles/15502, respectively.

20. Malley and Agha, "Camp David: The Tragedy of Errors."

21. Quandt, *Peace Process*, 368.

22. For reports covering the period of September 28, 2000 to December 2000, see "Illusions of Restraint: Human Rights Violations During the Events in the Occupied Territories, 29 September – 2 December 2000," published in December 2000 by the Israeli human rights organization, B'Tselem, http://www.btselem.org. See also "Lethal Force: Israel's Use of Military Force Against Palestinian Demonstrators," published by the Palestinian human rights organization, LAW (http://www.law-society.org), and submitted to the Special Session of the UN Commission on Human Rights, October 2000.

23. For text of UN Security Council Resolution 1322 (October 7, 2000), see UNISPAL, http://domino.un.org/unispal.nsf.

24. See reports by B'Tselem and LAW cited in note 22; see also Amnesty International, *Israel and the Occupied Territories: Excessive Use of Lethal Force*, October 19, 2000 (AI Index: MDE 15/041/2000), http://www.amnesty.org.

25. US Department of State, "Israel and the Occupied Territories," *Country Reports on Human Rights Practices – 2000*, February 23, 2001, http://www.state.gov/g/drl/rls/hrrpt/2000/nea/794.htm.

26. See Enderlin, *Shattered Dreams*, 313–17.

27. Ibid., 333–9; and Quandt, *Peace Process*, 371–2. Text of Clinton's speech is printed in Enderlin's discussion, and is available online at the Brookings Institution, http://www.brookings.edu/press/appendix/appen_z.htm.

28. Though not a UN document, the Taba Statement (January 27, 2001) text is available online at UNISPAL, http://domino.un.org/unispal.nsf. A year later, the European Union special envoy Miguel Moratinos prepared a document summarizing and describing the negotiations at the Egyptian resort, which were published in the Israeli daily, *Ha'aretz*: Akiva Eldar, "'Moratinos Document': The peace that nearly was at Taba," *Ha'aretz*, February 14, 2002, http://www.haaretzdaily.com. Present at the summit, along with his team, Moratinos interviewed and consulted negotiators on both sides. He released the document after presenting it to the Taba negotiators and gaining their approval of it.

29. All statistics regarding suicide bombing, extrajudicial killing, and home demolition are reported by B'Tselem, http://www.btselem.org. For detailed human rights reports on abuses both in Israel and the occupied territories, see Human Rights Watch, *World Report 2001* [and 2002, 2003], http://www.hrw.org; and US Department of State, *Country Reports on Human Rights Practices – 2001* [and 2002, 2003], http://www.state.gov/g/drl/hr/c1470.htm.

30. Akiva Eldar, "The Arafat–bin Laden equation won't stick," *Ha'aretz*, September 24, 2001.

31. The Security Council resolutions issued during this time were 1402, 1403, 1405; see also General Assembly Resolution ES-10/10. All resolutions are available on UNISPAL, http://domino.un.org/unispal.nsf. Quoted figures are from the "Report of the Secretary-General prepared pursuant to General Assembly resolution ES-10/10" (section III-E), available both on UNISPAL, and the UN's main site, http://www.un.org/peace/jenin/index.html.

32. Israel Ministry of Defense, http://www.seamzone.mod.gov.il. See also Israel Ministry of Foreign Affairs for more information on the barrier, http://securityfence.mfa.gov.il.

33. The General Assembly resolutions ES-10/13 (October 27, 2003) and ES-10/14 (December 12, 2003) appear on the UNISPAL site, http://domino.un.org/unispal.nsf. Resolution ES-10/14 is quoted.

34. The International Court of Justice's advisory decision (July 9, 2004) can be viewed on the ICJ's site, http://www.icj-cij.org. See follow-up reportage and commentary in the *Financial Times*, US edition, July 10, 2004, http://news.ft.com/home/us. It should be noted that the only member of the 15-judge panel to vote against the decision was the American judge, Thomas Buergenthal.

35. Alan Mairson, "Very Long Division," *National Geographic*, January 2004.

36. See Smith, *Palestine*, 507–10. See also Nicole Gaouette's series of articles ("Behind the Barrier"), which appeared in the *Christian Science Monitor*, and are available online at http://www.csmonitor.com/2003/0808/p01s05-wome.html.

37. The full text of the Sharm Al-Sheikh Fact-Finding Committee Report is available online at the US State Department's site, http://www.state.gov/p/nea/rls/rpt/3060.htm.

38. For a review of Sharon's settlement policies, see Daniel Williams, "Settlements Expanding Under Sharon," *Washington Post*, May 31, 2002, http://www.washingtonpost.com.

39. The text of President Bush's June 2002 Rose Garden speech ("President Bush Calls for New Palestinian Leadership") is available on the White House's site, http://www.whitehouse.gov.

40. "Bush calls for end to the Arafat era," *Ha'aretz*, English edition, June 25, 2002.

41. Ibid.

42. See Smith, *Palestine*, 515.

43. The full text of "A Performance-Based Roadmap to a Permanent Two-State Solution to the Israeli–Palestinian Conflict" is available on the UN site, http://www.un.org/media/main/roadmap122002.html.

44. The full texts of the speeches given by Bush, Sharon, and Abbas at the Aqaba Summit (June 4, 2004) are available on the Jerusalem Media & Communication Centre site, http://www.jmcc.org/documents/docs.html.

45. John Ward Anderson and Molly Moore, "Abbas Declares Victory in Palestinian Elections," *Washington Post*, January 10, 2005, http://www.washingtonpost.com.

46. Reported by BBC News, UK edition, November 28, 2003, http://news.bbc.co.uk.

47. The full text of the Disengagement Plan is provided online by the Prime Minister's Office, http://www.pmo.gov.il/PMOEng.

48. See Human Rights Watch, "Israel: 'Disengagement' Will Not End Gaza Occupation," October 29, 2004, http://www.hrw.org.

49. Ben Russell, "Palestinian malnutrition at African levels under Israeli curbs, say MPs," *Independent*, February 5, 2004, http://www.independent.co.uk. See also, Peter Hansen, "Hungry in Gaza," *Guardian*, March 5, 2003, http://www.guardian.co.uk. Hansen is the commissioner general of the UN Relief and Works Agency (UNRWA). The article also appeared in the *Journal of Palestine Studies*, XXXII, no. 4 (Summer 2003): 165–7.

50. US Central Intelligence Agency, *The World Factbook*, http://www.cia.gov/cia/publications/factbook.

51. Greg Myre, "4 Israeli Intelligence Experts Call for Political Solution," *New York Times*, November 14, 2003, http://www.nytimes.com.

52. Figures reported by B'Tselem.

Suggested Reading

BOOKS ON THE PALESTINE–ISRAEL CONFLICT

I've found the following general histories to be useful. Presented in increasing level of detail:

Ron David's *Arabs & Israel For Beginners* (New York: Writers and Readers Publishing, Inc., 1996), is the only other introductory work to emphasize the lack of involvement of ancient history in the conflict. David's primer is short, heavily illustrated and oftentimes entertaining. Another short primer on the Middle East, spending most of its time on Israel and Palestine, is François Massoulié's *Middle East Conflicts* (New York: Interlink Books, 2003). Massoulié's is easy to read, featuring many photographs. Ilene Beatty's *Arab and Jew in the Land of Canaan* (Chicago: Henry Regnery Company, 1957), albeit dated, is an easy read, under a hundred pages, and personably written. A book that recently re-emerged is T. G. Fraser's *The Arab–Israeli Conflict*, 2nd edn (New York: Palgrave Macmillan, 2004). Fraser's is another focused introduction, basically starting with World War I, that beginners will find helpful. Baylis Thomas's *How Israel Was Won: A Concise History of the Arab–Israeli Conflict* (Lanham, MD: Lexington Books, 1999), is the next level of detail and serves as a good follow-up to texts like David's and Fraser's. Thomas is still basic and doesn't assume prior knowledge, while presenting a more developed history.

Another good basic text, and a level up in detail from Thomas, is Ian J. Bickerton and Carla L. Klausner's *A Concise History of the Arab–Israeli Conflict*, 4th edn (Upper Saddle River, NJ: Prentice Hall, 2001). Their text is still quite manageable, with a good deal of documents and lists for further reading. Bickerton and Klausner, two professors, wrote this work as an introductory textbook. Theirs is a quality survey, both clearly written and very well organized.

Charles D. Smith's *Palestine and the Arab–Israeli Conflict*, 5th edn (Boston: Bedford / St Martin's, 2004), is a fully developed one-volume history of the conflict. It's a little over 500 pages, but a good deal of that is notes and documents. Smith's is an excellent history and is often used as a textbook for undergraduate courses on the subject. I would follow Smith with Benny Morris's *Righteous Victims: A History of the Zionist–Arab Conflict, 1881–2001* (New York: Vintage Books, 2001); and Mark Tessler's *A History of the Israeli–Palestinian Conflict* (Bloomington, IN: Indiana University Press, 1994). The Morris and Tessler texts are both lengthy, with Morris focusing more on military and war concerns, and Tessler on the political. Two older works still worth consulting are Christopher Sykes's *Crossroads to Israel* (Cleveland: The World Publishing Company, 1965), which covers from the Balfour Declaration (1917) to Israel's declaration of independence (1948); and Fred J. Khouri's *The Arab–Israeli Dilemma*, 3rd edn (Syracuse, NY: Syracuse University Press, 1985), which reaches the mid-1980s.

FOCUSED WORKS

For an Israeli perspective on the country and its people, I would suggest Amos Elon's *The Israelis: Founders and Sons* (1971; reprint, New York: Penguin Books, 1983); and the writings of Amos Oz, such as *In the Land of Israel*, translated by Maurie Goldberg-Bartura (1983; reprint, San Diego, CA: Harvest Books, 1993). For Palestinian concerns the writings of Edward W. Said are essential. His *The Question of Palestine* (1979; reprint, New York: Vintage Books, 1992) is a good place to start. David K. Shipler's *Arab and Jew: Wounded Spirits in a Promised Land*, rev. edn (New York: Penguin Books, 2002), provides a glimpse into how Israelis and Palestinians view themselves and one another.

GENERAL WORKS ON THE MIDDLE EAST

Avi Shlaim's *War and Peace in the Middle East* (New York: Penguin Books, 1995), is an excellent, brief overview of the modern Middle East, with an emphasis on US involvement. Another brief sketch of the US's role in the region, and its foreign policy in general, is Gabriel Kolko's *Another Century of War?* (New York: The New Press, 2002). Shlaim and Kolko generally write large analytical texts, but in these two examples they produced superb, short glimpses for the general reader – something more scholars should consider.

Arthur Goldschmidt Jr's *A Concise History of the Middle East*, 7th edn (Boulder, CO: Westview Press, 2002), is a larger general history of the Middle East and is commonly used as a textbook. Goldschmidt's writing is clear and engaging, it keeps the reader's attention, and has a good sense of balance. This is a first-rate general survey, and beginners will have no trouble. Another good general history is William L. Cleveland's *A History of the Modern Middle East*, 2nd edn (Boulder, CO: Westview Press, 2000).

PERIODICALS

Suggestions here will stray from the mainstream, as I assume the reader is familiar with *Newsweek* and the *New York Times*. My advice in the realm of periodicals, which also applies to all things in print, is read everything, and with a critical and skeptical eye. And don't be afraid to change your routine: If you're more conservative, try reading *Z Magazine*; if you consider yourself more liberal or left, consider picking up *Foreign Affairs*. (I recommend both.)

For analysis and coverage of the conflict in particular, the *Washington Report*, the quarterly *Middle East Report*, and *Tikkun* are all magazines worth looking at. The quarterly *Journal of Palestine Studies*, too, is an excellent source. For general news and analysis frequently addressing the Middle East, I suggest the monthly *Z Magazine*. I also tend to keep an eye on *National Geographic* for articles on various countries and topics relating to the Middle East.

Newspapers: My favorite newspapers are the *Christian Science Monitor* and the *Financial Times*. Despite its name, the *Christian Science Monitor* is a secular daily (Mon.–Fri.) and features some of the best journalism found in any daily. The *Financial Times*, though a financial paper, features first-rate journalism on world affairs. Another paper, the *Guardian Weekly*, is a good collection of what the British daily, the *Guardian*, has featured all week, and includes selections from the British *Observer*, the American *Washington Post*, and France's *Le Monde*.

INTERNET RESOURCES

Websites come and go and URLs change daily, but this is a fairly reliable list of sites. Again, I've strayed from suggesting things like CNN, and have provided some sites and sources that are less common and that I have found quite helpful. Needless to say, the content of these sites may not reflect my views.

News

Al Ahram (Cairo): http://weekly.ahram.org.eg

Christian Science Monitor (US): http://www.csmonitor.com
Democracy Now! (radio station with online archives): http://www.
   democracynow.org
The Guardian (UK): http://www.guardian.co.uk
Ha'aretz (Israel): http://www.haaretzdaily.com
Jerusalem Post (Israel): http://www.jpost.com
Link TV: http://www.linktv.org
Palestine Chronicle: http://www.palestinechronicle.com
Z Magazine / ZNet: http://www.zmag.org

Analysis, Human Rights

B'Tselem (Israeli human rights organization): http://www.btselem.
   org
Electronic Intifada: http://www.electronicintifada.net
Foundation for Middle East Peace: http://www.fmep.org
Human Rights Watch: http://hrw.org
Institute for Palestine Studies: http://www.palestine-studies.org
Middle East Institute: http://www.mideasti.org
Middle East Research and Information Project (MERIP): http://www.
   merip.org
Worldview, on Chicago Public Radio (with online archives): http://
   www.chicagopublicradio.org/programs/worldview/worldview.asp

Miscellaneous

CIA Factbook – Israel: http://www.cia.gov/cia/publications/factbook/
   geos/is.html
UN Information System on the Question of Palestine (UNISPAL):
   http://domino.un.org/unispal.nsf

Select Bibliography

Aruri, Naseer H. *Dishonest Broker: The US Role in Israel and Palestine*. Cambridge, MA: South End Press, 2003.

Beatty, Ilene. *Arab and Jew in the Land of Canaan*. Chicago: Henry Regnery Company, 1957.

Benvenisti, Meron. *The West Bank Data Project: A Survey of Israel's Policies*. Washington, DC: The American Enterprise Institute, 1984.

Bickerton, Ian J., and Carla L. Klausner. *A Concise History of the Arab–Israeli Conflict*. 4th edn. Upper Saddle River, NJ: Prentice Hall, 2001.

Carey, Roane, ed. *The New Intifada: Resisting Israel's Apartheid*. London: Verso, 2001.

Chomsky, Noam. *Fateful Triangle: The United States, Israel, and the Palestinians*. Rev. edn. Cambridge, MA: South End Press, 1999.

Churchill, Randolph S., and Winston S. Churchill. *The Six Day War*. London: Heinemann, 1967.

Cleveland, William L. *A History of the Modern Middle East*. 2nd edn. Boulder, CO: Westview Press, 2000.

David, Ron. *Arabs & Israel For Beginners*. New York: Writers and Readers Publishing, Inc., 1996.

Elon, Amos. *The Israelis: Founders and Sons*. 1971. Reprint, New York: Penguin Books, 1983.

Enderlin, Charles. *Shattered Dreams: The Failure of the Peace Process in the Middle East, 1995–2002*. Translated by Susan Fairfield. New York: Other Press, 2003.

Farsoun, Samih K., and Christina E. Zacharia. *Palestine and the Palestinians*. Boulder, CO: Westview Press, 1997.

Finkelstein, Norman G. *Image and Reality of the Israel–Palestine Conflict*. 2nd edn. London: Verso, 2003.

Fisk, Robert. *Pity the Nation: The Abduction of Lebanon*. 4th edn. New York: Thunder's Mouth Press / Nation Books, 2002.

Flapan, Simha. *The Birth of Israel: Myths and Realities*. New York: Pantheon Books, 1987.

Fraser, T. G. *The Middle East, 1914–1979*. New York: St Martin's Press, 1980.

—— *The Arab–Israeli Conflict*. 2nd edn. New York: Palgrave Macmillan, 2004.

Fromkin, David. *A Peace to End All Peace*. New York: Henry Holt and Company, 1989.

Glubb, Sir John Bagot. *A Soldier with the Arabs*. New York: Harper & Brothers, 1957.

Goldschmidt Jr, Arthur. *A Concise History of the Middle East*. 7th edn. Boulder, CO: Westview Press, 2002.

Green, Stephen. *Taking Sides: America's Secret Relations with a Militant Israel*. New York: William Morrow and Company, Inc., 1984.

Greer, Thomas H. *A Brief History of the Western World*. 5th edn. San Diego: Harcourt Brace Jovanovich, 1987.

Guyatt, Nicholas. *The Absence of Peace: Understanding the Israeli–Palestinian Conflict*. London: Zed Books, 1998.

Hayes, J. R., ed. *The Genius of Arab Civilization: Source of Renaissance*. 2nd edn. Cambridge, MA: MIT Press, 1983.

Herzl, Theodor. *The Jewish State*. 1946. Reprint, New York: Dover Publications, Inc., 1988.

Hitti, Philip K. *The Arabs: A Short History*. 1943. Reprint, Washington, DC: Regnery Publishing, Inc., 1996.

—— *History of the Arabs*. 10th edn. London: Macmillan & Co. Ltd, 1970.

Hourani, Albert. *A History of the Arab Peoples*. New York: Warner Books, 1991.

Ingrams, Doreen. *Palestine Papers, 1917–1922: Seeds of Conflict*. New York: George Braziller, 1973.

Khalidi, Rashid. *Palestinian Identity: The Construction of Modern National Consciousness*. New York: Columbia University Press, 1997.

Khouri, Fred J. *The Arab–Israeli Dilemma*. 3rd edn. Syracuse, NY: Syracuse University Press, 1985.

Kimmerling, Baruch, and Joel S. Migdal. *The Palestinian People: A History*. Cambridge, MA: Harvard University Press, 2003.

Lamb, David. *The Arabs: Journeys Beyond the Mirage*. Rev. edn. New York: Vintage Books, 2002.

Laqueur, Walter, and Barry Rubin, eds. *The Israel–Arab Reader*. 6th edn. New York: Penguin Books, 2001.

Mandel, Neville J. *The Arabs and Zionism Before World War I*. Berkeley: University of California Press, 1976.

Mansfield, Peter. *The Arabs*. 3rd edn. London: Penguin Books, 1992.

McCarthy, Justin. *The Population of Palestine: Population Statistics of the Late Ottoman Period and the Mandate*. New York: Columbia University Press, 1990.

Morris, Benny. *The Birth of the Palestinian Refugee Problem Revisited*. 2nd edn. Cambridge: Cambridge University Press, 2004.

—— *Righteous Victims: A History of the Zionist-Arab Conflict, 1881–2001*. New York: Vintage Books, 2001.

Neff, Donald. *Warriors for Jerusalem: The Six Days That Changed the Middle East*. New York: Linden Press / Simon & Schuster, 1984.

Peretz, Don. *Intifada: The Palestinian Uprising*. Boulder, CO: Westview Press, 1990.

Quandt, William B. *Peace Process: American Diplomacy and the Arab–Israeli Conflict Since 1967*. Rev. edn. Washington, DC: Brookings Institution / University of California, 2001.

Reinhart, Tanya. *Israel/Palestine: How to End the War of 1948*. New York: Seven Stories Press, 2002.

Rodinson, Maxime. *Muhammad*. Translated by Anne Carter. 1971. Reprint, New York: The New Press, 2002.

Rogan, Eugene L., and Avi Shlaim, eds. *The War for Palestine: Rewriting the History of 1948*. Cambridge: Cambridge University Press, 2001.

Rokach, Livia. *Israel's Sacred Terrorism*. 3rd edn. Belmont, MA: AAUG Press, 1986.

Sachar, Howard M. *A History of Israel: From the Rise of Zionism to Our Time*. 2nd edn. New York: Alfred A. Knopf, 1996.

Safran, Nadav. *Israel: The Embattled Ally*. Cambridge, MA: The Belknap Press of Harvard University Press, 1978.

Said, Edward W. *The Question of Palestine*. 1979. Reprint, New York: Vintage Books, 1992.

—— and Christopher Hitchens, eds. *Blaming the Victims*. London: Verso, 1988.

Schiff, Ze'ev, and Ehud Ya'ari. *Israel's Lebanon War*. Edited and translated by Ina Friedman. New York: Simon & Schuster, 1984.

Segev, Tom. *One Palestine, Complete: Jews and Arabs Under the British Mandate*. Translated by Haim Watzman. New York: Henry Holt and Company, 2000.

Shipler, David K. *Arab and Jew: Wounded Spirits in a Promised Land*. Rev. edn. New York: Penguin Books, 2002.

Shlaim, Avi. *Collusion Across the Jordan: King Abdullah, the Zionist Movement, and the Partition of Palestine*. New York: Columbia University Press, 1988.

—— *War and Peace in the Middle East*. New York: Penguin Books, 1995.

Smith, Charles D. *Palestine and the Arab–Israeli Conflict*. 5th edn. Boston: Bedford / St Martin's, 2004.

Smith, Huston. *The World's Religions: Our Great Wisdom Traditions*. 1958. Reprint, San Francisco: HarperCollins, 1991.

Sykes, Christopher. *Crossroads to Israel*. Cleveland: The World Publishing Company, 1965.

Tessler, Mark. *A History of the Israeli–Palestinian Conflict*. Bloomington, IN: Indiana University Press, 1994.

Thomas, Baylis. *How Israel Was Won: A Concise History of the Arab–Israeli Conflict*. Lanham, MD: Lexington Books, 1999.

Usher, Graham. *Palestine in Crisis: The Struggle for Peace and Political Independence After Oslo*. London: Pluto Press, 1995.

Vital, David. *The Origins of Zionism*. 1975. Reprint, Oxford: Oxford University Press, 2001.

Watt, W. Montgomery. *Muhammad: Prophet and Statesman*. London: Oxford University Press, 1961.

Index